Hacks, Blacks, and Cons

Hacks, Blacks, and Cons

Race Relations in a Maximum Security Prison

Leo Carroll
University of Rhode Island

WAVELAND
PRESS, INC.
Prospect Heights, Illinois

For information about this book, write or call:

Waveland Press, Inc.
P.O. Box 400
Prospect Heights, Illinois 60070
(708) 634-0081

Contents

List of Figures   vii

List of Tables   ix

Preface and Acknowledgements   xi

Chapter 1   **Introduction**   1

Prison Social Organization and Race Relations   2
Data and Methods   11
Summary   20

Chapter 2   **The Prison**   23

Physical Setting   23
Formal Organization   26
Goals and Resources   28
Compromise: Humanitarian Reform   30
Characteristics of the Inmate Population   33
Past Racial Conflict   39
Summary   45

Chapter 3   **The Hacks**   47

Conflict among the Administrators   47
Anomie among the Custodians   52
Adaptations of the Custodians   57

Chapter 4   **The Cons**   63

Social Types among the Cons   64
Humanitarian Reform and Convict Solidarity   85
Summary and Conclusion   89

Chapter 5   **The Blacks**   91

Black Perspectives: Soul and Nationalism   91
Social Types among the Blacks   98
Summary and Conclusion   112

Chapter 6   **Hacks, Blacks, and Cons: Discipline**   115

Racial Differences in Disciplinary Dispositions 116
Racial Bias of the Custodians 123
Black Resources 130
White Resources 137
Summary 143

Chapter 7   **Blacks and Cons: Routine Activities**   147

Work and Cell Assignments 150
Organized Recreation 156
Inmate Organizations 163
Hustling and Hanging Out 165
Summary 168

Chapter 8   **Blacks and Cons: Focal Concerns**   173

Drugs 173
Homosexual Behavior 178
Keeping the Peace 187
Meeting the Public 192
Summary and Conclusion 195

Chapter 9   **Conclusion**   197

The Aftermath of Attica 198
Some Implications for Further Research 212
Concluding Remarks 220

Epilogue 1988   **Race Relations in the Prison:**
Fifteen Years of Research   223

The Hacks 223
Blacks and Cons 228
Intergroup Relations 230
Conclusion 236
References 239

Notes   243

Bibliography   261

Index   273

About the Author   281

List of Figures

2-1	Map of the Prison	24
2-2	Table of Organization, ECI	27
4-1	Informal Social Organization of the White Prisoners	75
7-1	Racial Segregation of Prisoners in the Gym	160
7-2	Racial Segregation of Prisoners at the Movies	162
7-3	Racial Segregation in Informal Groupings in South State Wing	169

List of Tables

2-1	Authorized Positions at ECI for 1971-72 by Function	29
2-2	Authorized Expenditures at ECI for 1971-72 by Function	29
2-3	Offenses of Prisoners by Race	35
2-4	Length of Sentence by Race in Percentages	35
2-5	Number of Prior Commitments by Race in Percentages	36
2-6	Time Served on Current Sentence by Race in Percentages	36
2-7	Age of Prisoners by Race in Percentages	37
2-8	Years of School Completed by Race in Percentages	37
2-9	Chronology of Events at ECI, 1968-70	41
6-1	Reported Infractions by Race and Seriousness in Percentages	119
6-2	Percent of Infractions Reported by Officers to the Disciplinary Board by Race and Seriousness	119
6-3	Major Infractions Reported to Disciplinary Board by Race in Percentages	120
6-4	Dispositions of Major Infractions by the Disciplinary Board by Race in Percentages	121
6-5	Dispositions of Major Infractions by the Disciplinary Board by Disciplinary Record and Race in Percentages	122
7-1	Assignment of Prisoners to Work Details by Race	151
7-2	Assignment of Prisoners to Cells by Race	155
9-1	Chronology of Events at ECI, August-November 1971	200

Preface and Acknowledgements

A wave of violence, frequently with racial overtones, has drawn the attention of the nation to its prisons. In response to these outbursts some advocate more repressive institutions; others argue for the abandonment of prisons in favor of some more humane alternative. I am of the latter persuasion. Six years of experience in prisons, first as a guard and later as an observer, have convinced me that brutality and violence are the inevitable products of the current system of corrections. Further, I have become convinced that humanitarian reforms within prisons effect no substantial change in the level of brutality and violence, although they perhaps substitute psychological for physical measures. The material contained in this monograph—a study of race relations in a reform-oriented prison —provides, I believe, abundant evidence for each of these assertions.

A radical transformation of the correctional system is in order. But how likely is such a transformation in a society in which nearly half of the prisoner population are members of oppressed minorities? The analysis of race relations in the prison shows prisons to be a reflection of the society they serve. A humanization of American corrections thus presumes a humanization of American society. While not optimistic about the possibilities of humanization, I hope that this work will, at least in a small way, contribute to its realization.

Unfortunately, but necessarily, the people to whom I am most indebted must remain anonymous. These are the men—the hacks, the blacks, and the cons—of "Eastern Correctional Institution." Without their acceptance and cooperation the research could not have been done. To protect them I have chosen not to identify the institution or any of its personnel. All names used in this report are fictitious, and any resemblance to names of people working or confined in prisons is coincidental.

It is with a deep sense of appreciation that I acknowledge the assistance of Professors Harold Pfautz and Dietrich Rueschemeyer of Brown University, and Colin Loftin of the University of Maryland. While at times painful, their criticism was always constructive. Even more helpful than their technical assistance, however, was their unflagging support and encouragement.

Several people shared the tedious task of typing field notes and various drafts of the manuscript. To my mother, Mary Carroll, and to Sarah Zacks, Beth Underwood, and Gloria Tewhey I extend my warmest gratitude.

Words alone can never repay Carol, Jennifer and Gretchen whose emotional support sustained me through the difficult years of research and writing.

And, finally, there is Jeanne C. Moore whose unconditional love and gentle strength have, in the last several years, guided me in the way of wisdom and acceptance. To her, I dedicate this reissue marking a new chapter in our lives.

Grateful acknowledgment is made to the following for use of material reprinted herein:

Bantam Books, Inc. for quoting from George Jackson, *Soledad Brother: The Prison Letters of George Jackson*. Copyright © 1970 by World Entertainers Limited. Published by Bantam Books, Inc., and Coward, McCann and Geoghegan, Inc. Reprinted by permission of Bantam Books, Inc.

Columbia University Press for quoting from Ulf Hannerz, *Soulside: Inquiries into Ghetto Culture and Community*. Copyright 1969 by Ulf Hannerz.

Macmillan Publishing Co., Inc. for quoting from Robert K. Merton, *Social Theory and Social Structure*, revised and enlarged edition. Copyright 1957 by The Free Press, Inc.

Orlando (Florida) Sentinel Star, Inc. for quoting from James Bacchus, "Sumter Tense—Riots Could Happen Again" and from "Wainwright Says Black Prison Majority Feared," May 28, 1973.

Prentice-Hall, Inc. for quoting from John Irwin, *The Felon*, © 1970, p. 69. By permission of Prentice-Hall, Inc.

The New York Times Company for quoting from Michael T. Kaufman, "Troubles Persist in Prison at Auburn," May 17, 1971, and from Tad Szulc "George Jackson Radicalizes the Brothers in Soledad and San Quentin," *Magazine*, August 1, 1971. © 1971 by The New York Times Company. Reprinted by permission.

1 Introduction

"Nothing is more powerful than an idea, and they have the idea that they are victims of a racist society, repressed by racist pigs and racist institutions."[1] These are the words of Russell G. Oswald, former Commissioner of Corrections for the State of New York, who regards the issues posed by black prisoners as the most awesome challenge he has faced in his twenty-five years in corrections. Four months after he had spoken these words, Oswald confronted the issues head-on. On September 19, 1971 he ordered the New York State Police to retake the Attica Correctional Institution by assault. Thirty inmates were killed, most of them black.

More recently, following several weeks of disorder in Florida's correctional system, a white inmate filed a suit asking for a return to racial segregation in the state's prisons.[2] Commenting on this suit and the disorder that preceded it, Louie Wainwright, Director of Corrections, said: "It is an extremely hazardous situation. White prisoners are begging to be locked in cells because of the increasing aggressive activities by blacks."[3] Superintendent K.D. Conner of Florida's Sumter Correctional Institution observed that in a racially integrated prison, "the tension is directed more against the other race than against the staff."[4]

These are only two incidents in a wave of racial disturbances that has swept the nation's prisons in recent years. Most often this conflict has come to public attention in the form of violent disturbances in which black inmates are pitted against a predominantly white prison staff. The observations by Florida officials make clear, however, that these dramatic confrontations are only the tip of the iceberg. Beneath these outbursts, contained and hidden by the walls of the prison, are a myriad of conflicts that involve black prisoner against white prisoner as well as black prisoners against staff.

Despite the obvious racial tension in prisons, there has been no sociological analysis of the problem. Research in race relations tends to be guided by a melioristic interest. By and large it has concentrated on whatever has seemed to be the important problem of the moment. As the spotlight of public attention has illuminated one problem area after another, the focus of research has shifted. Thus, in succession since World War II research has concentrated on integration in the armed forces, discrimination in business and industry, residential segregation, school desegregation, and most recently urban violence. The importance and scale of these

1

issues dwarfed the problems surrounding the forced racial integration of the 600,000 incarcerated adults.[5] Moreover, until 1970 the prisons seemed to be islands of tranquility in an ocean swept by racial turmoil. Thus, while there have been a few studies of racial discrimination in law enforcement, there have been none of race relations in the prison.

There is a substantial body of sociological research on the prison. Yet, in all of this research there is only incidental reference to the fact that prisoners differ in racial identities. As will become clear later in this chapter, this oversight may actually be a reflection of the fact that until recently racial identities have been of little importance to prison social structure. Whatever the reason, however, the fact remains that studies of the prison offer virtually no information regarding race relations.

In view of the gaps in our knowledge concerning race relations in the prison, the research reported here was undertaken as an exploratory case study. By delving deeply into the situation of one prison, it seeks to provide some understanding of how race relations are organized in prisons. More concretely, the aim of the study is to describe the structure of race relations as it existed in one prison during the period of study, and to identify the conditions that maintained the structure and that may therefore cause it to change.

Prison Social Organization and Race Relations

I have observed that few of the many studies on the prison have considered the fact that inmates and staff alike differ in their racial identities. This omission may be an oversight due to the theoretical orientation of this research. Or, in fact, it may be an indication that race is of minimal significance within the prison. In this section, after reviewing the literature on inmate social organization, I offer an hypothesis concerning this question.

Prison Social Organization

Since the publication of Clemmer's study of a Midwest prison[6] in 1940 there has developed a rich body of scholarly literature on the social organization of the prison. Most of this research concerns the informal social organization of prisoners. Two questions dominate these research efforts: (1) the nature of prisoner organization, and (2) the origins of this organization. Some studies depict prisoner populations organized as collectivities; others characterize populations as organized into primary groups; and a few studies portray prisoners as unorganized. With regard to the second question some researchers view the prisoner subculture and social organization as emerging within the prison; others argue that inmate culture and social organization have their origins outside the prison. To a large extent the answers to these two questions are correlated. Those who portray prisoners as collectively organized in a symbiotic system are inclined to view this organization as indigenous to the prison. Those who portray prisoners as affiliated in primary groups usually argue that inmate culture is imported from outside the prison. In short, there are two models of inmate social organization: (1) a deprivation model and (2) an importation model.[7]

The Deprivation Model. The major premise of the deprivation model is that inmate culture and social organization are collective functional responses to the deprivations imposed by incarceration. Sykes and Messinger identified five such pains of imprisonment: loss of freedom, deprivation of material comfort, loss of autonomy, denial of heterosexual contact, and physical insecurity.[8] To this list McCorkle and Korn have added rejection by society.[9] Prisoners can never escape completely the impact of these deprivations, but inmate solidarity is one means by which the pain may be reduced for the greatest number. Thus, it is argued, there emerges within the prison an inmate culture, the major characteristic of which is a normative code of solidarity. The code enjoins prisoners to "do your own time," "don't rat," "don't bring heat."[10] These norms are articulated in a system of interdependent though not necessarily cohesive roles. "Real men" are those prisoners who exemplify the code in their prison behavior and enforce adherence to it. In opposition to "real men" are role types such as "merchants," "toughs," "fags," and "rats"—all of which stand in violation of one or more maxims of the inmate code.[11] Thus, the inmate social system stands in precarious balance between a collective solidarity founded upon conformity to shared norms and a state of complete disruption, a war of all against all.

Implicit in this model is a conception of the prison as a closed system, a total institution impermeable to influence from the outside. The inmate culture emerges through the interaction of prisoners within the walls and new prisoners are socialized into it.[12] Predisposing inmates to the socialization process is a ritual series of degradations that is part of the formal induction into the prison.[13] Through such defilements pre-prison identities are extinguished and a new identity, that of the convict, is conferred and continually affirmed.

Despite the hypothesis that prisoners are socialized into a pre-existing inmate culture, studies supporting the deprivation model have largely shown prisoner populations to be organized as collectivities rather than into primary groups. In Clemmer's study for example, only 18 percent of the population were affiliated in primary groups.[14] In Wheeler's study of socialization, only 43 percent of his sample were involved in primary groups.[15] Likewise, in four of the five institutions studied by Glaser there was a tendency for inmates to remain uninvolved in primary group relations,[16] and in a federal narcotics hospital studied by Tittle[17] less than half of the male patients reported having one or more good friends.

In sum, the deprivation model adopts a conception of the prison as a total institution. Life within the institution presents prisoners with a series of deprivations to which they adapt collectively by means of an indigenously developed code of solidarity. This code is articulated in a system of interdependent roles. While primary group affiliation may be present, the prevailing mode of organization is symbiotic rather than cohesive.

The Importation Model. A number of researchers have criticized what they regard as the restrictive scope of the deprivation model. While agreeing that inmate culture and social organization are adaptive responses to the problem of incarceration, these critics attack the conception of the prison as a closed system total institution. In essence, they argue that the quality of inmate adaptation is influenced by pre-prison experiences. From this perspective the existence of a well-developed and integrated inmate culture is an example of a latent culture.[18] It is one that has its origins and supports in groups outside the prison and is imported into the prison through the interaction of people from similar backgrounds in the face of common problems to which they must adapt.

Irwin and Cressey have provided the clearest statement of this position.[19] They argue that inmate culture is an accomodation among three diverse subcultural orientations: "thief," "convict," and "do right." Each of these orientations has its origins outside the prison. The "thief" subculture derives from the subculture of professional crime and extols the values of loyalty and trustworthiness. The "convict" orientation originates both in reform schools and the culture of the "hard core" lower class. The central value of this orientation is utilitarianism; "convicts" are oriented to achieving wealth, status, and power within the prison community. The "do right" orientation has its origin in the conventional values of the middle and working classes. In the prison it is characterized by an attempt to achieve the goals set for prisoners by the staff.

Irwin and Cressey hypothesize that in the typical prison the subcultural orientation of the "convict" is dominant, with those of "thief" and "do right" adjusting and accomodating to it.[20] As a result the prison population is organized as a congeries of cliques having diverse orientations and existing in some sort of balanced accomodation. Irwin, for example, has depicted convict social organization in California prisons in the following manner:

The convict population in California tends to be splintered. A few convicts orient themselves to the prison social system and assume roles in regard to the prison, and a few others withdraw completely, but the majority confine their association to one or two groups of convicts and attempt to disassociate themselves from the bulk of the population. These groups vary from small, close-knit primary groups to large casual groups.[21]

Additional support for an importation model is found in studies of prisons for women. Ward and Kassebaum characterized the female prisoners at Frontera, California as organized into primary groups and dyadic homosexual alliances, with little collective solidarity existing between groups.[22] At the Federal Reformatory for Women in Alderson, West Virginia, Giallombardo found the cornerstone of inmate organization to be pseudo-marriages linked together in an elaborate substitute kinship system.[23] Both studies interpret this form of adaptation as the result of prior socialization into the traditional female roles of wife and mother. It is the dispossession of these roles and the consequent absence of security, intimacy, and affection that women experience as the most deprivational aspect of confinement. Organization into dyadic homosexual alliances and close-knit primary groups evolves as a response to these pains. Thus, an ascriptive identity, sex, is viewed as structuring what is defined as deprivational about prison, and structuring the manner in which prisoners organize to alleviate these deprivations.

In contrast to the deprivation model, then, the importation model does not view the prison as a closed system total institution. It interprets inmate adaptations to imprisonment as conditioned by factors external to the prison. Within the prison inmates are organized into primary groups and cliques composed of prisoners sharing similar orientations, with little collective solidarity between groups.

Contradictions or Complements? The deprivation and importation models commonly are viewed as opposed models of inmate organization. But such a view may represent undue polarization. Rather than being contradictory, these models may in fact be complementary. Each may be a representation of the sources and form of inmate organization as it exists under different conditions. Prisons vary greatly in the balance of deprivation and control they impose upon inmates, and the balance of deprivation and control is a crucial condition in the deprivation model. As the argument runs, the greater the deprivation imposed and the more rigid and oppressive the authority to which inmates are subject, the more likely there is to emerge within the prison a normative code of solidarity. The converse of this argument is that the less harsh the deprivations and controls, the less likely it is that a code of solidarity will emerge. A worthy hypothesis, then, is that collective solidarity among prisoners is directly related to the degree of deprivation and control to which they are subject.

A low degree of deprivation and control is likely also to result in increased primary group affiliation. Humanitarian reform in prison usually includes such measures as extended and less supervised visiting privileges, less restrictions on access to the mass media, increased time for recreation, and the modification of prison uniform and hairstyles in the direction of styles current in the outside world. These and similar changes increase the permeability of the prison and facilitate the prisoners' continued attachments to external reference groups and their affiliation in cliques with other prisoners sharing similar orientations. In brief, lessened deprivation and control may weaken collective solidarity and simultaneously facilitate involvement in primary groups and continued attachments to reference groups external to the prison.

A close examination of the data presented in the few comparative studies reported in the literature provides support for this hypothesis. Berk's comparison of prisoner attitudes in three minimum security prisons varying in degree of their emphasis upon a treatment orientation revealed that prisoner attitudes toward the staff and program were the most positive in the treatment institution, the most negative in the custodial institution, and intermediate in the mixed goal institution.[24] Berk himself did not analyze differences among the institutions in the extent of primary group affiliation. A recomputation of data he presents, however, shows that 84 percent of the prisoners in the treatment institution received one or more sociometric friendship choices as compared to 71.5 percent in the mixed goal institution and to only 46.8 percent in the custodial institution.[25] Thus, if inmate attitudes toward staff are taken as indicators of collective solidarity, Berk's data are consistent with the hypothesis I have offered.

A similar pattern was observed by Street, Vinter, and Perrow in their comparison of inmate organization in six juvenile homes varying in the degree of their emphasis upon treatment. They found that collective solidarity as measured by loyalty to other inmates showed little variation by institution.[26] However, inmates in the treatment institutions had the most positive attitudes toward the staff and program, whereas those in the custodial institution had the most negative attitudes.[27] Further, inmates in the treatment institutions were the most highly involved in primary groups; those in the custodial institutions were the least involved.[28]

A study by Wilson compared staff-inmate relations and primary group affiliation among inmates in three units within one prison.[29] The units were characterized by different patterns of decision-making and degrees of deprivation. He reported that staff-inmate relations were most cooperative and primary group affiliations among prisoners were the most developed in the unit characterized by participative decision-making and high privileges. Prisoners in the unit characterized by bureaucratic decision-making and low privileges were reported as evincing the highest degree of alienation from the staff and having the lowest degree of primary group involvement.

Most recently, Tittle has reported on a study of inmate organization in a federal narcotics hospital having about as much deprivation and control as a minimum security prison.[30] Tittle characterizes inmate organization in this institution as weak and fragmentary. Both males and females were rather highly involved in primary group affiliation, and measures of opposition to staff and loyalty to other inmates indicated the presence of only a modest degree of collective solidarity.[31] Moreover, among the male prisoners collective solidarity and primary group affiliation were negatively associated, suggesting that at least for this segment of the population these are distinct forms of organization.[32] Further, while cohort analysis provided only limited support for the view that inmates were socialized into an inmate culture,[33] there was rather strong evidence indicating that pre-prison experiences, especially involvement in an addict subculture were determinants of inmate organization.[34]

In sum, evidence from the few comparative studies reported is consistent with the view that the deprivation and importation models are alternative representations of inmate social organization as it exists under different conditions. Conditions of maximum deprivation and control produce a symbiotic organization among the inmates characterized by high solidarity, interdependent roles, and low primary group cohesion. Decreased deprivation and control remove the impetus for collective solidarity and facilitate continued attachment to external reference groups and involvement in primary groups. Hence, under conditions of minimal deprivation and control inmate organization is characterized by low solidarity, limited interdependence, and high primary group cohesion.

Prison Reform and Race Relations

I noted above that the fact of racial differences is seldom mentioned in sociological studies of the prison, and I raised the question of whether this omission is an oversight of previous researchers or an indicator that racial differences are of little functional importance within the structure of the prison. The preceding review of studies on prisoner social organization suggests that the latter possibility may in fact be true, that the significance of race within the prison is a recent development brought about by the coincidence of prison reform and black nationalism. Before proceeding further, however, it is necessary to consider the sense in which the terms race and race relations are used by sociologists.

A Social Definition of Race. It has been common in the past to treat race relations as if they were a special and distinct form of human relationships. A perspective such as this, however, attributes an intrinsic social significance to a physical construct. Such a position is untenable. Comparative research clearly shows that the physical construct of race has no social significance in and of itself. In South Africa, for instance, race differences are the major axes of cleavage in a society ridden by racial conflict.[35] In contrast, racial differences are only one among many indicators of social class in parts of Latin America.[36] The ease with which the social significance of race may change was shown by Biesanz and Smith in their study of race relations in Panama and the Canal Zone.[37] On one side of the street, race relations were characterized by the segregation and discrimination common in the United States. It was found that people crossing from one side of the street to the other quickly adapted their behavior to conform with the prevailing mode of relations.

Cross-cultural variability in the social significance of race has prompted social scientists to adopt a social as opposed to a physical definition of the concept. Blumer has suggested that a workable concept of race for the social sciences is the following: "a class or group of human beings who are regarded and treated in social life as a distinct biological group with a common ancestry.[38] An acceptance of this or some similar definition of race leads to a conception of race relations as recurrent patterns of social interaction between groups, or individuals regarded as representatives of groups, which are defined as being biologically distinct and possessing a common ancestry.

Thus, whether or not a group constitutes a race in the physical sense is not the important question from the sociological point of view. What is important from a sociological perspective is whether a group is defined as a race by other groups with which it is in contact. Given this definition it is possible for race relations to exist between groups that are not in fact races in the physical sense. So, for example, Jews in the United States have been regarded as a race by a large segment of the Gentile population. Therefore, Jewish-Gentile relations in the United States may be regarded as race relations. Conversely, depending upon people's definitions, it is possible that ongoing relations between biologically distinct groups do not constitute race relations. Some writers, for example, maintain that Indian-Hispanic relations in many Latin American countries are more properly considered class relations than race relations. A similar situation may occur in custodially-oriented prisons.

Race in the Custodial Prison. Within a prison characterized by high deprivation and rigid, authoritarian control, the problems facing inmates may be so pressing and the range of available solutions so limited that the social significance of race is obscured by an overriding convict solidarity. Moreover, in a situation where prisoners regard themselves as a class united in their opposition to the staff, it is possible that the conflict will cause the staff to define themselves as a class united by their shared interest in controlling inmates. The interaction between staff and inmates thus may be structured in terms of perspectives derived from identities defined by reference to positions within the prison, rather than in terms of perspectives having their origins outside the prison. That is to say that, under conditions of high deprivation and regimentation, the structure of social relationships in the prison may conceivably be between "hacks" and "cons" and among "cons" rather than between blacks and whites.

As race is seldom mentioned in studies characterizing prisoner populations as collectively organized as a result of high deprivation, there is little basis for evaluating the social significance of race in prisons. Clemmer, however, after observing some structural differentiation by race among the prisoners he studied, noted that race prejudice existed only in the mildest form.[39] Moreover, his finding is consistent with social psychological research into the effects of both superordinate goals and shared threats upon prejudice and its expression in behavior.[40] Finally, it is consistent with observations of the decreased social significance of racial identities and the egalitarian patterns of race relations in military combat units.[41]

Prison Reform and Black Nationalism. The social structure of many, if not most, prisons today is quite different from that of the prisons studied by Clemmer in the 1930s and by Sykes in the 1950s. Since the wave of prison riots in the early 1950s, prison systems across the country have been moving from a custodial to a treatment orientation. In most cases this has not meant the abandonment of punitive and custodial goals in favor of a treatment ideal, however. Rather, the attempt to implement treatment goals has proceeded within the context of existing custodial structures through the introduction of measures such as indeterminate sentences, group therapy, academic and vocational education programs, work release programs and the increased use of probation and parole, along with extended visiting and recreational privileges. Such changes are best considered humanitarian reforms rather than treatment. At best they create conditions more conducive to treatment, but they do not constitute treatment in and of themselves.[42] Yet such changes do indeed have an impact upon the structure of prisons in the direction of alleviating deprivation, lessening regimentation, and facilitating contact with the outside world. And it is precisely such changes, I have argued, that erode convict solidarity and facilitate the emergence among prisoners of a fragmented social organization composed of numerous cliques with diverse normative and behavioral orientations.[43]

The recent era of prison reform has also been an era in which minority group resources have been mobilized in pursuit of political, economic, and social equality. It is the coincidence of these movements that has increased the social significance of race within the prison and altered the meanings associated with staff and inmate relations, increasingly transforming them into race relations.

Nowhere is the impact of the coincidence of these movements more evident than in the formation within prisons of religious and cultural activist groups such as the Black Muslims. Through extended litigation over the past twenty-five years, black prisoners have forced prison administrators to recognize the Muslims as a religion, and have secured rights to hold Muslim services within the prison, to have access to Muslim ministers even if the ministers are ex-felons, to receive Muslim literature, to wear Muslim medallions, and to have prison menus accomodate to the strictures of Muslim dietary practices.[44] The success of the Muslims has had consequences for freedom of speech and assembly within the prison far beyond the recognition of that particular religion, however. Largely as a result of the Muslim litigation, First Amendment rights have been extended to non-religious groups in prisons so long as they do not present a clear and present danger to institutional security; the burden of proving a clear and present danger falls upon prison administrations.[45] Thus, not only the Muslims, but also many other religious, cultural, and political groups are found within prisons today.

The existence of such groups within the prison increases the salience of racial and ethnic identities in at least two ways. First, conflicts between prison administrators and inmates associated with their establishment and continued operation stimulates racial awareness.[46] Second, once established, such groups serve as a base for the importation into the prison of perspectives having their origins outside the prison, and for articulating these perspectives in a manner giving a new meaning to imprisonment. As a result of their activities, even prisoners who never become formal members of the groups may nonetheless come to define themselves as political prisoners. As George Jackson, just before he was killed, was quoted as saying: these groups represent an organized "attempt to transform the black criminal mentality into a black revolutionary mentality."[47] To the extent that such attempts are successful, social relationships within the prison will be redefined as race relations.

Thus, while under conditions of high deprivation and control, race may be of minimal significance within the prison; as deprivation and control are decreased, race is likely to assume greater social significance. Today, as a result of the coincidence of humanitarian reforms within prisons and racial-ethnic social movements outside the prison, the structure of social relationships within prisons is increasingly taking on the character of race relations. It is with the nature and implications of this change within one prison that this study is concerned.

Data and Methods[48]

The data upon which this report is based were gathered by means of participant observation over a fifteen month period from October 1970 through December 1971 at Eastern Correctional Institution (ECI), a small state prison in a highly urban and industrial Eastern state. While there were a number of avenues into the prison open to me, most approaches—such as becoming a staff member or an unpaid volunteer in an inmate organization—had the potential disadvantage of aligning me with one or more factions within the prison community. Thus, I decided to enter the prison on my own and establish my identity as an interested observer writing a book about prison life. The strategy I adopted was, with the consent of the administration, to enter the more public areas of the prison such as the shops and the yard, to introduce myself and the project to prisoners I met in those areas, and to wait to be invited by them into the more private areas of prison life. Quite to my surprise most prisoners I met took an immediate interest in the project, readily introduced me to friends, and actively sought me out on later visits. Within the span of one month, then,I was able to meet a large proportion of the prisoner population, and to secure their tentative and somewhat suspicious cooperation.

To establish myself as a neutral observer of prison life, I had to develop somewhat different relationships with each of the different groups within the prison. There were two reasons for this. First, were my own status attributes. Among other things, I am free, white, and college educated. These attributes were of differential significance to each of the groups being studied. To the white prisoners, I was first of all free and interested in prisons; to the black prisoners, I was most obviously white; to the staff I was a "college student" and potential critic. With each group, then, there existed somewhat different impediments to interaction that had to be overcome by different tactics. Second, the groups themselves were in conflict, and as a result held conflicting behavioral expectations of my role. For example, where the inmates initially saw me as a potential ally in attacking the institution, the staff saw me as a threat for the same reason. In an attempt to minimize role conflict of this sort, I temporally segregated my relationships with each group, becoming involved first with the white inmates, then with the black inmates, and lastly with the staff.

Social Relations

White Prisoners. As I came to learn later, my initial contacts among the white prisoners were with low-ranking, marginal members of the prisoner population. Within a short time, however, my continued presence in the institution drew the attention of certain white leaders, and I was invited to meet with a group of sixteen white prisoners selected by the editor of the prison newspaper. In the meeting I explained my interest as an intent to write a book about how men adjust to the problems posed by imprisonment. As a result of this meeting, I was able to develop cooperative relations with six prisoners who were leaders of various inmate organizations. Over the next several weeks these prisoners acted as my sponsors, showing me around the institution, introducing me to prisoners, explaining my project as they interpreted it, and at times vouching for my trustworthiness. On a typical day during this period I would enter the prison, meet one or more of these individuals, and accompany them as they went about their daily routine. Gradually my network of relations expanded to the point where I was at least acquainted with members of most of the more enduring cliques in the white population. Throughout the study, however, my closest relationships among the white prisoners remained the relations with these six leaders and with another seven prisoners whom I developed as key informants, and who throughout the study provided me with numerous tactical suggestions as well as information about events I was either unable or not permitted to observe.

Black Prisoners. In contrast to my entry into white groups, my initial contacts with the blacks were with the leaders of the Afro-American Society. These contacts were made by introduction from white leaders of the prisoner organizations. For a considerable period of time, my relations with the black leaders remained cordial but distant. I explained my purpose to them as I had explained it to the white prisoners, and on occasion I spoke to them to get the black view of problems in the prison. However, black prisoners never sought me out as did white prisoners, and my involvement with white prisoners made it impossible for me to spend any appreciable time with black prisoners. After beimg in the prison for about four months, it had become clear to me that the development of close relations with the black population would require a disengagement from my white associates. I began a gradual process of disengagement at about this time, and my last three months of observation in the prison were spent almost entirely in the company of black prisoners.

Race, however, proved to be a more formidable barrier to interaction than did the distinction between being free and being a prisoner. I found myself to be more uncomfortable in my relations with the rank-and-file black inmates than I had been with the whites. Nor were these prisoners comfortable in my presence. As more than one black leader told me: ". . . the only whites they ever known have been cops, school teachers, and parole officers and they don't know how to relate to you." In retrospect, it appears to me that I was able to achieve only a limited acceptance among the rank-and-file black prisoners, although I came to know most of them and could freely move into their gatherings.

My relations with four or five black leaders, however, were among the most intimate I developed. One measure of the rapport was their confidence in me concerning the perpetration of a felonious assault in the prison. In the middle of a conversation about racial conflict three black leaders admitted to me that it was they, and not a white inmate, who had assaulted a black prisoner causing him to be hospitalized for a concussion and severe facial lacerations.

The rapport I was able to develop with this small group of black leaders was due largely to their dedication to self-improvement through reading and to our common interest in broad structural changes in American society. Hours were spent with them in the discussion of such matters as the state of national politics, the need for racial change, the possibilities of a black revolution, and ideological differences between writers such as George Jackson and Eldridge Cleaver. While I was often in disagreement with the views held by these black leaders, my genuine interest in and knowledge of such matters created a bond between us. And by means of such discussions I was able to gain insight into their perspectives on the prison, conflicts among the blacks, and eventually information on prisoner life comparable to what I received from white informants. Thus, while my contacts with black prisoners were not as extensive as were my contacts with white prisoners, I was able to gather comparable information through intensive contacts with a few black leaders.

Staff. Prior to entering the prison, I had decided that extensive and visible contact with the staff would jeopardize my ability to develop trust with the inmates. Thus, I avoided extended conversations with the staff unless I was in the company of one or more inmates respected by the others. When officers sought to engage me in conversation, as they often did, I was courteous but always sought to keep such interludes as brief as possible. There were other opportunities to talk with the officers, however, and I used these as fully as possible. Once or twice a week I ate in the officers' dining room, which is located outside the prison. During evening visits I would spend an hour or more in the captain's office having coffee with officers after the prisoners had been locked in their cells. Through these means I was able to become friendly with a good number of officers, and after leaving the prison I was able to tape record interviews with nine of them, the average interview lasting four hours.

Data Collection

Observation. Morris and Charlotte Schwartz have described two ideal typical observational roles: (1) the passive participant observer who minimizes his interaction with those he is observing, and (2) the active participant observer who maximizes his interaction with the research subjects by integrating his role with others in the setting.[49] In terms of the continuum established by these ideal types, the observational role I adopted was primarily that of an active participant. I dressed in clothing similar to that worn by prisoners, spoke prisoner argot, and engaged in the full round of institutionally sanctioned activities. So active was my participation in this sense that I was at times mistaken for a prisoner by prisoners and staff members whom I had not encountered previously. On numerous occasions, however, I adopted a passive role, although for only brief periods of time, to make intensive observations of selected settings and activities.

My early observations were essentially mapping operations.[50] As I entered settings in the prison I was careful to note their most salient physical features and later made sketches of each setting. As I met new prisoners I took note of who introduced me to them and who accompanied them, thus constructing maps of informal clique structures. Similarly, I noted both the formal and informal time schedules operative in the prison. During the first month of fieldwork my observations were almost entirely of this nature. Gradually, however, my observations came to be more selective. On the basis of past observations and information received from prisoners and staff, questions arose concerning differences in interracial interaction by setting and event. Answers to these questions often required a period of intensive observation. So, for example, I spent many Friday evenings in or near the restrooms of the auditorium in which movies were shown, charting movement in and out of the restrooms in an effort to determine the existence of a pattern of temporal segregation. At various times I made similar series of observations in the shops, the cell blocks, the dining hall, and at football and basketball games, parties, and banquets.

Interviews. As has been pointed out by Schatzman and Strauss, the distinction between participant observation and interviewing is rather arbitrary and artificial.[51] Of necessity, participant observation entails some type of interviewing, at least in the form of casual conversations. In the course of this study I made use of three types of interviews: (1) group discussions, (2) conversational interviews, and (3) formal, "unstructured" interviews.

A large amount of data was gathered by participating with inmates in spontaneous discussions about past, present, and future events. Such discussions provided insight into the meaning that events held for the prisoners, a comparison of racial differences in meanings and focal concerns, as well as factual information about the events being discussed. At times I was a passive participant in such discussions. At other times, however, I directed the discussion into areas that interested me by interjecting questions at appropriate points.

The interviewing technique used most frequently was the conversational interview.[52] These interviews served virtually the same purpose as the group discussions, but differed from group discussions in two respects. First, the interaction was usually between myself and only one inmate. Second, in these interviews I was always an active participant probing for quite specific information. Unlike formal interviews, however, conversational interviews took place in natural settings within the prison, were not pre-arranged, and were structured only by my conception of the information I desired. Further, in the course of a conversational interview, I often shared with the interviewee personal information about my own life as I probed for data concerning his life.

In September 1971, after being in the prison for a year, I withdrew for a two week period, offering the excuse that I was going on vacation. During this period, I reviewed my field diary and certain portions of my field notes, noting areas where I needed more material and the identities of staff members and prisoners who I believed were in a position to provide this information and would be willing to provide it. Matching the topics with the identities of prospective informants, I planned interviews to secure a complete coverage of the information I sought. Twenty-one interviews ranging from one to five hours in length were eventually completed: five with white inmates, seven with black inmates, and nine with staff members. The interviews with prisoners were conducted in the prison chaplains' office, as my key informants confided to me that this was the only office they believed to be free of electronic listening devices. The interviews with staff members were conducted in their homes and were tape recorded.

Documents. A third source of data was documents of various types. In the five years prior to my research, the prison had been evaluated by several different commissions. Before entering the prison, I reviewed the reports as well as newspaper accounts of the disturbances that had prompted the investigations. These documents provided me with a wealth of background material about the prison in general and about race relations in particular.

Midway through the research, I completed a census of the prisoner population by taking the names of inmates from the domicile records maintained in each wing. In the following weeks I read the file on each inmate, noting basic information such as race, age, offense, length of sentence, prior convictions, and the like. These data provided me with a means of verifying certain hypotheses concerning compositional differences between the white and black prisoner populations.

A third set of documents were disciplinary reports and dispositions.

From July through November 1971 I spent every Friday evening in the office of the Deputy Warden copying the disciplinary reports that had been submitted during the week and the action taken on the report by the Disciplinary Board, which met on Fridays. These data form the statistical basis for the analysis of race and staff-inmate relations in Chapter 6.

In addition to these documents, I was able to secure from informants essays and descriptions of events that occurred in my absence. Also, I secured staff reports and court transcripts on several of the crises that took place during the period of the study. In sum, the fifteen months of fieldwork yielded a massive amount of field notes, transcripts of interviews, and statistical and documentary material of different types.

Data Recording

Unrecorded information does not become data. The full meaning of this rather simple statement did not become clear to me until after the research had begun. My initial impulse was to remain in the prison for as long as I could, observing and experiencing as much as I could. I soon learned, however, that after four or five hours in the prison my ability to recall information diminished rapidly. Moreover, as it took longer to record data than it did to gather it, an eight hour period of observation did not leave sufficient time and energy for accurate and detailed recording. Thus, after a month or so in the prison, I limited my time there to between three and five hours per day, alternating among mornings, afternoons, and evenings. Data were recorded immediately after returning from the prison or, in the case of evening observations, on the following morning. Throughout the study two types of records were maintained: (1) field notes, and (2) a field journal or diary.

The field notes were detailed descriptions of what I had observed or heard during a period of observation. Basically, they were journalistic descriptions of who did or said what with whom, where it occurred, and who else was present. To the extent possible, these experiences were recorded verbatim, in the order in which they had occurred, and with no interpretation. I did not take notes in the prison, but immediately upon leaving the prison I would sit in my car for a half-hour or so and reconstruct my experience during the previous three to five hours, making notes of key words and phrases in a small notebook. Upon returning home, I worked this rough outline into a more detailed outline from which I typed the complete transcript, one original and three carbon copies.

Once a week the notes were reviewed, clipped, and sorted into three files: (1) a chronological file, (2) a concrete file, and (3) an analytic file.[53] As the title implies, the chronological file ordered the field notes by months and by weeks within months. The concrete file consisted of folders on key individuals, places, and activities within the prison. In the analytic file, the notes were sorted according to theoretical concepts—for example, "institutional change" or "black solidarity."

A separate set of notes was maintained in the form of a field diary. Included within the diary were both methodological and analytic notes.[54] Methodological notes consisted of my personal feelings on different days, my impressions of the reactions of others to me, critiques of my tactics, evaluations of how my presence may have affected an event or to what degree the report of an informant may be biased, and lists of tasks to be performed in the future. By comparison, the analytic notes consisted of questions that emerged in the process of gathering and recording data, tentative hypotheses, and more general formulations of prospective theoretical models. In addition to providing a check on the quality of the data collected, then, the diary also provided a bridge between the collection of data and the analysis of data.

Analysis of the Data

The complexity of qualitative data in conjunction with the non-standardized nature of the fieldwork enterprise have precluded the development of operationalized procedures for data analysis. Consequently, reports based on fieldwork frequently are characterized as impressionistic accounts, as if they represented nothing more than journalism. Fieldworkers react to such attributions with a sense of moral indignation, not only because they have spent a year or more of their lives collecting data under arduous circumstances, but also because they realize that their analyses were based upon the same logic as that underlying quantitative analysis. In contrast to survey research, fieldwork is more inductive than deductive. Nonetheless, fieldwork also entails the development of concepts and indices, the elaboration and evaluation of hypotheses, and the incorporation of findings into theoretical models.

Concepts. As a sociologist having done extensive reading of the research on prisons and in the field of race relations, I entered the prison with a body of concepts I assumed to be relevant to an understanding of race relations in that setting. Among these concepts were the following: conflict, cooperation, segregation, avoidance, integration, discrimination, organizational goals, solidarity, and power. These and other concepts provided me with a set of analytic questions. To answer the questions, it was necessary to develop indices of the concepts in terms of relevant data accessible to me. So, for example, the concept of organizational goals naturally raises the question: what type of institution is this? Is it a treatment institution, a custodial institution, or a mixed goal institution? For an answer I resorted to numerical measures drawn from documents such as budgetary statements and tables of authorized personnel. In similar fashion, I developed indices—sometimes quantitative but usually qualitative—of each of the concepts I brought with me into the institution. For example, one index of solidarity was the extent to which prisoners shared goods bought at the canteen; and segregation was measured by observations of spatial positioning in different settings.

Probably all people engaged in continuous interaction within distinctive social settings develop their own set of concepts to distinguish among things, persons, and events within those settings. Such concepts I refer to as empirical concepts. The language of prisoners is replete with a repertoire of empirical concepts: "hacks" refers to guards; "lugged" denotes being reduced or placed in segregation; "ratting" is the term applied to passing information to the guards; and "pitching" and "catching" respectively refer to the active and passive roles in homosexual activity. In addition to providing insight into the perspectives of prisoners, empirical concepts such as these point to patterns of activity likely to prove fruitful for analysis, and may also be used in the development of indices of social structure. Thus, the concern of prisoners with being "lugged" led me to use this process, operationalized through records of the disciplinary board, as an index of racial differences in staff-inmate relations. Similarly, the perceived incidence of "ratting," the number of prisoners regarded as "rats," and the severity of negative sanctions for "ratting" provide, I believe, valid and reliable indicators of solidarity. Finally, maps of prisoner social structure were developed by having informants place prisoners in one or another category of social types[55] identified in the argot of inmates.

A third category of concepts were developed in the course of the research to include properties and processes found to be significant for the analysis but for which no label was supplied by either the discipline or the population under study. An example of an analytic concept is a distinction I made among the black prisoners between "revolutionaries" and "half-steppers." "Revolutionaries" are black prisoners who exhibit a behavioral commitment to the ideals and goals of black nationalism. "Half-steppers," by comparison, verbally espouse these goals but deviate from them in their behavior through an involvement in drugs, homosexuality, and other activities. The black prisoners themselves make no such distinctions: black prisoners are either "brothers," loosely defined as members of the Afro-American Society, or "toms," non-members. Presumably to distinguish openly between "brothers" who are committed to black nationalism and those who are not would endanger the racial solidarity that the black leaders were attempting to build at the time. Nonetheless, such a distinction was vital to understanding the processes of conflict and change within the black population during the study.

Propositions. Numerous hypotheses were developed in the course of the fieldwork. These might be referred to as working hypotheses:[56] propositions of varying levels of abstraction that emerge from data collected and that serve to direct further data collection. On the most concrete level, I developed propositions such as "the majority of sexual assaults involve black aggressors and white victims," and "in comparison to white prisoners, black prisoners receive harsher penalties from the disciplinary board for similar offenses." Each of these hypotheses was developed on the basis of information gathered in group discussions and conversational interviews. Later information bearing on them was collected by analysis of records of the disciplinary boards, accounts of key informants, and by questioning staff members and prisoners selected for formal interviewing.

On a more theoretical level, I developed several hypotheses, including the following: "Humanitarian reform in the prison precipitates a decrease in convict solidarity among the white prisoners and facilitates the development of racial solidarity among the black prisoners." This proposition emerged from information gathered in group discussions, conversational interviews, and my observations of differences in the behavior of black and white prisoners. While it is not possible to actually test the causal relation posited in this proposition, retrospective accounts of long-term prisoners and staff members lend it a high degree of plausibility, as does the cumulative body of research done in other prisons.

It was possible to test other propositions, however, For example, on February 9, 1971 I wrote in the field diary that "a change in the leadership of the Afro-American Society will probably lead to increased internal conflict and perhaps conflict with the staff and the whites as well." This predictive hypothesis was based upon my observations that the high solidarity among the black prisoners was grounded in the perspectives of black nationalism which were articulated by a small group of "revolutionaries." In August 1971, the "revolutionaries" were displaced as leaders of the organization by "half-steppers." By the end of August, many programs of the organization had ceased to function; and conflict had increased, as could be seen from an increase in fights among the black prisoners and confrontations between black inmates and the staff. In November, confrontations with the staff reached a point where the administration deemed it necessary to transfer black leaders to other prisons.

Models. A third level of analysis was the development of models to conceptualize large portions of the material. Models were developed throughout the research and elaborated in analytic memos in the field diary. These were not fully articulated, however, until I left the prison and began a concerted analysis of the material, systematically relating it to sociological theory. So, for example, while in the prison I had observed that the officers were reluctant to perform their custodial functions, and I had hypothesized that their deviance was related to the process of humanitarian reform. It was not until after I had left the prison, however, that I was able to conceptualize their deviance—withdrawal from role performance—as a behavioral adaptation to an anomic situation created by conflicting organizational goals. Similarly, while in the prison I was well aware that certain activities were characterized by racial segregation and avoidance and that others were characterized by contact and cooperation. While in the prison I was however, more concerned with documenting the characteristics of various activities than with explaining them. Thus, it was not until I attempted to find a basis for differentiating among activities characterized by avoidance and those characterized by cooperation that I began to think in terms of the focal concerns of inmates and to relate this conceptualization to the theory of superordinate goals.

Summary

As there has been no previous study of race relations in this prison, this research was undertaken as an exploratory case study. The purpose of the research is to present an analytic description of race relations in one prison, identifying the conditions that maintain the structure, and thereby to generate hypotheses for further comparative research. To accomplish these goals, a flexible and open-ended research design was employed. Data were collected over a fifteen-month period by means of participant observation, formal and informal interviewing, and the analysis of pertinent documents. As data were collected and recorded, they were subjected to a preliminary analysis from which emerged analytic questions and working hypothesis that served to guide further data collection. Thus, throughout the research concepts and indices were developed, working hypotheses formulated and evaluated, and the findings finally incorporated into models at different levels of abstraction.

The early part of this chapter set forth what may be regarded as the central theme or hypothesis of this report: that race relations in the prison today are the result of both prison reform and black nationalism. The following chapters are organized around this theme. Chapter 2 presents a detailed description of the prison social structure. Chapters 3 through 5 are concerned with the informal collective adaptations to the prison structure made both by the staff and the inmates. These chapters focus on how reforms have decreased the power of the staff, and on racial differences in informal social organization among the prisoners. Chapters 6 through 8 present an analysis of the influence of race upon staff-inmate relations and relations among the prisoners. Of specific concern in these chapters is how racial differences in the collective adaptations made by prisoners affect intergroup relations. Finally, Chapter 9 is an analysis of how the structure of race relations was disrupted by one external event, the riot at Attica.

2 **The Prison**

Eastern Correctional Institution (ECI) is composed of three main facilities graded by custody. Set atop a small hill overlooking a major interstate highway is the medium-minimum security unit, which houses approximately 150 prisoners. Maximum security, containing a population of about 300,[a] is located one-half mile to the west. A small work-release cottage with a population of 50 is situated one-half mile to the northwest of the maximum security unit. For most purposes, each of these spatially separated units operates as a distinct entity. Each is administered by a Deputy Warden and has its own complement of staff. Inmates are classified and reclassified from one unit to another, but on a day-to-day basis there is little contact or communication among the three populations. For these reasons, and because it is the largest and most contained, I focused my research efforts on maximum security.

Physical Setting

Maximum security was built in 1878 and its physical structure reflects the premise of nineteenth century penology: inmates are to be punished and cannot be reformed until their spirits are broken. Constructed out of gray fieldstone, it resembles a decaying medieval fortress. An old country house extending out from the center of the front wall adds to this impression. Formerly the Warden's residence, this structure (1) now houses most of the administrative offices.[b] Directly behind the house, set in the center of the wall and rising 50 feet above it, is a large rotunda. On either side of the rotunda are two wings that at once constitute a massive front wall and house the men they confine. At each intersection of the walls is a stone tower manned by an armed guard.

Entrance to the institution is secured only by passing through three electronically controlled gates in the central rotunda. The third gate opens into a small hallway known as the "Rear Hall" (2). This is the nerve center through which all official communications pass, and from which all orders

[a]The institution also has a pre-trial detention unit. Of the approximately 300 men in maximum security on a given day, 200 are sentenced and 100 are awaiting trial. These two populations are kept segregated from each other, and the concern of this study is with the approximately 200 sentenced prisoners.

[b]Numbers in parentheses refer to Figure 2-1 p. 24.

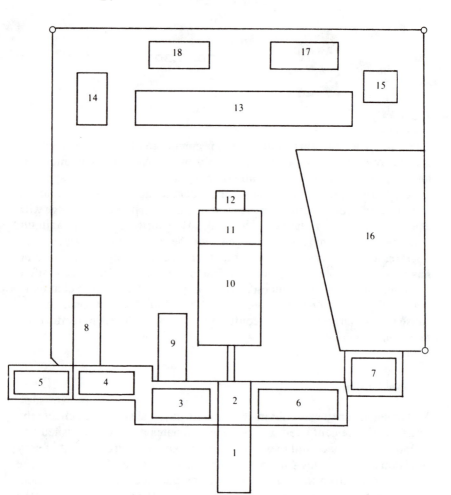

Key

1. Administrative Offices
2. Rear Hall
3. Upper South State Block
4. Lower South State Block
5. Awaiting Trial and Admission and Orientation
6. North State Wing
7. Behavioral Conditioning and Protective Custody Unit
8. "New Building"

9. Hospital
10. Inmates' Dining Hall
11. Kitchen
12. Officers' Coffee Shop
13. Industrial Building
14. Carpenter Shop
15. Machine Shop
16. Inmate Recreation Field
17. Basketball Court
18. Volleyball Court

Figure 2-1. Map of the Prison

are issued. Located here are the offices of the Deputy Warden, the Superior Officer for each shift, and the clerks who maintain an accurate record of all who enter, leave, or remain within the institution.

Two thick steel doors bar passage from the Rear Hall to the wings. One moves through these doors into a Kafkaesque world of dim lights, long corridors, metallic echoes, stale air, and dirty drab green walls. This is home for the men confined at ECI. Here they live in single-man cells arranged in blocks set in the center of the wing and rising 40 feet to the ceiling. The largest wing, South Wing, has two of these blocks (3,4). The smaller wing, North Wing (6), has only one.

At the rear of South Wing are two more steel doors. These segregate men awaiting trial and those undergoing admission and orientation (5) from sentenced prisoners. A similar area behind North Wing (7) is used for protective custody and behavioral conditioning: i.e., punitive segregation. If anything, conditions in these areas are more dismal than those just described. Cells are smaller and many amenities granted the general population are not permitted. Prisoners in these areas are confined to enforced idleness in a prison within a prison.

For most inmates, however, the cell, or "room" as it is called, serves mainly as place to sleep and rest. Each day presents an unchanging pattern of confinement, release, and reconfinement. Prisoners are released at 8 A.M. to eat and go to work, locked in at noon for a count, released at 1 P.M. for work, locked in at 4 P.M. for a count, released at 4:30 P.M. for recreation, and locked in at 9 P.M. for the night. Thus are days passed in a steady, monotonous rhythm.

The hours outside the cell are spent working or in recreation. Most of the work performed at ECI is directly concerned with institutional maintenance or production for the state. The largest number of inmates are employed in the Industrial Building (13), a massive two-story structure situated in the center of the yard. The first floor of this building houses the laundry and the license plate shop; a print shop, garment shop, and vocational training area are located on the second floor. All of these shops are open so as to facilitate surveillance by the custodians. On any given day some 100 inmates are employed in running presses, wash tubs, furnaces, paint sprayers, printing machines, sewing machines, and allied equipment. The impact is one of deafening noise, dirt, heat, and confusion.

From late May until early October prisoners are allowed recreation in the yard from 4:30 P.M. until dark. Between North Wing and the Industrial Building is a field (16) used for softball, baseball, football, and soccer, but adequate for none. Teams playing football must change positions frequently as the field is only 50 yards long. Behind the Industrial Building are a volleyball (17) and basketball court (18). These courts are scenes of constant activity, but the nature of the games precludes their use by more than 20 or 25 inmates at a time. Except for several benches and picnic tables at which inmates may play checkers or chess, these are the only outdoor recreational facilities. For most prisoners outdoor recreation, "yard time" in the language of the prison, consists of "tripping the yard" and fantasizing about what it is like to be free.

Still, "yard time" is highly valued by the inmates. The high valuation accorded it can only be understood by reference to its counterpart, "barn time," indoor recreation during the winter months. The only indoor recreational facilities are located in the "New Building" (8), a small structure built in 1956. The "New Building" contains several classrooms, a library and a cheesebox gym with two pool tables, a ping pong table, a set of weights, a punching bag, and an undersized handball court. For most inmates "barn time" consists of "hanging out" or "tripping the wings," talking and catching bugs in Dixie cups. Many just prefer to stay in their cells.

Formal Organization

ECI is only one facility within a State Department of Corrections. As shown in Figure 2.2, responsibility for the operation of the institution is vested in the office of a Warden, who is responsible to the Director of Corrections. Within the prison there exists a clear division of labor between the Warden and the Assistant Warden. The concerns of the Warden are largely broad policy-making and relations with external agencies and groups that have an interest in the prison. These agencies and groups include the Department of Corrections, the Office of the Governor, the Legislature, the State Budget Office, other law enforcement agencies, and a variety of interest groups. The concerns of the Assistant Warden are largely internal to the prison. It is the Assistant Warden who is responsible for the routine administration of the prison, and it is to the Assistant Warden that all department and division administrators within the prison are responsible.

The major administrative units within the prison are the three separate facilities graded by custody: maximum security, medium-minimum security, and work release. Each of these facilities is directed by a Deputy Warden (or the equivalent) and is organized in a quasi-military fashion. For example, in maximum security there are 103 correctional officers divided among three work shifts. Each work shift is commanded by a captain; each of the two day shifts has two lieutenants, the late night shift has one.

ECI performs a number of functions in addition to incarceration. It must administer its own budget, produce goods for use by other state agencies, maintain elaborate records on those confined, and provide both mainte-

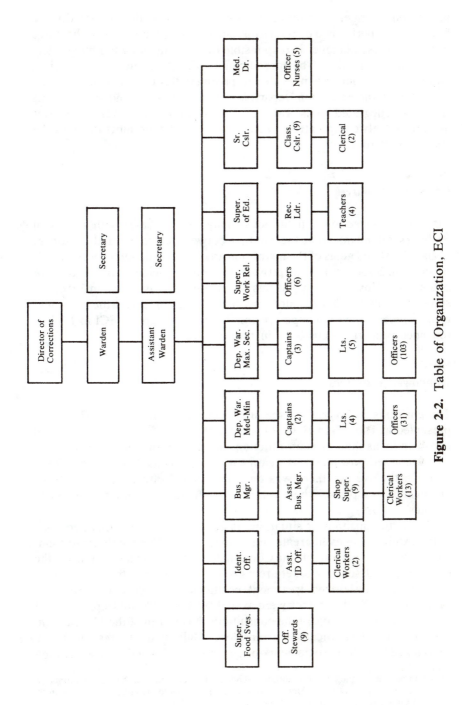

Figure 2-2. Table of Organization, ECI

nance and treatment services for the prisoner population. These diverse functions are performed by numerous small administrative units: the office of the Business Manager is responsible for administering the budget and organizing production. The Identification Officer maintains the records, and various services are provided to prisoners through the Classification Department, the Education Department, and the hospital and food services unit. As is suggested by the Table of Organization, these diverse functions are only loosely coordinated by means of their common supervision by the Assistant Warden.

Goals and Resources

Like many correctional institutions today, ECI is beset with structural problems attendant upon the conflict between custodial and treatment goals. The stated goals of the institution are "to provide security standards to safeguard society and to provide the most efficient rehabilitation of prisoners." However, beyond this statement of goals, made in 1956, the state has provided few resources with which to implement the treatment goal. As measured by manpower and financial resources, ECI in 1971-72 remained primarily a custodial institution.

Manpower Resources

The positions authorized by the state legislature for ECI in 1971-72 are presented in Table 2-1.[c] Fully 70 percent of the staff positions authorized had custody as their primary function. In comparison only 9.8 percent of the authorized positions had treatment or training as their primary function. On the average there was one correctional officer for every three inmates. By comparison there was only one treatment worker for every 21 inmates.

The actual manpower situation, as compared to the authorized positions, exhibited an even greater imbalance. Several key authorized treatment positions, for example the Coordinator of Education/Training and the one authorized social worker, remained vacant during the entire year. None of the authorized treatment positions were for psychiatrists or psychologists. Such services were available from the State Department of Health, but only on a part-time consultative basis. Ten of the 21 treatment workers were Classification Counselors. Only two of these had any specialized training in social work or psychology. While theoretically they

[c]The numbers in this table refer to authorized positions. At the time of the study a number of these positions were not filled. Hence the numbers in this table are larger than those in the Table of Organization which showed only positions actually filled.

Table 2-1
Authorized Positions at ECI for 1971-72 by Function

Function	Number	Percent	Inmate: Staff Ratio[a]
Custody	167	70.4%	2.8
Administration	47	19.8	10.0
Treatment	23	9.8	20.5
Total	237	100.0%	2.0

[a]The ratio is based upon an inmate population of 471, the average daily population for the last six months of 1971.

Table 2-2
Authorized Expenditures at ECI for 1971-72 by Function

Function	Amount	Percent
Custody	$1,735,636	54.2%
Administration	927,017	29.0
Treatment	150,559	4.7
Other[a]	387,174	12.1
Total	$3,200,386	100.0%

[a]Inmate salaries, employee benefits and debt service.

are treatment workers who are to "deal with inmate problems," the only problems with which they become involved are rather concrete and specific unrelated to underlying attitudes and values—phone calls, assistance in locating a job for parole, etc. For the most part, the job of the Classification Counselor involves the gathering of information on newly arrived inmates or inmates about to meet the parole board, and the preparation of summaries of this material. By way of manpower resources, then, the state in 1971-72 had allocated little with which an administrator might develop a treatment program.

Financial Resources

Nor did ECI receive much financial support from the state for treatment programs. The data presented in Table 2-2 point up this fact. At least as far as ECI is concerned, there is considerable truth to the dictum that prisons exist more for the benefit of their employees than for the benefit of inmates. In 1971-72, the funds allocated to ECI amounted to $3,200,386. Over half of this amount ($1,642,671) was for the salaries of the correctional officers alone. By contrast, only 4.7 percent of the authorized expenditures ($150,559) was for treatment purposes, and 93.4 percent of this amount was for the salaries of the treatment workers. Only $10,000, or a mere 0.3

percent of the total authorized budget, was allocated for the operation of treatment or training programs. These funds were to be used for the purchase of sorely needed educational and recreational equipment.

These figures refer only to positions and funds allocated to ECI by the state, however. In 1971, the prison received a grant of $160,000 from the federal government under the Manpower Development and Training Act (MDTA) to establish vocational training programs in drafting and printing. Even with the addition of these funds and the five positions for the program, however, ECI remained oriented predominantly to the single goal of custodial control.

Compromise: Humanitarian Reform

The social structure of an organization is only partially determined by the availability of resources to achieve specific goals. Goals themselves may affect the structure of an organization. They are mandates for action and provide administrators with an umbrella of legitimacy for decision-making of various sorts. Thus, the mere presence of a formally stated goal, even in the absence of resources to facilitate its attainment, may effect organizational change by legitimizing decisions that alter the nature of the internal structure of social relationships. With goals as diverse and contradictory as custody and treatment, this is especially likely to be true.

Implicit in the custodial goals of retribution, protection and deterrence is the assumption that prisoners are willfully evil and dangerous men. Translated into organizational terms these goals prescribe a rigidly authoritarian social structure.[1] Decision-making is highly centralized and governed by the concern for security and internal order. The staff are organized in a quasi-military hierarchy. Status distinctions between staff and inmates are sharply drawn and relations between the two are authoritarian and impersonal. The function of the staff is to enforce rigidly sets of rules serving to regulate even the most minute aspects of inmate behavior. Compliance with these regulations is achieved through the use of force and punishment.

A structure such as this contrasts sharply with that prescribed by contemporary treatment ideologies. From this perspective prisoners are "sick" or "maladjusted," rather than evil or dangerous. Through psychotherapy, group therapy, milieu therapy, or more eclectic procedures the inmate (client) is to gain insight into his feelings and behavior, and to be aided in changing his attitudes and responses. Accordingly, decision-making is decentralized and based on the welfare of the individual. Rigid regulations are discarded and inmates are permitted to be spontaneous and self-governing. Rank is deemphasized and relations between staff and inmates are expected to be warm, friendly, and emotionally supportive.

Custodial and treatment goals, then, imply radically different models of prison social organization. The addition of a treatment goal, such as occurred at ECI in 1956, is thus likely to have considerable impact upon the structure of an institution even without the provision of resources to attain it. Many of the conditions associated with the treatment model are not inherently linked to formal treatment programs. Rather, they are merely humanitarian reforms that are adjuncts to the treatment process. The relaxation of rules and regulations, the elimination of sharp status distinctions between staff and inmates, and the allowance of relative material comfort for inmates, for example, are not in and of themselves rehabilitative. They provide a climate conducive to gaining the cooperation of the client in the treatment program, and a means by which treatment efforts may be generalized and reinforced.[2] But such conditions may be, and in fact often are, introduced in the absence of formal treatment programs. Under the pressure of limited resources to achieve treatment objectives, the distinction between humanitarianism and rehabilitation becomes blurred. Changes that lessen the harshness and severity of imprisonment are introduced under the legitimation of the treatment goal.[3] It is such a policy of humanitarian reform in the name of treatment that has fashioned the institutional character of ECI.

Relaxation of Custodial Control.

The policy of reform was developed by Alfred King who was appointed Warden in 1956; he remained in that position until 1969. King characterized himself as committed to a 'habilitation' approach to corrections. As he saw it, the purpose of corrections is to provide prisoners with a sense of dignity they have never had. To this end, as he stated in his "Preface" to the *Inmate Guide,* ECI should be a "home away from home" for the men confined there.

Under King many of the more onerous custodial routines and rituals symbolizing inmate degradation and subordination were eliminated, and the level of material comfort permitted inmates was raised considerably. Prior to his appointment in 1956, ECI was a closely controlled and regimented institution. Inmates dressed in grey, wool uniforms and caps, and marched to and from work and meals in long columns. After the evening meal they were locked in their cells for the night. The only amenities permitted in the cell were a set of headphones with which to listen to the prison radio station, approved books, and a small amount of art and craft materials. Visits were limited to one a month, and they took place in the "tank," a small room divided by a pane of bullet proof glass. Even the most minute details of inmate behavior were regulated by rules such as that which prohibited staring at visitors, and the most severe punishments could be administered without a hearing.

Today, uniforms and formations are no longer required. Inmates have the choice of wearing their own clothes or those provided by the institution. Movement within the institution is only slightly controlled by a pass system. Out-of-cell recreation is permitted every evening from 4:30 P.M. until 8:45 P.M. There are virtually no regulations regarding what an inmate may keep in his cell, as long as it is not a threat to security and order. Most prisoners have televisions and radios, some have coffee pots and hot plates, and a few have stereos, record players, and even electric guitars. Visits are permitted twice a week, and they take place either in the dining hall where inmates and their visitors sit at small formica tables, or in a new well-appointed visiting room with a carpeted floor, wood paneling, and soft music. Most importantly, inmates accused of infractions of the few remaining rules are permitted a hearing with representation before any punishment may be administered.

Inmate Voluntary Associations

Perhaps the most significant of the reforms initiated by King, however, was the development of a number of inmate voluntary organizations. The rationale behind these organizations is to provide a means by which to channel and articulate volunteer resources from the community with inmate needs and interests. Each of these organizations has its elected leadership, and develops its own programs with the assistance of the volunteers. Staff supervision is kept to a minimum, existing usually in the form of a liaison officer, who may or may not be present at meetings. King referred to the organizations as semi-autonomous.

A number of these organizations have come into and passed out of existence over the past several years. Three, however, have been most durable and remain a significant part of the prison's program: a prison chapter of the state Junior Chamber of Commerce, the inmate newspaper, *The Beacon,* and the Afro-American Society. Others include a Yoga Society, an art club, a drama club, Alcoholics Anonymous, and a Lifers' Association.

The "Jay Cees" were established in 1966 with the cooperation of the state organization. In 1971-72, the membership varied between 60 and 75 prisoners. Like the national organization, the purpose of the ECI chapter is to develop leadership by involvement in activities of benefit to the community, in this case the prison. Since 1966, the organization has completed many such projects. They operate a canteen in South Wing and use the proceeds from this to subsidize expenses for Christmas parties for prisoners and their families, an annual Family Day, and a number of other banquets and parties. In addition, they raised funds to aid in the construction of the new visiting room, and are continuously involved in minor projects such as book drives to stock the prison library.

The Beacon also was started in 1966. Originally, the paper was circulated only among inmates and printed news of a sort in which only ECI prisoners would be interested. But in recent years it has developed a list of subscribers throughout the state, and a more editorial posture. The *Beacon* staff continually researches legal and penal developments throughout the country and presents articles proposing changes and reforms in the state's legal and correctional structure. As an offshoot of this program, they have been permitted to sponsor an annual Legislative Forum, a dinner to which the state legislators are invited and at which a series of legislative reforms are proposed by inmates. In 1970, they were successful in their efforts to change the law regarding parole eligibility for "lifers." "Lifers" previously had to serve twenty years before being eligible for parole; in 1970 this was reduced to ten years. Even more significantly, the *Beacon* has established a statewide organization concerned with prison reform, The Friends of *Beacon*. Through the efforts of this group, a privately operated halfway house for ex-felons was begun in 1972.

The Afro-American Society was begun in 1968. The organization, dedicated to "attaining and maintaining unity and dignity among the black brothers," provides a round of activities that nearly totally absorbs the majority of black inmates during the recreation hours. Through the assistance of several community organizations and a nearby university, the society has been able to secure several grants. With these funds they have established their own high school Graduate Equivalency Diploma (GED) program as well as courses in cultural anthropology, economics, business management, Afro-American history and art, and creative writing. Like the "Jay Cees," they also sponsor a series of parties and banquets for their membership.

Thus, while in terms of formal resources, ECI is a custodially-oriented institution, under the umbrella of legitimation extended by the goal of rehabilitation, the structure of ECI has been modified by a policy of humanitarian reform.

Characteristics of the Inmate Population

On March 19, 1971, there were 186 convicted felons confined in the maximum security section of ECI. As can be seen in Table 2-3, the offenses of which these men had been convicted ranged in seriousness from Breaking and Entering to Homicide. More than half (55.7 percent), however, had been convicted of either Breaking and Entering, Robbery, or Homicide. The data presented in Tables 2-4 and 2-5 indicate that the median length of sentence being served was 7.3 years, and the mean number of prior commitments was 1.6. The mean time served on current sentence, as indicated by the data in Table 2-6, was 1.8 years. As is common in most prisons, the prisoners in maximum security were young, the mean age being 29.3 years, and 39.2 percent of them were under age 25 (Table 2-7). Finally, as indicated in Table 2-8, more than half (53.8 percent) of the prisoners had completed some high school education. The mean number of years of school completed was 9.0 years.

Racial Differences

Of the 186 prisoners, 78 percent were white and 22 percent were black. In general, the characteristics of these two groups were similar. There were, however, some differences.

Offenses. Blacks as well as whites had been convicted primarily of Breaking and Entering, Robbery, and Homicide. Within these three offense categories, however, there were several differences. Most notable among these differences is that more than one-fourth (27.5 percent) of the black prisoners as compared to only one-tenth of the white prisoners (11.7 percent) had been convicted of Robbery.[4] Similarly, a larger proportion of black prisoners (17.5 percent) than white prisoners (4.9 percent) had been convicted of a Violation of Narcotics Laws. In the other direction, a larger percentage of white prisoners (28.3 percent) than black prisoners (17.5 percent) had been convicted of Breaking and Entering. Also, a larger proportion of white prisoners (18.0 percent) than black prisoners (10.0 percent) had been convicted of either Homicide or Manslaughter. A final observation is that the black prisoner population constitutes a slightly more homogeneous group with respect to offense characteristics than do the white prisoners. The four most common offenses of the black inmates —Breaking and Entering, Robbery, Homicide, and Violation of Narcotics Laws—account for 72.3 percent of the black population. In comparison, the four most common offenses of the white prisoners—Breaking and Entering, Robbery, Homicide and Assault—account for 63.5 percent of the white population.

Length of Sentence. The differences in offense characteristics between black and white prisoners appear to be reflected in differences in the

Table 2-3
Offenses of Prisoners by Race in Percentages

	Race		
Offense	White (N=145)	Black[a] (N=40)	Total (N=185)
Breaking and Entering	28.3%	17.5%	25.9%
Robbery	11.7	27.5	15.2
Homicide	15.9	10.0	14.6
Violation of Narcotic Laws	4.9	17.5	7.6
Assault	7.6	5.0	7.0
Sex Offenses other than Rape	5.5	7.5	5.9
Rape	3.4	7.5	4.4
Larceny	5.5	—	4.4
Conspiracy to Murder	2.7	5.0	3.2
Arson	2.7	—	2.2
Manslaughter	2.1	—	1.6
Kidnapping	2.1	—	1.6
Forgery	2.1	—	1.6
Other	5.5	2.5	4.8
Total	100.0%	100.0%	100.0%

[a]The offense of one black prisoner was not listed.

Table 2-4
Length of Sentence by Race in Percentages

	Race		
Length of Sentence	White (N=145)	Black (N=41)	Total (N=186)
Less than 1 year	3.5%	—	2.7%
1 - 3 years	26.9	19.5%	25.3
3 - 5 years	10.3	14.6	11.1
5 - 10 years	21.3	29.3	23.1
10 - 25 years	20.0	29.3	22.1
25 years or more	17.9	7.3	15.6
Total	99.9%	100.0%	99.9%

distribution of sentences between the two populations. The median length of sentence of the black prisoners (7.7 years) is slightly longer than that of the white prisoners (7.1 years).[5] This slightly longer median sentence among the blacks is attributable to their concentration in the sentence categories between 3 and 25 years. Nearly three-quarters of the black population (73.2 percent) are serving sentences between 3 and 25 years, as

Table 2-5
Number of Prior Commitments by Race in Percentages

	Race		
Number of Prior Commitments	White (N=145)	Black (N=41)	Total (N=186)
0	37.9%	34.1%	37.1%
1	18.6	19.5	18.8
2	15.9	19.5	16.7
3	13.1	9.8	12.4
4	9.0	9.8	9.1
5 or more	5.5	7.3	5.9
Total	100.0%	100.0%	100.0%

Table 2-6
Time Served on Current Sentence by Race in Percentages

	Race		
Time Served on Current Sentence	White (N=145)	Black (N=41)	(N=186)
Less than 6 months	24.8%	26.8%	25.4%
6 months - 1 year	23.4	17.1	22.0
1 - 2 years	24.1	26.8	24.7
2 - 3 years	12.4	19.5	14.0
3 - 5 years	9.8	4.9	8.6
5 years or more	5.5	4.9	5.3
Total	100.0%	100.0%	100.0%

compared to only one-half (51.6 percent) of the white population. Proportionately more whites, however, are serving both shorter and longer sentences. Nearly one of three white prisoners (30.4 percent), as compared to only one of five black prisoners (19.5 percent), is serving a sentence of less than three years. At the other extreme, almost one-fifth of the white population (17.9 percent), as compared to less than one-tenth of the black population (7.3 percent), are serving sentences of 25 years or more. Thus, with respect to sentence length, as with respect to offense characteristics, the black prisoners constitute a somewhat more homogeneous population than do the white prisoners. [d]

[d]The Quartile Deviation (Q) for length of sentence is 5.9 years for the black population and 8.5 years for the white population.

Table 2-7
Age of Prisoners by Race in Percentages

	Race		
Age	White (N=145)	Black (N=41)	Total (N=186)
Under 20	6.9%	9.8%	7.5%
20 - 24	30.3	36.6	31.7
25 - 29	22.8	19.5	22.1
30 - 34	18.6	19.5	18.8
35 and over	21.4	14.6	19.9
Total	100.0%	100.0%	100.0%

Table 2-8
Years of School Completed by Race in Percentages

	Race		
Number of Years Completed	White[a] (N=143)	Black (N=41)	Total (N=184)
0 - 5	6.3%	4.9%	6.0%
6 - 8	30.2	17.1	27.2
9 - 11	48.9	70.7	53.8
12 or more	14.6	7.3	13.0
Total	100.0%	100.0%	100.0%

[a]Data on two white prisoners could not be obtained.

Prior Commitments and Time Served. Tables 2-5 and 2-6 present data on the number of prior commitments and the amount of time served on the current sentence by race. In neither characteristic are there any significant differences by race. The mean number of prior commitments for whites was 1.6. For blacks it was 1.7. On the average, white prisoners had been in the institution for 1.9 years; for black prisoners the mean time served on the current sentence is 1.6 years. However, with respect to time served on current sentence, there is also a slight tendency for the black population to be more homogeneous. Where 46.3 percent of the black population had served between 1 and 3 years, only 36.5 percent of the white prisoners were in these categories.[e]

Age and Education. As can be seen in Table 2-7, the black prisoner popula-

[e]The standard deviation for time served on current sentence is 0.9 years for the black population and 2.7 years for the white population.

tion is both younger and more homogeneous with respect to age than is the white population. The mean age of the black prisoners is 28.1 years as compared to 29.7 years among the white prisoners. Nearly half of the black prisoners (46.4 percent) are under age 25, as compared to 37.2 percent of the white population. At the other extreme, 21.4 percent of the white convicts, as compared to 14.6 percent of the black prisoners, might be considered "senior citizens," being aged 35 and over.[f]

Table 2-8 presents data on the number of years of school completed upon entry into the institution by race. Here again, the greater homogeneity of the black prisoners is apparent. The mean number of years of schooling completed by the black prisoners (9.2) was slightly more than the average number completed by the white prisoners (9.0 years). Fully 70.7 percent of the black prisoners, as compared to 48.9 percent of the white prisoners, had attended but not completed high school. Before entering prison, proportionately more whites than black prisoners had both completed high school (14.6 percent v. 7.3 percent) and not completed grammar school (36.5 percent v. 22.0 percent).[g]

Summary and Conclusion

The white and black prisoner population tend to be more similar than different in a number of background characteristics. Perhaps the most notable demographic difference between the two populations is that of size. On March 19, 1971, there were 145 white and 41 black prisoners in maximum security. It is quite probably this difference in group size that is responsible for the second major difference noted: the greater homogeneity of the black population in such characteristics as offense, length of sentence, time served on current sentence, age, and education. Previous research has established a strong positive correlation between group size and heterogeneity, and an inverse correlation between size and such structural properties as cohesion, solidarity and centralized leadership.[6] In Chapters 4 and 5 I discuss racial differences in collective adaptations to imprisonment, noting that the black prisoners constitute a far more solidary group than the whites. It may well be that the greater solidarity of the black inmates was to some degree a function of the smaller size and consequent homogeneity of that group, rather than solely the result of the impact of black nationalism. The extent to which prisoner solidarity in general, and black prisoner solidarity in particular, are functions of group size would seem to be a worthy hypothesis for further research.

---

[f]The standard deviation for age is 8.8 years for the black population and 9.8 years for the white population.

[g]The standard deviation for years of school completed is 2.0 years for the black population and 2.6 years for the white population.

Past Racial Conflict

From 1956 until 1968 there were no serious disturbances at ECI. The policy of humanitarian reform instituted by Warden King appears to have placated the inmates, and King succeeded in gaining considerable public support for the reforms. He drew praise and honor not only from local groups and the state legislature, but also from national correctional associations. In this context the custodial staff, while discontented with the direction of King's policies, were unable to find an issue with which to mobilize support. Thus, from the outside at least, ECI appeared to exist in a state of equilibrium from 1956 to 1968. But beneath the surface there existed a large measure of discontent.

Admirable as the reforms were, they left larger issues unresolved and aggravated other problems. From the inmates' perspective there remained the crucial questions of adequate food and medical services, psychiatric and psychological services and academic and vocational education as well as the cramped and dirty conditions in which they are forced to live. From the perspective of the custodial staff, the reforms stripped them of many of the coercive means by which they maintained control and indeed increased their problems by extending greater freedoms to inmates. All it took was an issue to bring their discontent to the surface. That issue came in the form of racial conflict.

Collective Disturbances

In 1965, only some 14 percent of the inmate population was black. By 1969 the black population represented almost 25 percent of the inmate body. During this same period, the attention of the entire nation was riveted on the conflicts surrounding civil rights demonstrations and urban riots. It was in the aftermath of these riots that black consciousness emerged among the expanding black population at ECI. As one black leader related it to me:

I came here in '67 just before we had all them riots. Like I couldn't believe it after seeing what was going down in the streets. Every brother in here was still processing his hair. Every Saturday morning they'd go to the shower room and work on their hair till it was all straight and slick. They wanted to be like them white gangsters we got in here. But them riots in Watts (sic) and Newark and Detroit changed that. It was after them that we began to get ourselves together in here.

There is general agreement at ECI that prior to 1967 the black inmates constituted a small and docile segment of the population. They were inclined toward integration and participated extensively in both the "Jay Cees" and *The Beacon*, which had been established in 1966. From 1967 through the end of 1968, however, several conflicts attendant upon the increase of the black population and the emergence of black consciousness polarized the inmate population along racial lines.

Early Conflicts. The first of these conflicts emerged in *The Beacon*. A number of articles expressive of the newfound black identity were rejected by the predominantly white editorial board. The blacks charged the whites with racism, but the whites steadfastly refused to publish these articles on the stated grounds that the paper should reflect only interests and problems common to all inmates, and not those peculiar to one group. In the face of this refusal, the two black editors resigned, and all black inmates ceased submitting pieces for publication.

Shortly after this incident, a black leader who had been elected Vice President of the "Jay Cees" succeeded to the presidency after the unexpected parole of the President. A small group of white leaders who occupied key committee positions resisted his succession. At first their resistance was passive, taking the form of negligence in their duties. But when the President moved to replace them with black inmates, they in turn moved to impeach him and resorted to physical coercion in an effort to secure the necessary votes. Once again, the blacks resigned, and at this time they petitioned King to establish the Afro-American Society. He reluctantly agreed.

These burgeoning racial tensions within ECI first came to public attention in the summer of 1968. That summer a group of 75 inmates went on a brief rampage, causing considerable damage in several shops and the dining hall and injuring five correctional officers. Coming as it did before the problems in the "Jay Cees" and the formation of the Afro-American Society, the disturbance reflected the incomplete racial polarization at that time. Most of the participants were black, but there were some whites, and the demands made by the rioters concerned food, living conditions, parole procedures, and training programs—demands of concern to all inmates. This fact diverted attention from the racial nature of the action. One investigation released to the press a week after the disturbance stated ". . . all agree that no strictly racial problem exists at ECI."

In fact, however, the disturbance did have a racial basis, and its major consequence was further racial polarization among the inmates. One of the black leaders recalled the incident to me in the following way:

We were trying to get some black representation on the parole board and in the higher ups. We sent something to the Warden about it and he turned it down without even talking to us. All the brothers then started in talking about messing the joint up seeing as they didn't want to talk to us like human beings. Some brothers went over to the whites and they said they'd go down with us 'cause they had a lotta beefs too . . . . We set it up for exactly 1:00 P.M. when everybody would be going into the shops. But when the time came most just stood around watching. Not more than 50

Table 2-9
Chronology of Event at ECI, 1968-70

Date	Events
May 1968	Black prisoners withdraw from *The Beacon*
July 1968	Disturbance: prisoners against staff
September 1968	Black prisoners withdraw from the "Jay Cees"
October 1968	Formation of the Afro-American Society
January 1969	Disturbance: black prisoners against staff
January 1969	Cells of black prisoners set on fire
February 1969	Black prisoners verbally assault white female visitors
Feburary 1969	White prisoners storm segregation unit
March 1969	Disturbance: black prisoners against white prisoners
March 1969	Report of commission investigating January riot
May 1969	Fire in maximum security: 6 prisoners escape
May 1969	National correctional figure criticizes administration
June 1969	Warden King resigns; Flint appointed interim Warden
July-Sept. 1969	Work stoppages and strikes by white prisoners
September 1969	White leaders placed in segregation; court petitions
April 1970	Knott appointed Warden; Flint named Director of Corrections
April-Aug. 1970	Expansion of inmate privileges; black prisoners reintegrated into population
August 1970	Reestablishment of Afro-American Society
August 1970	Court decree establishing new disciplinary procedures
October 1970	Court decree abolishing mail censorship

guys actually went down behind it and these was mostly blacks. The whites punked out at the last minute.

This incident generated racial antagonism among both black and white inmates. For their part, the black inmates felt themselves betrayed and scapegoated by the whites. The whites, having been locked in their cells for several days, viewed it as a senseless act that served no purpose other than to "bring heat." It was in the context of these antagonisms that the incidents in the "Jay Cees" arose and the Afro-American Society was founded.

A Racial Confrontation. Racial grievances that went unspoken during the 1968 disturbance were articulated rapidly by the Afro-American Society. Almost immediately the organization petitioned the Warden for permission to wear Afro haircuts and dashikis, and to have soul food included on the prison menu. Further, the organization began to develop proposals that the parole board be expanded from three to five members and that the new members be black, that several black Classification Counselors be hired as well as a black Coordinator of Education and Training.

King at first was unresponsive to these requests. But when the Afro-

Americans requested a dance at which they would wear African style clothing and the guards would be in civilian suits, he called a meeting to discuss with them the direction the organization was taking.

Reports on the meeting vary. Apparently, King arrived late and took exception to the seating arrangements, which placed him in front of the organization's officers as if being interrogated. When he protested, the black inmates took offense and walked out of the room. At this point, King announced that the organization was disbanded.

Later that day, the organization held another meeting in the library. King interpreted their action as insubordination and ordered the gate separating the library from the rest of the prison locked and all other inmates placed in their cells. The black inmates, along with several white prisoners, found themselves locked in the "New Building." They proceeded to break up furniture, to arm themselves, and to barricade the gates. King summoned the State Police, who surrounded the building and filled it and South Wing with tear gas. After 90 minutes of gassing, the black inmates surrendered and were placed in segregation.

Racial Polarization. This outbreak was only the first in a series of disturbances that rocked ECI during 1969. Locked in their cells for several days, seeing other white prisoners treated as "hostages," having been tear-gassed, and seeing the only indoor recreational facilities destroyed, the white inmates became extremely agitated. One week after the disturbance, a number of cells belonging to black prisoners who had been placed in segregation were set afire. Their belongings had been left in their cells and were totally destroyed. The blacks sought retaliation in one of the few ways open to them. The wing in which they were segregated overlooked the walk along which visitors passed coming into the institution. White female visitors were met with a steady stream of obscenities from the black inmates. The effect on the white prisoners was predictable. A group of white prisoners attempted to storm the segregation unit. Failing in this, they were placed in segregation themselves, on the side of the wing opposite from the black inmates. Tension built rapidly as both blacks and whites hurled epithets and threats back and forth 24 hours a day. The situation climaxed when fifteen white prisoners returning from outside recreation stormed across the cell block and assaulted four black prisoners doing maintenance work. In the resulting melee several prisoners and officers were severely injured, one white inmate leader requiring hospitalization for serious abdominal wounds.

Generalization of Conflict. This incident brought to an end conflict of a specifically racial nature. The black inmates were transferred to the segregation unit in medium-minimum security, where most of them remained for the next year. But conflict did not cease with the removal of the black inmates. The anger and hostility of the whites was redirected onto the administration and the issues of food, living conditions, and the absence of treatment programs.

In May of 1969, several prisoners set fire to the roof of maximum security, destroying a large portion of it. Approximately 50 prisoners were transferred to temporary quarters. Within two weeks six inmates, all serving long sentences, escaped.

Those prisoners remaining in maximum security after the fire began to stage several well-organized work stoppages to call attention to the above-mentioned conditions. Work stoppages of several days each occurred in July, August, and September. Finally, in September, the administration selected 24 inmates believed to be responsible for these insurrections and placed them in Administrative Segregation for an indefinite period. This action promptly brought to an end the one year of collective disturbances. But it also was the starting point of a new inmate protest strategy, appeal to the courts. I shall return to this below. At this point, I turn to the official reaction to these inmate protests.

The Official Response

The response to these disturbances took three forms: (1) official investigations and recommendations, (2) the appointment of a new Warden, and (3) judicial decisions in favor of inmate interests.

Investigations. Immediately after the disturbance by the Afro-American Society in 1969, the newly elected Governor appointed a commission to investigate conditions at ECI. The report of this commission was delivered in March, and was followed in May by a second report prepared by one of the leading national figures in corrections. Both of these reports were sharply critical of the institution, and together they recommended a complete restructuring of ECI. Thse recommendations included the establishment of vocational and educational programs, the development of a clearly defined administrative structure, numerous improvements to the physical plant, stricter rules regarding inmate behavior, and increased pay for correctional officers. In making these recommendations, both reports only thinly veiled their criticism of King's administration. For example, the second report made the following statement:

Many of the problems affecting staff morale, rehabilitation of inmates, community aftercare, work programs, and vocational training that now beset the institution are the result of a policy of indecision and drift. They have not been dealt with constructively over a considerable period of time. They can no longer be neglected.

A New Warden. Until the publication of these reports, King was able to ascribe the disturbances to black militants and a small group of white discontents. The wide publicity given the reports belied these interpretations and eroded King's support. When the escapes occurred in June of 1969, a prominent legislator publicly branded King's administration as irresponsible. Shortly after, King submitted his resignation.

King's interim successor was Vincent Flint, who had served twenty years at ECI as a Classification Counselor and Assistant Warden. Flint saw the restoration of order as his first priority, and it was his action in placing 24 inmates in Administrative Segregation that brought the disturbances to an end. In April of 1970, Flint was named Director of Corrections and Charles Knott was appointed Warden.

Unlike King or Flint, Knott came to the position from outside the state. He had previously been a correctional officer and then administrative assistant to a well-known reform warden. Just prior to becoming Warden at ECI, he had served as a Parole Officer in a predominantly black area of a major city. Publicly, he characterized his correctional philosophy as "liberal, left of center, progressive" and committed himself to the development of a "therapeutic atmosphere" at ECI. Soon after assuming the position he was openly critical of the previous administration, claiming that "there's been very little rehabilitation going on. It's been all talk and no performance." He called upon the people of the state to decide if they want "ECI to be a modern, progressive institution or to revert to a repressive Alcatraz-type institution."

Knott's open espousal of the treatment goal and the initial changes he made in this direction helped to quiet inmate protests. A grant for vocational training was secured, the work release program was expanded and moved to separate quarters outside the prison, visiting privileges were increased from one to two days per week, and regulations such as those regarding haircuts and beards were further relaxed. In a short time inmates were proclaiming "he's done more in three months than the other bastard did in five years."

This new climate of victory and optimism among the inmates appears to have dissipated the racial antagonisms of the previous year. Soon after taking office Knott began a program to gradually reintegrate the black inmates into the prison population. This program proceeded without incident, and in August the black inmates were permitted to reestablish the Afro-American Society.

Court Decisions. Adding to the spirit of renewed optimism among the inmates were two court decisions in 1970. The 24 prisoners placed in segregation by Flint in 1969 had immediately filed a suit challenging his action on the grounds that it was arbitrary and capricious, and that they had not been provided with the minimal procedural safeguards of due process of law. After nearly a year of negotiation by the court, a consent decree was entered, establishing a new set of disciplinary and classification procedures at ECI. These procedures sought to protect the rights of inmates from undue interference through a variety of safeguards including representation at disciplinary hearings. The court placed ECI on eighteen months probation, and commissioned an outside study group to evaluate the implementation of these regulations.

Later in 1970 the same court ruled that the system of mail censorship in operation at that time was beyond the legitimate role of prison authorities. This ruling virtually prohibited the prison administration from censoring outgoing mail and limited censorship of incoming mail to inspection for contraband.

These responses to the inmate disturbances served to accommodate the conflicts among the inmates and between the inmates and the administration. From the inmates' perspective, the reports and decisions constituted official legitimation of their protests. The appointment of Knott, with his announced commitment to rehabilitation and the initial changes he made, raised their hopes concerning the future direction of ECI. Amid this climate of renewed optimism, Knott was able to reintegrate the black inmates into the prison population and to permit them to reestablish the Afro-American Society. Temporarily, at least, tension was abated.

Summary

Eastern Correctional Institution (ECI) is a small state prison in an Eastern state. The maximum security section of ECI was constructed in 1878 to support a system of regimented custodial control. The normal population in maximum security numbers some 200 men. Approximately 78 percent of this number are white; the remaining 22 percent are black. The white and black inmate populations are similar in a number of background characteristics: offense, length of sentence, prior commitments, time served on current sentence, age, and education. There is, however, a discernible tendency for the black population to be more homogeneous in these characteristics.

Despite having a charter to rehabilitate inmates, the resources available to ECI in 1971-72 were committed predominantly to the single goal of custodial control. The character of an institution is not shaped by resources alone, however. Under the legitimation of the treatment goal, a program of humanitarian reform has been in operation at the prison since 1956. This policy has alleviated many of the more onerous deprivations of imprisonment, and prisoners have been permitted to form a number of semi-autonomous voluntary associations. Among these organizations are a chapter of the state "Jay Cees" and an Afro-American Society.

From 1956 to 1968 ECI was marked by stability. However, the compromises embodied by the policy of humanitarian reform left many issues unresolved and aggravated other problems. In 1968, an increase in the number of black prisoners and in black consciousness precipitated a series of disturbances in which the underlying discontent came to the surface. There were several investigations recommending a complete restructuring of the institutions, the appointment of a new warden, and two court decisions further curtailing custodial powers. These responses placated the inmates. When this study began in September 1970, the conflicts of the previous two years had been accommodated, and the institution had regained a semblance of order.

3

The Hacks

Fully 70 percent of the institutional staff at ECI have custody as their primary function. Officially these men are correctional officers; they refer to themselves as guards; to the inmates they are "hacks." The hacks stand on one side of a caste line that is the fundamental feature of the prison social structure. They are the lower echelon members of a dominant group possessing a monopoly of the legitimate means of coercion. Supported by the authority of the state, granted the power to punish nonconformity and to reward conformity to their expectations, with their positions buttressed by walls, bars, and weapons, the custodians might appear to be both absolutely and securely dominant. But, as Sykes has shown, the nearly total power of the hacks is more illusion than reality.[1] At ECI the reforms have dispelled even the illusion of total power. In eliminating many of the rules, rituals, and routines by which inmate behavior was regulated, the reforms destroyed many of the symbols and supports of coercive power. In granting inmates access to the legislature and courts, in eliminating censorship of mail, and by extending certain safeguards of due process of law to prisoners, the reforms have provided inmates with the capacity to develop a significant degree of countervailing power. Finally, and of direct concern in this chapter, the changes and reforms of the past few years have induced a state of anomie within the administrative/custodial hierarchy itself.

As anomie has become an increasingly popular concept it also has become increasingly ill-defined. As developed originally by Durkheim[2] and later elaborated by Merton[3], however, anomie refers to a state of relative normlessness in a group or society.[4] It is in this sense that I shall use the term. At ECI there are two primary sources of anomie. First, the inherent contradiction between custodial and treatment goals has created conflict among the top administrators and resulted in ambiguous role definitions for the lower echelon personnel. Second, the policy of humanitarian reform has undermined the capacity of the officers to maintain security and internal order, a primary responsibility to which they remain committed. The result of these strains has been a fragmentation of social relationships at all levels of the custodial/administrative hierarchy and a rebellion of the officers against the prison administration.

Conflict Among the Administrators

The problem of goal conflict had long been present at ECI when this study began. During the period of the study, the clearest manifestation of this problem was the unsuccessful attempt of Charles Knott to solidify his position as Warden and to mobilize the staff under his direction.

The Problem of Administrative Succession

The replacement of administrative personnel often presents problems for bureaucratic organizations. In *Patterns of Industrial Bureaucracy*, Gouldner presents an incisive analysis of these problems and of how they were resolved in one factory.[5] Entering a plant that had been characterized by an "indulgency pattern," a system of lenient and flexible rules and close personal relations and favors between supervisors and workers, the new plant manager, Vincent Peele, was confronted with a number of problems. Among these were the implementation of efficiency goals set by the central office, the resistance of middle management personnel who held ties of loyalty to his predecessor and viewed Peele as an illegitimate heir, the resistance of rank and file workers who derived many benefits from the indulgency pattern, and lastly his own personal anxiety in the face of the challenge he confronted. To cope with these problems, Peele resorted to several courses of action that resulted in a bureaucratization of the plant. He enforced previously dormant company rules, thus eliminating many of the characteristics of the indulgency pattern. He adopted a pattern of close personal supervision of production both by personal observation and a system of written reports. Most importantly, he made several "strategic replacements." He demoted or fired several of the old lieutenants and replaced them. He filled new positions that opened as a result of new machinery and operations in the plant with new managers who, like himself, were committed to production goals and formalized procedures and who were tied to him by bonds of personal loyalty. Through such means Peele was able to establish his position as manager.

A prison is not a gypsum plant. Nonetheless, the situation faced by Charles Knott at the beginning of this study was analogous to that of Vincent Peele. Like Peele, Knott was a successor to a man who had occupied the position for a number of years, and he was a successor from outside the organization, to some extent a stranger among friends. In assuming the position of Warden, he entered an institution that, by virtue of the policies of his predecessor, was characterized by a system of lenient rules and relaxed discipline akin to the indulgency pattern. Moreover, as a result of the disturbances and investigations of the preceding year, Knott was mandated to change the character of the institution, to move it in the direction of a treatment orientation. And finally, in approaching the position, Knott also exhibited a great deal of anxiety. He was a political appointee whose position was dependent upon the maintenance of security and order and the whims of the electorate as much as upon the implementation of treatment programs. That he saw himself in a probationary status was symbolized by the fact that he maintained his residence in his native state some 50 miles from the prison.

Lack of Options. That Knott was unable to establish himself as Warden may be understood in terms of several conditions associated with his position that made it different from the gypsum plant studied by Gouldner. First, there exist no bureaucratic rules that Knott could impose to facilitate attainment of the treatment goal. Unlike the production of gypsum board, the process of rehabilitating offenders cannot be precisely defined and specified. It requires professional expertise rather than bureaucratic authority and a relaxed and relatively comfortable atmosphere. The implementation of bureaucratic rules and regulations, then, was not seen by Knott as a means of solidifying his position, as it was antithetical to the goals set for him and to which he himself was committed. The priorities Knott set were (1) the procurement of professional treatment personnel and the establishment of treatment programs, (2) the education of his staff in the perspectives of treatment ideology, and (3) a further relaxation of custodial measures.

The first two of these priorities were never realized. As I noted in the previous chapter, soon after he became Warden Knott secured a federal grant to establish a new vocational training program, but he received no additional resources from the state. In the first budget he submitted to the legislature in 1970, he requested additional funding for several new positions. Among these positions were a psychiatrist, a clinical psychologist, three social workers, two teachers, a deputy warden for treatment services, a drug addiction specialist, and a coordinator of inmate activities. Not one of these positions was funded, and the same response was given to a similar budget request in 1971. Thus, despite his mandate to implement a treatment approach, Knott was unable to secure the essential resources to achieve this objective, and the changes he was able to make were by and large an extension of the policy of humanitarian reform—increased visiting privileges, the permission to form additional inmate organizations, permission for long hair and beards, and so forth.

The lack of resources for new programs and positions had implications beyond the immediate consequence of the failure to develop a treatment orientation. It denied to Knott the only means available to him to make "strategic replacements," to establish his own inner circle of assistants who shared his orientations and were loyal to him. As it was, his immediate subordinates were men who had worked their way up through the ranks at ECI, who did not share Knott's orientation to treatment, who viewed him as a usurper of their prerogatives for advancement, and whose positions were secure by virtue of civil service. O'Toole, the Assistant Warden, had begun work at ECI in 1946 as a guard and had been successively promoted up the custodial hierarchy, becoming Assistant Warden in 1969. Smalley, the Deputy Warden, had also come to ECI in 1946 as a guard; and Dick White, the Director of Classification, had been in his position for over twelve years.

Administrative Conflict. Despite considerable difference among these three men, they frequently acted in concert to thwart Knott's programs. One example of their resistance is the area of work release. Knott openly espoused the concept of "community-based corrections," and one of the accomplishments of which he was most proud was the procurement and renovation of a cottage off the prison grounds as a residence for 50 prisoners on work release. As he saw it, this was to be the first step in the development of several such cottages. But the placement of individuals on work release required the approval of the Classification Board composed of Knott, O'Toole, Smalley, White, and one other member. Inmates were frequently denied work release by 3-2 or 4-1 votes with the result that although the cottage could accommodate 50, there were seldom more than 20 or 25 inmates on work release at any one time.

Knott might have been able to overcome such resistance had he been able to secure additional personnel similarly committed to his orientation, or if he had the support of his superiors. He had neither. His one opportunity to make a "strategic replacement" occurred when Smalley resigned as Deputy Warden. Knott sought to replace him with a man with whom he had worked prior to coming to ECI. This effort was vetoed by his superior, however, and Smalley was replaced by Boucher who, like the others, entered his position after fifteen years as a guard, lieutenant, and captain.

Knott's superior was Vincent Flint who, as we have seen, had worked at ECI for nearly twenty years as Director of Classification and Assistant Warden. He had close personal ties with both O'Toole, whom he had favored for Warden, and White, who had succeeded him as Director of Classification. Knott thus found himself entrapped by a network of informal ties between his superior and his subordinates. "I'm in a squeeze between the guy above me and the guys below me, and I can't move a thing," was the way he put it.

Goal Dissensus

The strain in the relations between Knott, Flint, and the others was not merely a clash of personalities but a reflection of the dual goals assigned to the institution: to protect society and to rehabilitate the offender. Both goals are granted equal legitimacy but decision-making requires administrators to accord a priority to one or the other. Knott accorded priority to the treatment goal. He characterized his correctional philosophy as "liberal, left of center, progressive," and was willing to sacrifice an appreciable degree of security in the interest of rehabilitation. Flint and the others, while not in diametric opposition to Knott, espoused a more conservative view. Flint for example, characterized himself as a reformer. But he contended that reform programs would be destroyed by adverse community reactions if the reforms jeopardized institutional security. Thus, in Flint's view, treatment efforts had to be limited by custodial concerns.

In attempting to develop a plan of action for the prison, then, Flint and Knott were brought into frequent conflict. In these conflicts neither party had complete power over the other. On the one hand, Knott's attempts to promote treatment goals were limited by the power of Flint. On the other hand, Flint's commitment to security was limited by the investigative commissions that had strongly recommended the development of treatment programs, by the decrees of the court, by the attention of outside groups that had become interested in prison reform, and by the possible threat of inmate disturbances if changes were not forthcoming.[6] The relations between the top administrators was thus contained within a system of checks and balances; Knott was able to develop a variety of reform programs within the institution, but Flint was able to exercise a veto on any changes that in his view threatened security or that might incur an adverse reaction from the community. Among the programs implemented by Knott were the following: a vocational training program, a work release program, an inmate advisory council, the expansion of visiting privileges and a relaxation of custodial rules regarding dress, haircuts, and the like. Among the programs proposed by Knott but vetoed by Flint were the following: the expansion of the work release program into a system of halfway houses, home furloughs for selected prisoners, and an in-service training program in treatment techniques for correctional officers.

Such continuing conflicts among the top administrators created a situation of organizational drift, a situation in which the resources of the institution were not clearly committed to any goal beyond that of self-maintenance and in which administrative decisions frequently had the effect of neutralizing one another. As one officer expressed it:

It's like having a ship without a rudder. . . . If you say we're supposed to rehabilitate people, we don't do that. If we're supposed to produce things, we don't do that either because we don't work them enough. And all these changes mean we don't punish them either. Nobody knows what we're supposed to do so we don't do anything.

As suggested by this comment, one result of goal dissensus and conflict among the administrators was an absence of policy direction that exacerbated a pre-existing state of anomie among the lower level custodians.

Anomie Among the Custodians

Prior to 1956, the officers were "guards," and their role was precisely defined. The sole functions of the guard were to maintain security and internal order. A detailed set of rules regulated even the most minute aspects of inmate life, and a complementary set of written procedures guided the guard in his surveillance of inmate behavior and enforcement of the rules. Today the official title of the custodial staff is "correctional officers," a title that both incorporates and symbolizes the conflicting and ambiguous definitions of their current role.[7] As the term "officer" connotes, the custodians remain organized in a military hierarchy, the function of which is to ensure security and order. But the adjective "correctional" connotes an additional expectation of equal priority. In some way the officers are expected to be agents in a rehabilitative process in addition to maintaining security and internal order. How this is to be accomplished has never been, and probably cannot be, precisely defined. The only guidance given the officers are the general guidelines that the maintenance of security and order is to be accomplished in a manner consistent with the "home away from home" atmosphere that has been the goal of the reforms, and that they are to contribute to this atmosphere by being relaxed and friendly in their relations with inmates.

To a large extent, the home away from home atmosphere has been created by the abolition of specific rules regarding inmate behavior. The *Inmate Guide Book,* for instance, specifically states that "we refrain from listing a series of do's and don'ts." This absence of specific rules for inmate conduct does not mean that inmates are permitted to act in any manner they desire. Rather, while inmates are granted considerable freedom of action, it remains "understood" that their conduct will not be a threat to security and order and that behavior constituting such a threat is subject to punishment. But what types of behavior constitute such a threat? Clearly, an attempted escape or the possession of a knife does. But what about loud hollering, rough horseplay, or other forms of seemingly innocuous behavior that may nonetheless result in a fight or possible disturbance? On such matters there is no consensus. Decisions of this nature are left to the common sense and discretion of the officer, which results in considerable inconsistency in rule enforcement, as well as a sense of futility and frustration among the officers.

That's the biggest problem today. There's no policy, no guidelines. You know I consider myself to be a well-balanced person and I try to understand what they mean by not listing the 'do's' and 'don't's'. But you just can't run an institution without a written policy of some sort. But fantastically enough that's what we're doing. There is no written policy. . . . It's frustrating, damn frustrating. You're just never sure what it is you're supposed to be doing, and the next guy might be doing the exact opposite of what you're doing.

Goals and Means

In part the anomic state of the custodians is a result of ambiguous and contradictory role definitions, which in turn are a function of the contradictory goals assigned to the prison and the resultant conflict among the top administrators. There is a second source of anomie, however. As elaborated by Merton, a major source of anomie is "disassociation between culturally prescribed aspirations and socially structured avenues for realizing these aspirations."[8] Seen in this light, anomie among the custodians at ECI also is the result of their continued commitment to the goal of custodial control in the face of institutional changes that made the attainment of that goal by traditional means increasingly more difficult.

The officers do not accord equal legitimacy to the conflicting and muddled definitions of their role. In the absence of treatment programs and professional treatment personnel, there has been no attempt made to convert the officers to the perspectives of modern treatment ideology. They continue to refer to themselves as guards, to view their primary function as security and control, and to hold a custodial perspective on the nature of crime and the proper treatment of inmates. In their view, crime is the result of the laziness, greed, or immorality of the individual offender. Criminals deserve to be punished for their wrongdoing. Nor, in their view, is there any conflict between the goals of punishment, custody, and rehabilitation. Quite to the contrary, these are seen as complementary and consistent goals. Punishment and custody are ensured by the strict enforcement of rigid rules. These same measures are necessary to the success of treatment efforts. An austere prison existence will instill in inmates a fear of return. By learning to conduct himself in accord with the rules of the prison, the inmate will find it easier to abide by the less stringent rules of society after his release. Moreover, to be successful education and training programs must insist on attendance and attention to the instructional program. And finally, introducing such programs, as well as the many volunteer programs, when custodial rules are being relaxed is an abdication of the responsibility to protect the community. The increase in traffic in and out of the institution is a threat to security and order that necessitates more rules rather than less.

But in fact, as has been pointed out, as a result of the policy of humanitarian reform inmates have been granted increasing freedom, and written rules regarding inmate behavior have been replaced by unwritten "understandings." Moreover, as a result of the court decrees in 1970, the power of the officers in enforcing these understandings has been restricted. One ruling, it will be remembered, extends certain minimal safeguards of due process of law to inmates. Consequently, officers may lock an inmate in his cell only if he presents a clear and present threat to the security and order of the institution, terms which are left undefined. Further, an officer reporting an infraction must first notify the inmate that he is being reported and tell him the reason for it. He must then submit the report to his superior for investigation, and be prepared to answer questions at a disciplinary hearing at which the inmate has the right to counsel. From the viewpoint of the officers, these rules are a serious infringement upon their authority and make it impossible for them to perform their duties. Further, the ruling ignores the very vulnerable position in which they find themselves, a situation in which an aggrieved inmate might easily assault them. One result, then, according to the officers, has been an increased reluctance to take action against an inmate unless absolutely necessary.

Deterioration of Relationships. The result of these intrusions upon the coercive powers of the custodians has not only been normlessness in the area of job performance, but also a deterioration of the working relationships among the custodians. Like the police in the case of the Miranda decision, the officers view the court decision as placing the law and the courts on the side of the inmate and in opposition to them. By extending legal rights to inmates, restricting the power of the officers and placing the institution on eighteen months probation, the decision makes the prisoners the "good guys." In short, the officers feel themselves betrayed and "sold out" by agencies that should support their authority. These agencies are not only the courts but the Department of Corrections itself. The nature of the court ruling was in the form of a consent decree, a compromise agreement between counsel for the plaintiffs and the Department of Corrections. The officers interpret this action as a betrayal by their own superiors.

I'm thoroughly disgusted by the whole thing. And the main thing that disgusts me is that it was our own people that was supposed to be down there fighting for us that dreamed up that catastrophe. . . . They're the ones that wrote it. The Legal Aid Society, or whatever it was, they just read it and of course they were delighted! But it was our own people, Flint and the state's attorneys, they're the ones that sold us down the drain.

In the eyes of the correctional officers, the court decision is only the most recent example of betrayal by their superiors. Given their commitment to custodial values and the need for strong external controls in rehabilitation, the entire series of reforms has been a "sell out." As they see it, the decisions to relax controls and grant greater freedoms to prisoners have not been made in an effort to develop a rehabilitative approach. They have been made to pacify the inmates so as to protect the positions of the top administrators. In their eyes, the interests and welfare of the officers have been sacrificed to the self-interests of their superiors and the inmates.

Flint and them other big shots, what do they care? They can't go any higher up now unless they was elected governor. So all they want is a quiet can. Their attitude is 'keep it cool, boys. Don't have any trouble out there. Don't hit the papers. Keep the lid on. If you have to give a little, give a little'. It keeps the inmates happy but we're the ones that have to come in here and put up with all this shit. No one gives a damn about us.

The feeling of not being supported by one's superiors pervades the entire chain of command and is fed by many daily incidents. On one occasion I witnessed an officer break up a fight between two inmates. He waded in among some 25 spectators and separated the two combatants. He informed each that they were to be reported for fighting and ordered them to return to their cells. At this point he was accosted by the spectators who argued that there was no reason for reporting them as it had merely been a friendly argument. Nonetheless, the officer stood his ground, reported the inmates, and returned them to their cells. Later that day, he learned that the captain had returned them to normal status, and that no Disciplinary Board was recommended, as there had been no animosity involved.

Such incidents are not uncommon. The superior officer and the Disciplinary Board confront a violation from a different perspective than the officer on the scene. Inmates hostile and perhaps violent at the time of report may be quite calm by the time the superior officer conducts his investigation. Thus, an incident that may have appeared serious at the time, and perhaps was, may appear to have been not so serious several hours later. Moreover, the investigation by the superior officer and the evidence brought forward by the inmate and his counsel at the hearing may uncover mitigating circumstances unknown to the officer who submitted the report. Such was the case, for example, of one inmate who assaulted another and was merely reprimanded. The investigation revealed that he had been unable to see the doctor that day to receive his dosage of Thorazine. Then, too, the Disciplinary Board is obliged to consider the welfare of the inmate and the effect of a disciplinary action on the general population as well as the facts of the matter. There may be evidence that segregation or solitary confinement may be unduly harmful to the physical or mental health of the prisoner, or it may be feared in some cases that a severe action may incite a disturbance. Finally, and perhaps most importantly, superior officers regard the reports of many officers with a high degree of suspicion.

There is a widespread belief among the superiors that many officers exaggerate their reports so as to ensure a punishment. Nor is this belief altogether unjustified. On one incident I was able to follow, the officer reported the inmate for "refusing an order to come down off the tier and using profanity and threatening me when I informed him of the booking." In fact, the inmate had refused the order but accepted the report without complaint except to attempt to explain why he had failed to come off the tier when so ordered.

For several reasons then, the disposition of a disciplinary report is often less severe than that deemed just by the officer submitting the report. Ideally, the officer is not expected to concern himself with the disposition of the case. His function ends with the submission of the report. In fact, officers take an intense interest in such dispositions and can relate to a questioner how many reports they've "won" and "lost" over a specified period of time. But because they are not expected to be concerned with the disposition, they are seldom informed of the reasons for whatever decision is made. The result is a general feeling that they are unsupported by their superiors, and that the disciplinary process makes them look like fools to the inmates they are expected to supervise.

Most of the time the inmate just gets a reprimand, and a reprimand is the most menial form of punishment you can inflict. An officer can be abused to such a degree that he can't take it anymore so he files a disciplinary report and the thing gets watered down so much by the process that follows that it's insulting. . . . By the time the report is dispensed with, the officer is a laughing stock to the inmates and a sadist with a pen to the Board.

The absence of a specified set of impersonal rules in combination with the belief that one's "common sense" decisions will often be unsupported by his superiors has resulted in a deterioration of the working relations among the lower level custodians themselves. Under such conditions, to exercise custodial control is to place oneself on the line. The submission of a disciplinary report may in fact result in the questioning of the integrity or competence of the officer. Moreover, the fact that another officer may overlook or permit the same behavior, means that to enforce a rule may also draw the personal vindictiveness of an inmate. In consequence, the officers define their rule enforcement function in a highly personal manner. Each officer constructs his role in a manner so as to cause himself the least trouble. They view themselves not as a team working together to ensure security and control, but as individuals whose function is to minimize disorder and trouble in their individual areas of responsibility even at the expense of overall institutional security. One evening, for example, I was in the gym after evening recreation in the yard. Sentenced men are allowed to use the gym at this time, but men awaiting trial are to return to their wing. In the gym at the time were some 25 prisoners, eight of whom were men awaiting trial, conspicuous by their khaki shirts and trousers. It was inconceivable that the officer in charge of the gym, posted by the door, did not notice these men. Yet he made no attempt to remove them. Some fifteen minutes later the officer in charge of the A/T wing came into the gym, and without a word to the gym officer, set about gathering his charges. To do this meant that he had to leave a wing containing some 100 prisoners unsupervised.

One of the areas in which the lack of cooperation in rule enforcement among officers is most evident regards the pass system. It is understood that no inmate is to be permitted to go from one area of the institution to another, say from the shop to the wings, without a pass from his supervisor, and that officers are to issue passes only for good and sufficient reason. Again, however, this is not a written rule nor are the "good and sufficient reasons" delineated. The result is that many officers are reluctant not to grant a pass. One shop officer explained:

If there was a clear policy on it and everybody enforced it, they'd be no problem. I could just say 'no it's against the rules.' But that ain't the way it is. So if I say 'no' then I got an argument or a fight. So usually I just let them go. That way I don't have the argument or the fight, just the worry that he might be getting into something.

A similar response was given to me by a wing officer when I noted a number of men in his wing who should have been in the shops.

To tell the truth, I don't care if they have passes or not. As long as they ain't troublemakers I'll let 'em in. The way I figure it is that it's the shop officer's job to know where his men are. That's what he's getting paid for. And if he let's 'em out, why should I set myself up by saying 'no.' Then he's an angel and I'm a prick. I can do without that kind of grief.

Thus, as a result of contradictory organizational goals and conflict among the top administrators, the role definitions of correctional officers at ECI are ambiguous and to some extent conflicting. Further, the policy of humanitarian reform has stripped the officers of much of their coercive power while increasing the problems surrounding the maintenance of internal order and external security. In response to these pressures, there has developed among the officers a state of normlessness regarding their job performance that has deteriorated working relationships.

Adaptations of the Custodians

Merton has identified several modes of deviant behavior as adaptive responses to anomie: innovation, ritualism, retreatism, and rebellion.[9] Two of these modes of adaptation were most in evidence among the custodians: innovation and rebellion. Innovation refers to the attempt to secure goals by proscribed means. This mode of adaptation characterized the job performance of the custodians. Rebellion refers to collective efforts to modify the social structure. This mode of adaptation was manifest in the organization and the activities of the officers' union.

The Corruption of Authority

Among the custodians at ECI innovation takes the form of a widespread corruption of authority, a pattern of relations wherein the officers seek to maintain control and minimize their personal trouble through personal ties and illicit exchanges with prisoners.[10] A central thrust of the reform emphasis has been to decrease the social distance between keeper and kept. One of the most striking aspects of institutional life at ECI is the extent to which in fact this distance has been minimized, and the extent to which officers are enmeshed in friendship relations with prisoners. On a random tour through the wings one may find one officer engaged in conversation or even horseplay with a group of inmates, and a second watching television with another group. At the same time the officer in the gym may be playing pool or ping pong, and upstairs the officer in the library may be engrossed in a game of chess. Similar patterns exist in the shops where officers may provide coffee for inmates at their own expense and work alongside them. Throughout the institution officers and inmates, particularly long-term white prisoners, are on a first name basis.

Presumably such relationships are an aspect of the rehabilitative process, a means by which prisoners may be reformed through positive relationships with law-abiding citizens. In some instances these relationships may in fact serve this purpose. More often than not, however, they are indicative of the corruption of the officer rather than of the reform of the inmates. The corruptive nature of these arrangements becomes clear in such instances as when on a hot August day three inmates are drinking Kool-aid under the shade of a tree while their supervisor mows the lawn. Or, as on another occasion, when an officer aids an inmate in making picture frames and shadow boxes from state owned lumber for sale to other inmates, the officer thus making himself an accessory to grand larceny. Or, as is frequently the case, information of a vital nature to the performance of custodial duties is not relayed to officers to whom it is of the most immediate concern for fear they will forewarn inmates of some impending action.[a] One senior captain candidly informed me:

It's gotten so that I cannot tell an officer things that I should be telling him. I can't tell him anything serious that I might think is going down because he runs right to the inmates. And it might be in his area. . . . I'd say there's only five or six officers that

---

[a] Shortly after the study was completed, four prisoners escaped from maximum security despite the fact that their plan was known in advance. One factor that facilitated the escape was the decision not to inform the officers in charge of the wing from which the escape was made, presumably for fear they would warn the inmates.

I can really communicate with, that I can say watch this guy, let me know where he goes, who he's with 'cause I think he might be into drugs. With most, if I tell 'em they'll go to the inmate and put him onto it. . . . I can't figure it out. But one thing I do know, most of 'em ain't working for me, they're working for the inmates.

In fact, according to our interpretation, the officers are not working for the inmates; they are working for themselves. Unable to secure compliance with their directives by the enforcement of a set of impersonal rules, they seek to secure compliance by means of friendship, overlooking infractions, and providing highly desired information to inmates. Their behavior is not so much a repudiation of the goal of custodial control as it is an attempt to maintain order, and at the same time to protect themselves, in the face of institutional changes that have made order more difficult to maintain and their position more vulnerable.

The Rebellion of the Hacks

With reference to rebellion as an adaptive response to anomie, Merton has written:

When the institutional system is regarded as the barrier to the satisfaction of legitimized goals, the stage is set for rebellion as an adaptive response. To pass into organized political action, allegiance must not only be withdrawn from the prevailing social structure but must be transferred to new groups possessed of a new myth. The dual function of the myth is to locate the source of large-scale frustrations in the social structure and to portray an alternative structure which would not presumably give rise to the frustration of the deserving.[11]

As we have seen the reforms at ECI have been experienced by the officers as barriers to the achievement of goals to which they are strongly committed. The apathetic performance of their duties represents not only a response to a situation they perceive as futile, but a withdrawal of allegiance to the structure established by the mixed goals of custody and rehabilitation. While I have no direct evidence on this point, statements by officers indicate that this has long been the case, that the officers have from the beginning been frustrated by the gradual extension of privileges to inmates and the incursions upon their own authority. But the relative quietude which pervaded the prison from 1956 to 1968, and the widespread popular support given to the reform program, deprived the officers of any issue by which they might hope to generate public support for their own position. The inmate disturbances from 1968 through 1970 provided them with such an issue. In 1969 the rebellion of the officers began.

Work Stoppages. In the midst of the disturbances in April 1969, the officers staged a "sick out" and held a press conference to protest the absence of rules and regulations at the institution, and to demand an improved pension plan and pay raise. In response to their protest, the legislature granted the officers a substantial increase in salary, an increase that still left their salaries considerably below those of correctional officers in other states, however. Moreover, no action was taken on an improved pension plan nor their demands for the reinstitutionalization of custodial rules. The real significance of the protest, however, lay in demonstrating to the officers that they could expect to achieve some gains by independent action of this nature.

After the court rulings in August 1970, the officers again staged a "sick out." This time they sought the support of the state employees' union in gaining a revocation of the rulings. However, the union not only refused to support the officers but chastised them for irresponsible action. Following this unsuccessful attempt to gain union support, 116 officers resigned from the state employees' union, and a petition was submitted to the state Labor Relations Board to hold an election on prison employee representation. The petition was signed by 184 of some 240 ECI employees in the bargaining unit. The petition was granted and at an election in December, 1970 the ECI employees established their own independent bargaining unit, The Fraternal Order of Correctional Officers.

The Officers Union. The new union immediately embarked upon an aggressive strategy to secure its interests. In the eleven months from January through November, the union organized five walkouts to publicize their demands. Each of these walkouts occurred in the wake of an inmate disturbance used to dramatize the plight of the officers, and each followed a similar strategy. On each occasion the press was notified of the impending work stoppage, and the morning shift, on which most officers work, congregated on the grounds outside the prison rather than reporting to work. There, against the background of obscenities and catcalls from inmates, who remained locked in their cells, spokesmen recounted the reasons for the walk out and reiterated demands for higher pay, an improved pension plan, more officers, and the reestablishment of written rules regarding the conduct of both inmates and officers.

On the first three issues the officers had the support of both Flint and Knott, and the new union was successful in securing a considerable increase in salary and a special pension plan permitting retirement at age 50 after 20 years of service. But the re-establishment of written rules remained in contention until November 1971. Knott openly opposed such a policy on the grounds that it will "put us right back where we were 30 years ago." In the wake of the uprising at Attica, the officers' demands for written rules became more strident, and following an incident in which some 30 inmates refused to enter their cells one evening, the union organized a three-day walkout in November. Under pressure of this sort, Knott was forced to relent and a five-man commission of officers was appointed to develop a set of written rules for both inmates and officers.

For the better part of the period of this study, then, the lower level correctional officers, the ''hacks,'' were engaged in a minor rebellion. By organizing themselves into an independent union they were able to secure better pay, an improved pension plan, and most importantly a commitment by the administrators to their ''myth'' that written custodial policies would eliminate their frustrations.

Summary

The intent of this chapter has been to portray the social situation of the custodians at ECI. From our perspective they constitute the dominant group, standing above and controlling the subordinate inmate population. As we have seen, however, the dominant position of the custodians has been eroded by several factors. First, the contradictory goals assigned to the institution along with goal dissensus among the top administrators has resulted in ambiguous role definitions for the officers and a lack of effective leadership. Second, the officers have retained a commitment to the goal of custodial control in the face of institutional changes that have stripped them of much of their coercive power, thus making the attainment of this goal by traditional means more difficult. As a result of these pressures the administrative/custodial hierarchy is characterized by a state of normlessness and deteriorated working relationships. On the job, officers attempt to maintain order and protect themselves by allowing their authority to be corrupted. Off the job, they are engaged in a minor rebellion against the prison administration in an attempt to secure more stringent custodial regulations. Thus, not only have the resources at the disposal of the custodians been depleted by the reforms, but also their capacity to mobilize their still considerable resources has been impaired by their anomic state.

4 The Cons

The concern of this and the following chapter is with differences in the informal social organization among the white and black inmates at ECI. More specifically, our attention is directed to differences in the focal concerns and interests of these collectivities, their structure of leadership and control, and the relative degree of cohesion and solidarity within each collectivity.

A mode of analysis uniquely suited to this problem is that of isolating indigenous social types. As elaborated by Samuel Strong,[1] social type analysis is based upon the assumption that collectivities live within different social worlds, each world having its own distinctive problems and objects of attention. Social types are shared characterizations of behavioral patterns that emerge as adaptive responses to these distinctive problems and concerns. According to Strong, individuals are typed by others in their social world on the basis of conduct the individual displays in relation to the "axes of life"—"the crucial lines of interest in the group."[2] Thus, social types may be viewed as roles that are defined in terms of perceptions and evaluations of actual behavior, rather than in terms of normative expectations, and as roles that are conceptualized and labeled by the members of the group under observation, rather than by the observer.

Klapp has noted that social type analysis is a valuable tool for the study of informal social organization.[3] Social types make a finer discrimination of roles than is recognized by the formal structure, and thereby provide "a chart to role-structures otherwise largely invisible and submerged."[4] The utility of social type analysis in this respect has been demonstrated in previous studies of prisoner social organization. Sykes, for example, identified several "pains of imprisonment" and analyzed the informal social organization of prisoners by reference to roles defined in terms of differential adaptations made to these deprivations.[5] Giallombardo made a similar use of social type analysis in her study of the inmate population at a Federal Women's Reformatory.[6] The real value of this methodology is seen in the fact that the roles identified by Sykes and Giallombardo, and the ways in which they were related, differed greatly, thereby suggesting that the "axes of life" differ for male and female prisoners, as do the ways in which they organize collectively to cope with the problems of institutional life.

Like the prisoners in the institutions studied by Sykes and Giallombardo, those at ECI also label each other in terms of the behavioral responses made to the prison situation. The analysis that follows, then, relies primarily upon the isolation and description of indigenous social types to present a map of the informal social structure of the black and white inmate populations. As will be shown, the primary "axes of life" differ by race, as do the predominant modes of collective adaptation.

At one point in the following chapter I depart from social type analysis to present a distinction constructed from my own analysis. This is necessary because the roles identified and labeled by the black prisoners represent only a partial description of the empirical state of affairs. That is to say that not all distinctive behavioral adaptations received a consensual label from the black prisoners. Klapp hints at this problem when he observes that small, solidary groups such as religious sects may transform one social type into an ideal type applied to all members in an effort to recruit and socialize new members and minimize internal conflict.[7] Such was the case with the black prisoners organized in the Afro-American Society. Thus, to avoid the bias that would follow from accepting the ideal as the real, I must introduce a conceptual distinction of my own construction in the analysis of the informal organization of the black prisoners.

Social Types Among The Cons

Imprisonment presents those confined with a rather standard set of problems. Thus, it is not surprising that the crucial "axes of life" reflected in the social types identified by the white prisoners at ECI are quite similar to those identified previously by Sykes.[8] The focal concerns of the white prisoners at ECI include the following: relations to staff and the social world they represent, loss of freedom and autonomy, deprivation of material comforts including drugs, sex, and physical security. Inmates are typed in terms of which of these several concerns serves as the primary referent for their behavior. Labels with respect to one interest, however, carry implications for behavior in regard to other concerns as well. For example, a "stand-up guy" is defined primarily in terms of the staff-inmate axis, but the label also connotes a low interest in drugs because involvement in drugs makes a prisoner vulnerable to the power of the staff and is thus inconsistent with the behavior of a "stand-up guy." At ECI, then, inmates tend to play one role with respect to the entire prisoner population.[a]

Stand-up Guys and the Mafia

Stand-Up Guys. At ECI the "stand-up guy" is the counterpart to the "real

---

[a]This is perhaps a function of the small size of the population. In large institutions, especially those with 3,000 or more inmates, it would seem likely that few prisoners would be known by most others and that individuals may be able to segregate their behavior and thus be labeled differently by different audiences.

men" described by Sykes. A "stand-up guy" is mentally and physically tough. He "takes his time" without complaint. To attempt to exploit or manipulate him in any way is to invite direct and personal retaliation. At the same time he is loyal. He does not abuse or exploit other inmates, nor will he betray another inmate, consciously or unconsciously. Were he to see two inmates fighting, for example, he would pass by rather than possibly draw the attention of an officer by stopping to watch or break it up. Most of all, a "stand-up guy" can be counted on "when anything is going down," when there is a collective disturbance. Disturbances, however, are not his preferred style. In his relations with the staff, the "stand-up guy" is cool and aloof. His behavior is artfully designed to display his personal integrity and autonomy without "bringing heat." Rather than refuse to stand for the count, he leans against the wall with his back to the cell door.

Of the 145 white inmates at ECI, no more than fifteen are recognized as "stand-up guys."[b] For the most part, the backgrounds of these individuals reflect an involvement in professionalized and organized crime. Five had been convicted of Armed Robbery and were serving sentences averaging eleven years. Five others were reputedly high-ranking members of an organized crime syndicate, having been convicted of Conspiracy to Murder and/or Murder and were serving sentences of close to twenty years on the average. For these individuals, their confinement represents "dead time," and their overriding interest is to do their time as quickly as possible. Speaking of his time, one of those convicted of Armed Robbery made the following comment:

I been a thief all my life and I ain't about to change now. But if I flat out the bid I got (complete sentence without parole) I'll be too old for any big jobs. So I figure I gotta make parole so's I can make one more big score and retire.

The prison behavior of this particular individual, whom we shall call Sal, is fashioned by this interest in making early parole and is typical of most "stand-up guys." He has several acquaintances with whom he shares a particular interest—cards and dominoes—and spends much of his leisure time engaged in such activities or in his cell reading war novels. He works as a porter in one of the wings, a job with few duties and considerable freedom to move about the institution. Several evenings a week he works in the "Jay Cees" canteen. His presence there profits the "Jay Cees," as few inmates will attempt to "beat the stand"[c] while he is working. Through his

[b]My estimates of the number and characteristics of various types is based on two sources. In many informal conversations with inmates I asked them to define various types and to provide examples of each. Somewhat more precise identification was made with the aid of three informants from a list of all the white inmates present in Maximum Security on March 19, 1971. A particular inmate was included in a category if all three agreed on the identification.

[c]"Beating the Stand" is a game by which inmates secure commodities from the stand without payment. This is done directly by looting or indirectly by charging the purchase to another inmate.

work at the stand he is able to secure enough food to meet his own needs and to exchange for other commodities and services. So, for example, he has a "kid" with whom he occasionally engages in sexual activities. In return for this service, the "kid" is permitted to "beat the stand" when Sal is on duty.

He does not regard any of these acquaintances as friends, however, and is fond of saying, "If you want a friend you can trust, go to the cemetery." Other "stand-up guys" express similar attitudes toward friendship: "If you don't know a guy for fifteen or twenty years, you can't trust him 'cause you don't know who he is." A friend is someone whom the "stand-up guy" has known for a long period of time and who, by his actions, has proven he can be trusted and relied upon to "go all the way with you." Most inmates do not meet these criteria. They are "rats" and "punks," and the "stand-up guy" sees himself as above the petty and routine concerns that occupy them. For some "stand-up guys" the forced association with other inmates develops in them a sense of contamination.

You got a low caliber of men in here. When I get out if anybody ever asks me if I was here I won't tell 'em. They might just know what this joint is like and then I'd be a 'rat' just 'cause I was here.

Among the "stand-up guys," then, there is little sense of any positive identification with the inmate body. In their behavior they remain nearly as aloof from the inmates as they do from the staff. Still, they personify the ideal of solidarity, are highly respected, and in the few inmate activities in which they become involved they are opinion leaders. One such activity was a committee established by the "Jay Cees" to improve the operation of the prison library. Murphy is a "stand-up guy" who, while not a member of the "Jay Cees," was asked to be on the committee because he had been a librarian at another institution. The following incident occurred during one of the meetings concerned with library policy.

The problem arose as to what to do if inmates lost or refused to return books. After some discussion Lyons (Vice-President of the 'Jay Cees') made a motion to the effect that the administration be informed and the inmate be made to pay for the book out of his account. This seemed to reflect the majority view in the preceding discussion. But Murphy got very angry. Standing up, he shouted, "And what the hell are they gonna do? They'll start having shakedowns, that's what. I ain't gonna be part of nothing that brings heat on other guys. I say we just give him a notice and if he don't bring it back we talk to him. If he ain't got the book we rip up the card and forget it." At first Lyons and the others objected, claiming that most inmates were treacherous and should be made to pay. But Murphy stood his ground, arguing that even if they were treacherous, they were still inmates and to betray them was to make oneself as treacherous as them. In the end a motion was passed that the 'Jay Cees' establish a special fund to pay for lost books.

In this incident we see the opinion forming influence of the "stand-up guy." Not an active member of the organization, Murphy nonetheless was able to effectively oppose the Vice-President of the organization by interpreting the decision within the framework of a code of solidarity. Murphy, and other "stand-up guys," however, are only infrequently involved in such activities, usually becoming involved only when the activity meets some interest of their own. This fact, and their aloofness from most inmates, limits their influence as opinion leaders.

The Mafia. Both the ability of "stand-up guys" to exercise power and their limited use of it is most evident with respect to the five members of the organized crime group. Within the institution the individuals formed a cohesive clique variously termed "the mafia," the "purple gang," or the "untouchables". All inmates regard them with a mixture of respect, awe and fear.

All the guys in here idolize 'em. All they have to do is suggest something and it'll be done right away.

. . . .

Everybody knows who they are and they respect 'em for it. Nobody would think of crossin' 'em 'cause they'd put the kiss of death on 'em.

. . . .

It ain't so much a power or influence thing. They got that all right. But the reason they got it is 'cause the other guys respect 'em. It's more respect than power, if ya know what I mean.

The deference shown to these individuals is evident in many small ways. Soon after they arrived, for example, one of them let it be known that the noise after lights out was disturbing his sleep. Thereafter, there was little noise in his block after 10:30 p.m. On summer evenings most of the yard is cast in shadow except for a small area against the rear of the Industrial Building. This spot belongs to them and is seldom occupied by other inmates, even if the "mafia" are not in the yard at the time. At the periodic banquets sponsored by the 'Jay Cees' and the *Beacon,* they are provided with a corner table complete with tablecloth, silverware, salt and pepper, and their food is brought to them and their guests while others, including the Warden, have to stand in line.

At one of these banquets, attended by some 100 prisoners and 200 guests, a popular inmate assaulted an officer who had apprehended him attempting to bring in a bottle of liquor. The inmate was removed from the dining hall to the Deputy Warden's office. Several of his friends then began to threaten a disturbance if any disciplinary action were taken against him. Faced with a difficult situation in which he would set a dangerous precedent were he to accede to the inmate demands, but would run the risk of a serious disturbance in which outsiders might be injured if he did not, the captain in charge requested the intervention of one of the "mafia." Through this intervention a compromise was reached. The captain permitted the offending inmate to return to the banquet in return for his assurance, guaranteed by the inmate mediator, that he would accept whatever disciplinary measures might be forthcoming. The banquet proceeded without further incident, and the next day the inmate and three of his friends were transferred to another institution.

On another occasion, the influx of drugs into the institution reached such a level that it began to cause considerable custodial concern. To avoid a general shakedown of the institution, the "mafia" and a group of their associates conducted their own shakedown and turned a large supply of drugs over to the custodians.

It is only in infrequent crisis situations such as the above that the influence of the "mafia" is brought into the open. More commonly their influence is spread beneath the surface. None of them, for example, are members of the "Jay Cees" or other inmate organizations. But when the "Jay Cees" held their annual election, it was widely known whom the "mafia" wanted for President; he ran unopposed although he had been only a marginal member. They maintain rather close personal relations with another group of inmates, the "wise guys," and through them exert some control over the illicit activities within the institution.

It is not dominance of the inmate population nor control of illicit activities that concerns the "mafia." Their interests are in maintaining a degree of stability and order within the population so that they may do their time with comfort and ease. Their leadership role is one of mediation rather than control. Their identities as members of organized crime place them above the level of suspicion of betrayal of inmate interests. Their demonstrated lack of interest in and lack of dependence upon most illicit prison activities eliminates any question of ulterior motives. Because of "who they are" they are in a position to arbitrate disputes and conflicts both between staff and inmates and among inmates. By mediating such conflicts, they regulate the population to a degree sufficient to achieve their purposes.

Wise Guys and Politicians

In contrast to the "stand-up guys," there exists at ECI two loosely knit cliques that do attempt to dominate and control different aspects of inmate life. The "wise guys" are a loose confederation of some twelve or fifteen inmates whose major concern is personal aggrandizement through the use of force and the control of illicit activities. The "politicians" are those inmates who form the leadership of the "Jay Cees" and the *Beacon*.

Wise Guys. In their background and prison behavior, the "wise guys" resemble closely the "young toughs" mentioned by McCleery[9] and the "state raised youth" described by Irwin.[10] Slightly younger than the white population as a whole (29.3 years vs. 29.7), they had twice as many prior convictions (3.4 vs. 1.7), and were serving sentences averaging some eighteen years.[d] In several cases their long sentences were the result of "parlaying their bids," convictions for crimes committed during imprisonment. "Wise guys," in the argot of the prison, are doing "life bids on the installment plan."

By several measures the "wise guys" are loyal and tough. Their hostility towards the staff is open and intense, they openly espouse the virtue and necessity of inmate unity, and they are likely to be in the forefront of any disturbance. In some ways, then, they resemble "stand-up guys." Like the "stand-up guy," they also see the majority of inmates as weaklings. But where this perception inclines the "stand-up guy" to avoidance, to the "wise guy" it is a license for exploitation. Prison, in their view, is the ultimate test of manhood. A man in prison is able to secure what he wants and protect what he has: "In here a man gets what he can," and, "Nobody can force a man to do something he don't want to," are key elements of their belief system. Any prisoner who does not meet these standards is not a man, "has no respect for himself," and is therefore not entitled to respect from others. Sharing such definitions, the "wise guys" work together in loose and shifting combinations and alliances to aggrandize themselves at the expense of those who prove themselves to be weak.

Several of them operate a betting pool on sports events. Bets are placed with cigarettes or order forms for various commodities at the inmate store, and winners are paid with the same. Losers who fail to make good on their bets are coerced into giving up a portion of their store orders for a considerable period of time or, failing this, are "piped."[e] When the "bank" runs low, i.e., the supply of cigarettes and store commodities controlled by the "wise guys", it is replenished by "shaking down" newly arrived inmates. None of the "wise guys" appear to have the necessary outside connections to provide a steady flow of drugs into the institution. Nonetheless, they are able to realize a profit from the available supply. For the most part, drugs are brought into the institution by individual inmates through their visits. An individual who has been able to "connect" in this manner may be hijacked. Other inmates having frequent visits may be pressured into requesting their visitors to bring in drugs. And the occasional prisoner with the necessary connections to secure a regular supply may have to buy the "protection" of the "wise guys" by providing them with a portion of his supply or profit.

---

[d]These figures are based on twelve inmates whom my informants agreed were in this clique.

[e]Assaulted with a lead pipe or some other heavy, blunt weapon

The exploitation of white inmates by the "wise guys" extends into every facet of prison life. Prisoners are forced to provide them with coffee or sandwiches from the kitchen, to do their laundry, or to satisfy their sexual needs. Perhaps the most blatant form of exploitation in which they engage involves the "Jay Cees" snack bar. Each month inmates are allowed to purchase cards for use at the snack bar. These are kept at the stand, and as purchases are made the amount is deducted from the individual's card. "Wise guys," however, do not need cards. They enter the stand at will and take whatever they want. Often this is done in full view of 20 or 30 inmates waiting in line to be served.

"Wise guys" are hated and feared, but the average white inmate feels powerless to oppose them. Where the "wise guys" are aligned in a rather large clique, most white prisoners remain relatively isolated from each other and are unable to mobilize a significant counterforce to them. Nor, for several reasons, can they turn to the staff. First, many of the exploitive activities of the "wise guys" are not in direct violation of any regulation. Such is the case with the looting of the snack bar. As the custodians see it, the "Jay Cees" established and operate the snack bar, and it is a "Jay Cee" responsibility to protect its operation. Second, other of their activities involve the exploitation of inmates who themselves are engaged in some illicit activity such as drugs. To seek the assistance of the staff in such instances is to invite official sanctions against one's self. Third, to "rat" on a "wise guy" is to risk probable physical retaliation from other members of the clique. The only means of escaping this threat is to enter protective custody, which is highly punitive, necessitating nearly continual cell confinement.

All of this is not to say that the "wise guys" operate with complete impunity. They do not. Some inmates do "rat" and enter protective custody. Officers do occasionally come upon them in the commission of some act and report them. Moreover, there are prisoners, the "stand-up guys," who will retaliate, who are "men" and cannot be exploited. As noted above, when Sal is running the snack bar, the "wise guys" stay out. Nor are they likely to interfere with his sexual partner or other acquaintances. The existence, then, of some ten "stand-up guys," each with several acquaintances, excludes a portion of the population from direct, personal exploitation. It is the new inmate, the young and unaffiliated, those doing short time, who are the prime targets of the "wise guy's" tactics.

Another restraint upon the "wise guys" appears to be their close relation with the "mafia." Members of the "wise guys" and the "mafia" spend considerable time together playing cards, tripping the yard, and engaging in conversation on the steps of one of the cell blocks. The precise meaning of this relationship is difficult to determine. Some staff and inmates believe that in fact the "mafia" control the rackets in the institution, and that the "wise guys" are their "leg men." What appears more likely, however, is that the relationship is one of co-optation. From their association with the "mafia," the "wise guys" derive considerable status, and there may also be the hope of some more secure future criminal employment. There are also more tangible rewards. Members of the "mafia" have been known to deposit money in the accounts of "wise guys," and on at least one occasion they have secured a job for a "wise guy" with a local union. Through their acceptance and favors the "mafia" are able to control the "wise guys" at critical points. Several such instances have been mentioned. The threatened disturbances at the banquet involved key figures in the "wise guy" clique. Despite the fact that "wise guys" profit from drugs, it was with their assistance that the drugs were collected to avoid a custodial shakedown. When the looting of the snack bar reached a point where the bar was operating at a loss, the leaders of the "Jay Cees" brought the matter to the "mafia," and the looting was promptly curtailed.

Such incidents are by no means conclusive evidence. But they do suggest that the close personal relations between the "mafia" and the "wise guys" are perhaps a means used by the "mafia" to control and restrain disruptive behavior in critical situations, whether the threat be from the "wise guys" themselves or some other element of the population.

Politicians. From the viewpoint of those outside the institution and some staff as well, the leaders of the white prisoner population are those who occupy elected offices in the "Jay Cees" and on the *Beacon*. This group of some fifteen prisoners represents the inmate body to outside organizations and to the Warden and the staff. When the Warden was presented with a petition from another group to elect an inmate advisory council, he denied it on the grounds that he already had such a council in the elected leaders of the inmate organizations.

But, as the label "politician" implies, there is considerable alienation between this group of elected representatives and the majority of white inmates. While on the one hand they are accorded respect for their organizational abilities and accomplishments, on the other hand they are looked upon with considerable suspicion, envy, and jealousy. For one thing, despite their elected position, they are not representative of white inmates in terms of demographic characteristics. They are considerably older than the white population as a whole (32.4 years), have a far longer median sentence length (23.5 years), and slightly more than 50 percent of them are convicted of Murder.[f]

The ambivalence with which the "politicians" are regarded, however, stems more from a perspective implied in their activities than from the

---

[f]These figures are based on fifteen inmates who held elected positions as officers or board members of the "Jay Cees," or were members of the editorial staff of *Beacon*.

demographic differences between them and their constituents. Many of their activities are of direct benefit to the entire inmate population. As I have noted before, the organization sponsors a variety of banquets and parties, a family day, and a number of other functions that make time easier. Further, as I have also noted, they are actively engaged in prison reform. *The Beacon* is a vehicle to educate the public concerning abuses of the legal and penal systems. The "Jay Cees" sponsor an annual legislative forum by means of which they have been able to secure passage of some progressive legislation.

Throughout these legal activities, however, is a perspective that has been termed censoriousness.[11] The "politicians" attempt to achieve changes in the penal system by means of criticizing the administration for deviating from their own stated commitment to rehabilitation. In effect, this implies an acceptance of the label society has placed upon the inmate. By implication, it is a perspective admitting that inmates are criminals or are sick and require rehabilitation. The "politicians" do not "reject their rejectors." They accept this rejection, grant its legitimacy, and seek to use it as a weapon to achieve change within the system. Statements indicative of this perspective appear in every issue of *The Beacon*.

The fact is that 80 percent of the men who are incarcerated in our prisons will eventually be free. Therefore, society must ask itself several basic questions such as: How do we want these men to return to the community? Do we want them to return the same way they went in, or do we want them to return as productive citizens?

The hardest lesson for over half the men incarcerated today is learning how to adjust to society's way of living. Odd as it may seem, a great majority of men in prison do not know how to act in the surroundings of people other than the environment of that in which they were brought up in. . . . Once taken out of that environment and introduced to a strange atmosphere of people who have lived on the right side of the street and learned how to conduct themselves, the first impulse is panic for fear that whatever he may say or do is not going to be up to the standards that good people abide by.

Many of the activities of the "politicians" seem to be an attempt to prove to society and themselves that they and other inmates are capable of rehabilitation. For instance, the general membership meetings of the "Jay Cees" take place in a room decorated with both the federal and state flags. Meetings are begun with a prayer by the chaplain, a pledge of allegiance to the flag, and a recitation of the "Jay Cee" creed:

We believe that faith in God gives meaning and purpose to human life. That the brotherhood of man transcends the sovereignty of nations. That economic justice can best be won by free enterprise. That government should be of law rather than of men. That earth's great treasure lies in the human personality. And that service to humanity is the best work of life.

Of a total membership of some 60 inmates, no more than 20 attend a typical general membership meeting, and the discomfort of those attending in reciting this creed is overwhelming. Where the "politicians" stand and recite these incantations in a loud voice, the others bow their heads, scuffle their feet, look out the window, or engage in some action to place distance between themselves and the words they mutter.[12]

"Politicians" exhibit great concern about proper decorum in their meetings with outside guests. Most of these meetings occur in a room in which a table is set with a white cloth. Name cards are placed around the table, an agenda is prepared and distributed, and meetings are run in strict accordance with parliamentary procedure. To ensure proper appearances, only certain members, generally the "politicians" themselves, are admitted to these meetings. The majority of inmates probably could not care less about the content of the meetings, but the meetings often involve female visitors from surrounding colleges, and there is thus considerable resentment among the prisoners at their exclusion. After one such meeting an inmate commented angrily to another: "They musta had ten broads in there. The least they coulda done was send one or two out for us, them bastards."

The "politicians" are also resented because of the privileged positions they occupy. While they, like other inmates, have assigned jobs, they are able to schedule their organizational activities so that they seldom work. Because of their positions, they are granted considerable freedom of movement within the institution and are almost continually engaged in meetings with outside groups, the staff, or themselves. Thus, the "politicians" have a vested interest in protecting their position, and it is often apparent to other inmates that their actions are more self-serving than in the interests of the inmate population. An example of this occurred with respect to securing official permission for inmate representatives to attend monthly meetings of the Executive Board of the state "Jay Cees" and the Board of Directors meeting of Beacon House, a halfway house allied with *The Beacon*. The Warden agreed to permit representatives to attend these meetings and requested a list of the candidates from which he would select two. Over a six-month period, no inmate was selected because of the unwillingness of the "politicians" to submit names of inmates whom the Warden could approve. He would not approve any of the "politicians" because of the length of their sentences, and they refused to submit the names of any inmates who were not within their group.

Actions such as the above, their concern with appearances, and the perspective from which they view themselves and other inmates account for the ambivalence with which the prisoners regard the "politicians." Inmates are uncertain about what side the "politicians" are on. Their loyalty is always in question.

I just don't trust them guys. If something was to go down tomorrow they might just be in here swinging clubs with the hacks.

The position of the "politicians" is thus quite vulnerable. Lacking a committed following, they do not themselves possess the necessary resources to maintain their position if opposition to their leadership were to arise. For this reason they are drawn into a cooperative relation with the "mafia." Many of the programs and activities of the "politicians" are in accordance with the interests of the "mafia." Legislative changes such as the bill to make "lifers" eligible for parole after ten years, administrative changes such as increased visiting privileges, and less stringent criteria for minimum custody and work release, and the yearly round of parties and banquets at which the "mafia" are honored guests have the potential for making time both shorter and more comfortable. The "mafia" recognize that there are few prisoners other than the "politicians" with the motivation and ability to achieve such changes and to sponsor such programs. Thus, the "mafia" use their influence to ensure the continued election of the "politicians" and at times to prevent opposition to some of their more controversial programs.

The informal social organization of the white prisoner population is depicted in Figure 4-1. As can be seen there, leadership is vested in the "mafia," but their influence is exercised largely through the "wise guys" and the "politicians," the physical power of the "wise guys" being used to control other prisoners when necessary, and the organizational abilities of the "politicians" being used to achieve desired changes through negotiation and arbitration with the staff.

Administration Men and Hippies

Administration Men. Some fourteen white inmates are known as "administration men." Where the loyalty of the "politicians" is suspect, that of the "administration men" is clear. They identify with the values of legitimate society. They see themselves as conventional people who, perhaps through being a victim of circumstances, are now forced to live among criminals. To the "administration men" the institution is "a vicious place," "a jungle," and "most of the guys in here are animals." To some extent the differences the "administration men" see between themselves and other inmates is borne out by their backgrounds. For twelve of the fourteen, their current confinement is their first. Eight have been convicted of Homicide, two of Manslaughter, three of Assault, and one of Sodomy. Despite lack of prior criminal involvement, however, "administration

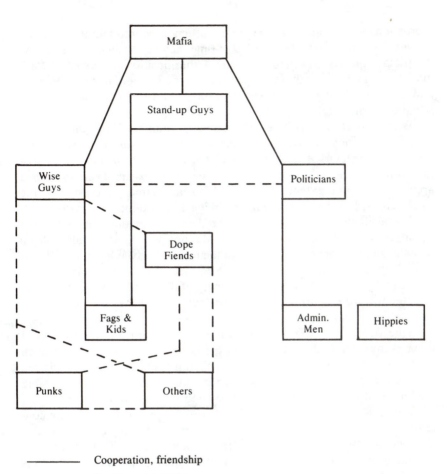

Cooperation, friendship

— — — — — Conflict, exploitation

Figure 4-1. Informal Social Organization of the White Prisoners

men'' are serving long sentences because of the seriousness of their offences. Their median sentence length is 35.5 years.

The prison behavior of the "administration men" is a self-conscious attempt to set themselves apart from the other inmates. One of their central concerns, and that which earns them the label of "administration men," is to develop a close relationship with the staff. This is most evident in the jobs they secure. Most have jobs that in some way place them in an intermediate position between the staff and other inmates. Two are proofreaders in the Print Shop, working in the supervisor's office correcting and often rejecting the work done by other prisoners. Two others work in the recreation office and, in the summer, officiate at intramural sports activities. Another, over a long period of time, has established himself as the unofficial supervisor of the Plate Shop. Other positions occupied by "administration men" are those of first cook in the kitchen, inmate librarian, and "Rear Hall" porters, who are responsible for the maintenance of the administration offices.

With respect to other inmates, "administration men" are loners. They do not form close friendships either among themselves or with other prisoners. The focus of their non-job related activities is their case. Much of their time is spent in their cells studying law and preparing a variety of legal appeals. To some extent, this gives them a common interest with the "politicians," many of whom have similar backgrounds and with whom they occasionally share newly discovered legal information. But, unlike the "politicians," "administration men" do not use their acquired legal knowledge to advance the interests of the inmate body as a whole. "Politicians" file class actions; "administration men" file personal appeals.

Apart from his case, the prison activity of the "administration man" is directed toward preparing himself for release. While they do not consider themselves criminals, most see in themselves some character flaw that must be overcome. The "administration men" form the core of those inmates involved in the few formally sponsored treatment programs such as Alcoholics Anonymous and group therapy. Others turn to religion, becoming near fanatics who spend large amounts of time in prayer and bible reading, and who surround themselves with religious objects.

The prison behavior of the "administration men" earns them the contempt of other inmates, who see them as adjuncts to the custodial force. But the fact that most of the "administration men" have killed or violently assaulted another person is not lost on other inmates, and their contempt is tinged with fear. It leads to avoidance rather than dominance or exploitation. Murphy, a "stand-up guy," expressed this reaction clearly in recalling an incident involving Hank:

I hate every one of them punks. I'd like to see every one of 'em dead. But to tell the honest truth there ain't too many I'd wanna tangle with myself. You know Hank? . . . Well him and me came into the joint about the same time and we worked in the laundry together for a while. I remember I used to think, how the hell could that ass kill two guys? Then one day I seen how. Some sheets he was doing got ripped up in the mangle. He went right outta his fucking skull. He ripped up the mangle with his bare hands and then he started on the rest of the place. . . . It took ten or eleven hacks to stop him and you shoulda seen the damage he done there. . . . Guys that flip out like that, though, they're crazy. The best thing to do is just stay away from 'em.

Hippies. Another group of white prisoners whose normative orientations lie beyond the prison are some eight inmates identified as "hippies." If, in some sense, "administration men" are the extreme right wing of the white population, the "hippies" are the extreme left. Their external identification is not with the values of legitimized authority but with the counter-culture. Like the "administration men," they also do not define themselves as criminals. They are political prisoners, victims of an inequitable and illegitimate politico-economic structure. From their perspective, it is not only they who are not criminals; no inmates are criminals except perhaps the "mafia." Committed to this perspective, they experience a curious mixture of solidarity with and alienation from other white inmates. On an ideological level, they feel a sense of unity as a result of their common oppression. On a personal level, however, they feel estranged due to what they perceive as the false consciousness, the lack of political awareness, and continued commitment to materialistic values of the average prisoner.

The "hippies" form a close-knit clique who remain detached from other inmates. Despite the definition of themselves as political prisoners, their prison behavior is devoid of any overt and immediate revolutionary direction. Most of their time is consumed in reading a diverse body of literature in philosophy and social science, and in extended "rap sessions" in these areas. In the summer of 1971, yoga became a way of life for the "hippies." They formed a Yoga Society and each evening gathered in a circle in one corner of the yard to perform their exercises and chants. To "stand-up guys" such as Sal and Murphy the "hippies" are "creeps."

Fags, Punks, and Kids

If one were to judge the intensity of the deprivations of incarceration by the frequency of topics that arise in inmate conversation, sexual deprivation would top the list. At ECI one cannot move about the yard or the wings for any length of time without coming upon a group of prisoners entertaining each other with stories of their sexual exploits. Generally these conversations are in the form of performances in which one inmate recounts, in explicit detail, glowing tales of the number of sexual conquests he has made, the particular acts at which each partner was most adroit, and of his own sexual endurance. The nature and content of these performances suggests that it is not merely the absence of heterosexual release that is frustrating for the prisoner, though this is undoubtedly true. Equally and perhaps more important seems to be the fact that the absence of heterosexual contact deprives the prisoner of a major means by which he may affirm his masculinity.[13] The inmates at ECI, like those in all prisons, are drawn predominantly from segments of the population in which dominance and conquest in heterosexual relations are of heightened significance in the assertion of claims to masculine status. Heterosexual deprivation, then, is frustrating for the prisoner not merely because of the absence of this form of sexual release, but also because its absence is experienced as a severe threat to masculinity.

This two-pronged nature of the sexual problem defines the form of sexual relations in the prison. A prisoner may find some measure of sexual release through masturbation. Activity of this sort resolves only one dimension of the problem, however, and may itself generate a threat to a prisoner's image of himself as a "man." Ritualized sexual conversations, as noted above, may partially resolve the problem of masculine identification. Beyond these outlets, however, there exists the opportunity for homosexual contact, which, accorded appropriate definitions, may resolve both problems. Within the culture of the prison, such a definition exists. The label homosexual is attached only to those prisoners who assume the passive role in a sexual act. A prisoner who assumes the active role, who does not reciprocate in the sex act, is not a homosexual. By acceptance of this definition, then, it is possible for prisoners to obtain some measure of sexual release in a non-solitary manner without threatening, and perhaps even enhancing, their claims to status as a male.

Fags. At ECI, as elsewhere, two major types of homosexuals are identified, "fags" and "punks."[14] "Fags" are admitted homosexuals, prisoners who engaged in homosexual activity prior to their incarceration and for whom this is the preferred form of sexual relationship. Prior to his imprisonment, the "fag" may have played a "butch" or "fem" role, but in the prison he adopts only the passive role. A "queen" is a "fag" whose role-playing extends into every facet of his (her) behavior. "Queens" display exaggerated feminine mannerisms, wear tight pants, have long hair, a female name, and, in one case, simulated female breasts by silicone injection. Most "fags," however, confine their passive role to the sexual act itself.

"Fags" desire sexual contact within the prison and actively seek it. Their interests in these relationships, however, extend beyond the desire for sexual satisfaction and include needs for affection, intimacy, and security. Such interests complement many needs of prisoners with long sentences, and the typical relationship for a "fag" is a pseudo-marriage with an older long-term inmate. They may live in cells next to each other, work in the same shop, eat together, and engage in most activities in common. Such relationships are subject to enormous strain, however. One strain derives from the inability of the active partner to commit himself wholly to the role. To be engaged in a pseudo-marriage and at the same time to preserve his image of masculinity, he must at least publicly demonstrate some degree of disaffection from the relationship. Often this results in the active partner publicly degrading and demeaning the "fag." He may force his partner to engage in homosexual play activities as the butt of jokes for a group, or he may coerce the "fag" into providing sexual services for several of his friends. He may also exploit the "fag" for other interests. One "fag" described the breakup of a recent marriage in the following way:

At first it was good, you know. We was having sex and that was good. But it was more than that. We were sharing everything and doing everything together. We was close and the best part was that he didn't have to keep that tough guy mask on. He told me things about himself that he wouldn't tell anybody else, and it made him feel good to have somebody to talk to. But them other guys he hangs with got into it, and he started coming outta that tough guy bag. He began to treat me like dirt and he even tried to get me to put out for all them and beat the shit out of me when I wouldn't. One day he came into my cell. I had a diamond ring on the table. He grabbed it and put it on his finger and walked out. I think he was bullshitting me, he meant to give it back. But then he met Vic and Vic said, 'Why give it back? We could cop some dope with it', and that's what they did. When that happened I said the hell with him and moved over to the side I'm on now.

Strain in the relationship also arises from the activities of the "fag." By prostituting himself, a "fag" may secure virtually any luxury available in the prison, and such covert activities are common. The common knowledge that "fags" are treacherous in this manner further crowds the relationship with mistrust and suspicion, adding to its instability. While "marriages" occur, then, they are usually of short duration, and within a year a "fag" may be involved in several of them.

Punks. Of the 145 white inmates in the institution on March 19, 1971, only three were identified as "fags," and all three were involved in pseudo-marriages. The available supply of willing "passive" sex partners is, then, considerably less than the demand, and there is a constant tension to effect some balance between active and passive role players. This balance is effected by means of seduction, coercion, and threat. A "punk" is a young inmate who, at least initially, adopts the passive role as a result of force. Eleven white inmates were identified as "punks." The average age of the eleven was 21.3 years. Their average sentence length was 4.1 years, and only three of the eleven had a prior commitment. On the average, then, "punks" are young, serving short sentences, and are on their first sentence. Compared with other inmates, they also appear to be physically underdeveloped for their age, though this is only an impression.

The process by which a "punk" is made may begin prior to his arrival in the prison. Other inmates being transported to the prison with a potential "punk" may prepare him for his role.

When I first came in I was scared. I'd never been in a jail before and I didn't know no one here. I didn't know what to expect. Coming up in the van all the others was pullin' and tuggin' at me, and laughing about what was gonna happen. They kept tellin' me how many lifers they got here and how they all like to have kids and what would happen if I didn't go along with 'em. I was scared, I didn't know what to do.

Soon after he arrived, this inmate was approached by two others carrying a jar containing some orange liquid. They told him the liquid was acid and threatened to throw it over him if he did not "come across" for them, which he immediately did, only to find out the liquid was orange juice. Thereafter he was repeatedly coerced into performing sexual services, and eventually placed himself in protective custody. After several months of continual confinement, however, he accommodated himself to his role and returned to the general population.

Anything was better than that. I couldn't take being locked up 23 hours a day, never getting outta that wing, never being able to go to the movies or anything. So I decided if that's what they wanted, I'd give it to 'em. And after a while it got so I could tell who'd bang me in the head if I didn't come across and who wouldn't. So I just give it up to the "wise guys" and them but if the others want it, they gotta pay in advance.

By thus accommodating himself to the role forced upon him, by developing an ability to discriminate between real and non-real threats, the "punk" is able to gain some measure of physical security as well as material reward.

Kids. An occasional "punk" may be able to manage his sexual activities even further, confining them to a relatively small group. "Stand-up guys" shun entry into a pseudo-marriage as a sign of weakness. They may, however, offer protection and favors to a particularly attractive "punk" in return for his regular performance of sexual acts. The "punk" is then known as their "kid." Sal, the "stand-up guy" who works in the "Jay Cee" stand, was looking for a "kid":

I gotta find me a kid, but it's hard, ya know. I don't want nothing to do with any of them "punks" we got here now. But if some nice looking, clean punk comes in then I might just do something for him. . . . Well, like sorta take him under my wing and give him things from the stand. . . . It's just kinda nice to have a "kid" around, ya know, one that you can count on and that's pretty much yours. I hate like hell to have to use one of them "punks" that's "catching lobs" [fellatio] from everybody else.

The relationship between "kids" and other inmates are distinct from both those of the "fag" and the typical "punk." Unlike the pseudo-marriages to the "fags," the "kid" relationship does not extend beyond the sex act itself, nor is it an exclusive relationship. It is a contractual exchange of sexual services for protection and material reward, and is devoid of emotion and intimacy. "Kids" do not necessarily live next to their sex partners, nor do they work, eat, or "hang out" together. Several inmates, usually known to each other, may share the same "kid." As long as the "kid" is able to fulfill his sexual obligations with respect to each one, there is no conflict. In contrast to most "punks," on the other hand, the "kid" is not coerced. "Kids" have already been "made" and are now offered assured compensation for their services. From a narrow point of view, then, they enter the relationship voluntarily and by means of it are protected from coercion or threat by others. As there is little emotional investment in the relationship, however, protection remains uncertain and "kids" in fact are often betrayed.

Dope Fiends and Others

Dope Fiends. Drugs have replaced liquor as the most desired illicit commodity at ECI. Even inmates who were not users prior to their imprisonment become occasional users in an effort to escape the realities of life within the walls. But inmates make a clear distinction between such occasional users and the "dope fiend." "Dope fiends" are inmates who were addicts prior to their incarceration and for whom "scoring drugs" and "getting high" remain their consummate interest while in prison. Despite this rather clear distinction, however, most "dope fiends" remain rather indistinguishable from the majority of the white population. My informants, for instance, were in general agreement that some 20 to 30 percent of the white inmates were "dope fiends," but they exhibited considerable disagreement over the identification of specific inmates as "dope fiends."

There are several reasons for this confusion. First, few inmates have been convicted of violations of narcotics laws. Most "dope fiends" have been convicted of Breaking and Entering, Larceny, or some similar property offense related to their addiction. Thus, most "dope fiends" are not labeled as such by the nature of their offense. Second, the offenses of "dope fiends" are usually of a minor nature, and they receive relatively short sentences. Being in maximum security for a relatively short period of time, they remain unknown to the majority of inmates. Third, not enough drugs enter the institution for the "dope fiend" to maintain his physical addiction. They are therefore distinguishable from the occasional users only by the degree of their desire for drugs and the effort they expend to obtain them. Finally, because of the risks involved and the high demand for drugs, "dope fiends" attempt to conceal their activities from inmates as well as from officers.

Despite their relative anonymity, "dope fiends" are deeply involved in the underlife of the institution. They stand at the center of a complex network of relationships that has arisen around the procurement, sale, and usage of drugs. Occasionally, a "dope fiend" may receive drugs as a gift from a visitor. More commonly, however, drugs must be purchased, whether from a visitor or another inmate, at highly inflated prices. A "nickel bag" ($5.00 worth) of heroin, for example, costs between $15.00 and $20.00 at ECI. And, unlike other transactions, drugs are sold only for cash. To secure drugs, then, "dope fiends" frequently form alliances with other inmates to raise the necessary cash. Even if they have the money, however, they may not have a set of "works," a hypodermic needle and syringe. Another inmate without money but with the "works" may then be brought into the combination. The effort to secure drugs thus drives "dope fiends" into symbiotic relationships with at least three or four other inmates.

An occasional "dope fiend" is able to maintain his street connections and thus secure a rather constant supply of drugs exceeding his immediate needs. He may then turn to "dealing" within the institution. By cutting a "nickel bag," purchased at $15.00 from a street connection, into rather minuscule portions sold for $5.00, the "dealer" can realize a considerable profit. "Dealing," however, is a risky business. Not only must the "dealer" protect himself from the staff, but if he is to realize a profit he must protect himself from inmate predators, such as the "wise guys," who will convert his profit into their own. To protect himself, the "dealer" may form a confederation with four or five other inmates. A non-user is given a portion of the profit in return for receiving the drugs from a visitor and "stashing" them. Two or three others, in return for a portion of the supply, act as "runners." They spread the word that drugs are available, collect the cash, and return it to the "dealer." The "dealer" secures the drugs from the "stash," who remains unknown to the "runners" and who turns the drugs over to the "runners" who distribute them.

It is a well-known fact that when it comes to narcotics, "dope fiends" have no friends. The relationships described, whether based on selling or consuming drugs, are not cohesive. They are symbiotic relations that hinge upon the common interest in "scoring" and "getting high." As such, the membership of the various combinations is constantly shifting, depending upon who has the necessary connections to secure drugs and who has the money to purchase them. Pervading these relationships is the fear of "getting beat." A "dope fiend" may be "beat" in various ways. The "dealer," for instance, is highly vulnerable. His operation may be, and often is, uncovered by the "wise guys," in which case he takes all the risks for little or no profit. Apart from that, his "stash" may use the supply to begin "dealing" himself, or his "runners" may hijack his supply or profits. Users may likewise be "beat." One of the major confidence games within the institution is for "dope fiends" to present themselves as "runners" and then use the collected cash to make their own purchases. Or they may in fact be "runners," but fail to make the contracted delivery. In both cases, they may claim to have been "hijacked" by the "wise guys." A variant of this game is for a "dope fiend" to collect cash to make a purchase from a street connection, use the drugs himself, and then claim the connection failed to deliver.

Others. Confidence games and petty hijacking activities such as these are by no means the sole province of the "dope fiends." As was pointed out in Chapter 2, nearly one-third of the white population are serving sentences of three years or less. Inmates at ECI are eligible for parole after completing one-third of their sentence, and it is a common practice to place prisoners in minimum security several months prior to parole. This makes for a high rate of population mobility among the white population. Close to one-third of them remain in maximum security for only three to six months. They exist only as nameless faces to the majority of whites and are not identified by any distinctive label. They are "others."

The steady flow of "others" through maximum security presents a difficult control problem for both the custodians and the long-term inmates. "Others" are generally an impoverished class and are not in the institution long enough to gain access to positions that would provide them with a "hustle," a means of engaging in informal exchange relations. Their very transiency and anonymity, however, afford them a measure of protection for a variety of disruptive activities. They form small cliques and hijack each other, and steal cigarettes, televisions, and other commodities from open cells. They use their anonymity to "beat the stand" by making purchases and charging them to another inmate's account. These and other exploitive activities serve to increase the level of suspicion with which the white inmates regard each other, and they contribute to the general absence of any sense of inmate solidarity.

Rats

Nowhere is the absence of white inmate solidarity more evident than in white views on "rats" and "rattings." A "rat" is an inmate who communicates information concerning inmate activities to the custodians. Among the white prisoners there is no clearly definable class of inmates termed "rats." With the exception of the "mafia" and "stand-up guys," any inmate not in the circle of one's immediate associates is an actual or potential "rat." From the standpoint of any particular inmate, then, nearly all others are "rats."

The norm against "ratting" remains an ideal but is not often realized in practice. Inmates do not expect another inmate to endure any pain or suffering without "ratting." Ideally, he should; realistically, few will. As one old-timer put it quite candidly: "The rule here is don't rat, but don't let your conscience kill ya." The norm against "ratting," then, is not seen as a moral absolute demanding unthinking and automatic compliance. It is relative and admits of many exceptions, one of which may be if another has "ratted" on you. The following conversation among three inmates occurred in my presence in the yard. Harry was dreading the fact that he was going to court in the morning and was seeking advice from Sam and Joe:

Harry: They want me to testify against the guy that put me in here. I don't know what to do. I sure would like to get that bastard.

Sam: Wait 'till ya get out and then stick a shiv in him.

Joe: Don't be a fool, man. That'll just get ya more time. They got anything else on ya?

Harry: Yeah, passing some paper.

Joe: Then, make a deal. You help them if they help you. That way you get the bastard now and get a break yourself. What you think, Sam?

Sam: It's one way of doing it, I guess.

In a solidary inmate group with a strong consensus on the norms against "ratting," the incidence of "ratting" may strengthen group solidarity. Strong group sanctions, including physical assault and death, imposed upon the "rat" may serve to unify the group against a common internal enemy. But, given the definition of "ratting" at ECI, sanctions against "rats" weaken the group further.[15] Accepting the norm as situationally specific, the inmates define "ratting" as a personal rather than a group concern. If one inmate "rats" on another, it is their "beef," to be settled by themselves.

As long as he don't "rat" on me why should I care? Why should I stick my neck out when the other guys don't give a shit and one of 'em might even "rat" on me.

If we view the interest of third parties in punishing proscribed behavior as an indicator of the degree to which a norm is institutionalized, then this comment indicates that the norm proscribing "ratting" is not institutionalized at ECI. "Ratting" often is not penalized. Moreover, when it is penalized, the penalties are in the form of personal vendettas that, rather than unifying the group against a common enemy, fragment it into cliques in conflict with each other. This makes "ratting" even more likely. Anonymous "ratting" on the activities of another is another means of revenge, of evening the score. "Ratting," and the sanctioning of "rats," constitutes a vicious circle undermining and eroding the solidarity of the white population.

Humanitarian Reform and Convict Solidarity

In Chapter 1, I distinguished between two models of prisoner social organization, the deprivation model and the importation model. The deprivation model, it will be recalled, views inmate social organization as a system of roles that articulate a normative code of solidarity, a code that emerges within the prison in response to the deprivations of incarceration. In contrast, the importation model views prisoner social organization as being fragmented into primary groups possessing diverse normative orientations that have their origins in subcultures outside the prison. While these models are frequently considered contradictory, evidence from comparative studies was cited suggesting that they may in fact be complements, representations of inmate organization under varying conditions of deprivation and control.

Except for a similarity in the labels by which white inmates are identified, the informal social structure of the white population at ECI bears little resemblance to that depicted by the deprivation model. It is not a system of interlocking roles defined by reference to a shared normative code of solidarity. Commitment to such a code is found only among the "stand-up guys" who, while influential and respected by all prisoners, exhibit little sense of positive identification with the inmate body. To the extent that solidarity exists among other white inmates, it is a calculated solidarity resting upon mutual need satisfaction rather than conformity to a set of norms defined as moral imperatives.[16] White inmates evaluate each situation from the perspective of their own needs and interests, and solidarity exists only to the extent that one's personal needs and interests are satisfied by the situation or activity in question. The coincidence of personal and group needs and interests occurs most commonly only within small cliques, and the basic unit of the white inmate social structure is the three to five member clique. Even within these cliques, the bonds are more symbiotic than cohesive and memberships are continually changing. Rather than a social system, the social organization of the white population might better be described as a congeries of cliques with diverse orientations. Some of these orientations such as those of the "mafia," "stand-up guys," "dope fiends," "administration men," and "hippies" have their origins in subcultures outside the prison. Others such as those of the "wise guys," "politicians," "punks," and "kids" appear to be indigenous products. On balance, however, the social organization of the white prisoners at ECI is more in line with the importation model than the deprivation model.

Whether in fact the current organization of the white prisoners at ECI represents a change in response to the policy of humanitarian reform cannot be tested with data available from the study. Nonetheless such an interpretation is in accord with the perspective of long-term inmates. Retrospective accounts are undoubtedly fraught with nostalgia. Even so, there is still a remarkable consensus among the long-term residents at ECI that there is far less solidarity among convicts today than previously, and that the loss of unity is due to the reforms that have been introduced. John, a "lifer" who has been at ECI since 1953, noted:

This was a tough can then. . . . I ain't sayin' we was all buddies or nothing. It never was like that. Back then everybody stayed pretty much to themselves, but they knew where they stood. We was all cons and there was respect for a con. That's what's changed. There's no respect for a con anymore. . . . All them changes is what did it. They broke down all the old barriers. There's nothing to fight anymore. The hacks ain't enemies, not really. How can you consider a guy who gives your wife a ride home or lets you make an extra phone call an enemy? And without an enemy there's no need for unity.

In John's view, the reforms, by restricting custodial powers and encouraging positive staff-inmate relations, have destroyed the basis of convict solidarity. This, however, is only the most obvious way solidarity is undermined. The extension of privileges, in combination with the relaxation of regulations, results in frequent minor conflicts between inmates. For example, an inmate who desires to take a nap at noontime may be disturbed by the stereo of his neighbor. As a result of the reforms, such incidents are frequent and recurring, and the inmate must settle the matter himself or suffer the discomfort and aggravation. In either case, incidents such as these serve to alienate the inmates involved.

Hostile feelings are also generated through competition for positions in the vocational training and work release programs. A position in the MDTA program is valued by many inmates because it pays $20.00 per week—far more than other jobs, and work release is valued for the access it provides to the free world. Inmates believe that if their institutional record is "clean," they are entitled to participate in these programs as soon as they become eligible. Only 30 can participate in the MDTA program at any one time, however, and work release can accommodate only 50. Thus, many of those eligible are denied and are resentful of those who receive the positions.

Resentment also rises from the disparities in material comfort resulting from the reforms. Color televisions, stereos and other luxuries are permitted, but must be purchased by the inmate himself. An inmate usually accomplishes this with the aid of his family or other visitors. Not all prisoners receive visits, however, and the families of many are unable or unwilling to provide such amenities. In this way, the relative comfort of some increases the felt deprivation of others.

Max, a long-term inmate and veteran of sentences in several institutions, points to yet another frustration attributable to the reform:

Compared to the other cans I been in this place is a country club. It's gotta be the easiest joint in the country but it's the most aggravating too. . . . Ya can't keep your mind off the streets.

Time is made easier by severing all emotional ties with the "streets" and involving oneself completely in the life of the institution. Attainment of this psychological state becomes more difficult as the institution becomes more permeable to outside influences, and the reforms at ECI have made the institution highly permeable. Previously, visits were permitted only once a month and took place in the "tank," a small room in which the inmate was separated from his visitor by a pane of bulletproof glass. Today, visits are permitted twice weekly, and there is no physical separation between an inmate and his visitor. At one time, all mail and newspapers were closely censored; today, there is no censorship. In the past, the only communication medium permitted inmates was the institutional radio station. Today, virtually all inmates have their own radios and perhaps the majority have television. Until recently, few non-staff personnel entered the entrails of the institution. Today, scores of volunteers, male and female, enter the institution daily and interact with inmates relatively free from the surveillance of the custodians. Nearly every month there is a banquet, party, or some other occasion when the family and friends of inmates enter the institution and socialize in a rather festive spirit.

Through these and other channels opened by reforms, the world of the "streets" flows freely through walls and bars that were once impermeable barriers. In one sense, this makes the time easier. It is less deprivational, less monotonous, and more pleasurable. But, in another sense, it is harder. Prisoners are less able to escape from an awareness of what they have lost. They are less able to sever the emotional ties with friends and families and to identify completely with their fellow captives. The muffled sobs one hears from cells after parties and banquets are a testimony to the pain imposed by the maintenance of these attachments.

This identification with external reference groups is not only psychological; it is behavioral as well. As a result of the reforms, the institution makes little attempt to "strip away" pre-prison identities. Inmates are identified by name, not number. There is no uniform beyond the required green or khaki trousers. Shoulder length hair and even beards are permitted. Through distinctive styles of dress, personal ornaments, cell decorations, music collections, and innumerable other means the white prisoners are able to give expression to aspects of their pre-prison identities. Moreover, in organizations such as the "Jay Cees," the Yoga Society, the Art Guild, and in classes (creative writing, speaking, etc.), inmates are able to associate on bases other than their common identity as inmates. The result is to splinter the white population into small cliques with shifting memberships depending upon the felt needs or interests of the moment. John, the lifer quoted above, also commented on this change:

It used to be that everybody was the same. We had uniforms and numbers, everybody had the same haircut, and we had the bell system so everybody went together in line. Now every guy in here's an individual and there's no unity.

Summary and Conclusion

The intent of this chapter has been to portray the informal social organization of the white prisoner population. Toward this end I have made use of social type analysis, the isolation of roles defined indigenously in reference to the "axes of life"—the crucial lines of interest in the group. A number of focal concerns and interests are reflected in the social types identified and labeled by the white prisoners: relations with staff, loss of freedom and autonomy, material deprivation, sexual deprivation, drugs, and physical security. Inmates are characterized by which of these concerns serves as the primary referent for their prison behavior. Typing in terms of one concern, however, carries connotations for behavior with respect to other concerns, with the result that white inmates tend to play one role in regard to the entire population.

At ECI a small number of white prisoners whose behavior displays the ideal of convict solidarity are termed "stand-up guys." "Stand-up guys" are mentally and physically tough, loyal, and non-exploitive in their relations with other inmates. Most of them, however, regard the majority of their fellow captives with disdain and remain aloof from them. For this reason, most "stand-up guys" wield relatively little influence, despite being highly respected. A small clique of "stand-up guys" do function as leaders, however. This clique, known as the "mafia," consists of five prisoners drawn from the ranks of organized crime. As with other "stand-up guys," the prison behavior of the "mafia" represents an adaptation of the subculture of professional crime to the problems of imprisonment. The interest of the "mafia" is to do their time as quickly and as comfortably as possible with a minimum of disruption. The influence they exert is oriented to the attainment of these interests. Their leadership style is largely the covert exercise of influence and the mediation of disputes among inmates and between inmates and staff.

Allied with the "mafia" are two loose confederations of prisoners with quite dissimilar orientations, the "wise guys" and the "politicians." The "wise guys" are a band of young toughs whose primary interest is the aggrandizement of themselves through the exploitation of other inmates. The "politicians" in contrast, are older inmates, prone to non-violence, whose interests are the achievement of institutional change by means of negotiation with the staff. The relation between each of these groups and the "mafia" is symbiotic. In return for status, material favors, and perhaps the promise of future criminal employment, the "wise guys" submit to the control of the "mafia" and assist them in controlling disruptive behavior on the part of other inmates. In return for protection of their position, the "politicians" make the "mafia" honored guests at their parties and banquets and work for changes of benefit to the "mafia."

The ability of the "mafia" to control disruptive behavior usually is exercised only in situations that threaten their interests in some way. In consequence, conflict and exploitation is a way of life among the white prisoners. At the center of this web of conflict stand the "wise guys," who operate the largest rackets in the institution, rob inmates of drugs, money, and material goods, and coerce or seduce others—"punks"—into providing them with sexual services. On a smaller scale the interest of "dope fiends" in securing drugs and the material deprivation of the anonymous one-third of the population I have termed "others" result in a never-ending series of confidence games and petty hijacking activities. Even the voluntarily provided sexual services of the "fags" produces conflict as "fags" are degraded by their partners and in turn prostitute themselves to other inmates.

In short, the informal social organization of the white prisoners may be best described as a non-solidary congeries of cliques. Leadership is exercised mainly to further and protect the self-interests of the leaders. Cooperative relations exist only within small cliques, and the prevailing relations between cliques are competition and conflict.

This fragmentation of the white prisoners may be attributable to the policy of humanitarian reform. In lessening deprivation and the power of custodians, the reforms removed the major impetus to convict solidarity. Further, the increased permeability of the prison as a result of the reforms facilitates the continued attachment of prisoners to external reference groups. The result is an aggregation of individuals having little sense of loyalty to others beyond their immediate associates and exhibiting diverse behavioral orientations that have their origin and support both within and outside the prison.

The Blacks

In the preceding chapter I argued that the reforms at ECI have eroded the bases of convict solidarity and splintered the white population into small cliques with diverse orientations. Just the reverse is true of the black prisoners. The increased permeability of the institution and the greater freedom of interaction accorded inmates have facilitated the development and maintenance of a racial solidarity among the blacks. Nearly the entire black prisoner population are members of the Afro-American Society, the purpose of which is "to attain and maintain unity among the black brothers and to uplift our standards of dignity." As the statement suggests, racial identification is the primary axis of life for most black inmates, the deprivations of incarceration being subordinate to this concern. As a result of their interaction within the Afro-American Society, the black prisoners have been able to import into the prison perspectives having their origin in an external black culture, and to adapt and specify these perspectives to the context of confinement.

Black Perspectives: Soul and Nationalism

In the past decade, a dramatic cultural change has occurred among Afro-Americans, particularly with respect to shared perspectives on their heritage, identity, and relation to American society. At the risk of over-simplification, two perspectives at the center of this change may be isolated: "soul" and nationalism. "Soul" reflects the celebration of a black American culture that has developed as an adaptation to conditions imposed by racism. Nationalism refers to a belief that blacks share a distinct ethnic heritage having its roots in Africa; that they should control their own social, economic, and political institutions; and that perhaps they should possess their own country.[1] Neither of these perspectives is new, but in the past decade they have assumed the character of conspicuous social movements. These movements have permeated the walls of the prison and inform the collective adaptations made by black prisoners to the circumstances of incarceration.

Soul

Earlier researchers such as Frazier[2] and Glazer and Moynihan[3] have argued that Negroes, unlike other American racial and ethnic groups, have no values and culture of their own to guard and protect. In their view, the experience of slavery stripped black people of their African heritage, and they are thus nothing more nor less than black Americans whose values represent only "pathological" elaborations on general American values. More recent research in urban black ghettos, however, inclines toward a different view. Singer,[4] for example, claims that there has been an ethnogenesis on American soil, that through three centuries of oppression by, and isolation from white Americans, black Americans have developed and elaborated a distinct culture of their own. Hannerz[5] and Blauner[6], while agreeing that black culture has much in common with the lower class culture of poverty, nonetheless argue that there exists a set of shared perspectives and modes of action that are the products of black experience and that may be viewed as a distinctive black-American culture.

A full explication of the arguments concerning the existence of a truly black American culture distinct from a lower class culture is well beyond the scope of this chapter and unimportant for the purposes of this study. What is important for this study is that black urban ghetto dwellers share a set of common understandings that they define as distinctly black and that they view as marking them off as a distinct collectivity from whites. The many themes and correlates of this perspective are subsumed under the concept of "soul." As described by Hannerz, "soul" is:

A black folk conception of the "national character" of black people in America—to have soul or to be a soulful person is to share the conventional understandings unique to black people and to be able to appreciate them and express them in action.[7]

Used only by ghetto dwellers, and then only in relation to their own experiences and life styles, the precise referents of "soul" remain unclear. One clue to them, however, was provided by bluesman Al Hibbler. When asked by Charles Keil what it takes to have "soul," Hibbler listed three criteria: "Having been hurt by a woman," "being brought up in that old time religion," and "knowing what that slavery shit is all about."[8]

Traditionally, "soul" is a religious term. Its selection today to designate what is believed to be essentially black indicates at least one aspect of its contemporary meaning. Divested of religious connotations, "soul" refers to the essential moral, spiritual, and emotional nature of the person. Through centuries of suffering and persecution black people see themselves as having developed a humanity not shared by whites. A "soulful" person is one who experiences strong feelings and emotions, and who expresses these essential aspects of self in his behavior, dress, and language. "Rapping," for instance, a colorful and lively way of talking characterized by a high degree of affectation is a manifestation of "soul." As

Kochman describes it, one "raps" to a person rather than with a person.[9] It is a performance more than a verbal exchange, a means of projecting one's personality onto a situation to evoke a favorable response. The individual who is adept at "rapping" is held in high esteem. Conversely, in interaction with one's peers, one should make no pretense at being other than he is. He should not "shuck" or "jive," and "sounding" and "signifying" are highly stylized verbal formulas by which peers attempt through insult and aggression to strip away any attempt at pretense.[10]

"Soul," then, relates to the expression of one's being in action, a being seen as forged through perseverance in the face of suffering and oppression. Herein lies another "soul" theme: perseverance. "Soul" is a celebration of the ability of black people to survive and to "keep on struggling" in the face of white oppression; and it is a belief that the white race would not have survived under similar circumstances. To survive, to "make it with dignity" in the face of circumstances over which one has no control is also the mark of a "soulful" person.[11]

Implied in this perspective, however, is a view of life as a jungle in which only the tough and the smart survive. One way to survive is to "hustle", to utilize one's personal skills in the manipulation and exploitation of others. Within the "soul" perspective is a view of life as a game in which individuals are forever seeking to corrupt contexts and relationships for personal profit.[12] Thus, while "soul" relates to a pride in group survival and continuance of the struggle, it also implies a suspicion of the motives of others in an effort to protect oneself from exploitation.

One context in which one may be exploited is sex. "Soul" involves a frank and open appreciation of sex as a highly expressive relationship involving intense emotion and the mutual validation of masculinity and femininity. At the same time the circumstances of black life make sexual relationships highly unstable, a fact reflected in the high incidence of broken families, common law unions, and illegitimacy. To be hurt by the opposite sex is then a common and perhaps expected aspect of lower class black life. The experience of being hurt by the opposite sex and allied conceptions of the opposite sex as treacherous and deceitful are basic ingredients of "soul."[13]

Many commentators have remarked upon the present orientation of black life, the absence of a deferred gratification pattern.[14] "Soul," by indirection, relates to a concept of time. "Soul time" is time consonant with the high valuation of expressive activity and the chance nature of such activities in the ghetto.[15] "White time" is standardized and synchronized so as to facilitate the performance of instrumental activities. "Soul time" is personal, informal, and relaxed so as to facilitate the performance of expressive activities. A "dude" must be ready to "move where the action is"; and the action, be it a party or some other form of expressive activity, must be allowed to run its course.

What I have presented thus far is an all too brief and inadequate description of several themes that inform the "soul" perspective. There is little in this description to distinguish "soul" from the culture of poverty. Nor should there be. The black experience in the United States has been one of poverty and oppression, and the perspectives of "soul" may best be interpreted as an adaptive response to that situation. But it is a response that has been shaped within socially defined racial boundaries, and there are other elements of "soul" that reflect this fact. Involved in "soul" is a celebration of the Southern experience. The South is the "home country" in the minds of many black ghetto dwellers, and the South provides one of the clearest symbols of "soul." The food which black slaves ate —blackeyed peas, chitterlings, fried chicken, mustard and collard greens, grits, corn bread, and so forth are now celebrated as "soul food."[16] Linked as they are to the nadir of the black experience, such foods are now interpreted as sustenance for the essential humanity of black people, a humanity forged through poverty and oppression. Similarly, as the term "soul" itself suggests, despite the loosening grip of churches upon black ghetto dwellers, the "old-time religion" is still very much a part of the "soul" perspective. As Powdermaker observed 35 years ago, a black church service bears little resemblance to a poor white one despite the fact that the two share some common origins and institutional forms.[17]

A third distinctly black element of "soul" is music. If there is any one aspect of contemporary popular culture in America that may be claimed by black people, it is music. And it is in music that the various themes of the "soul" perspective receive their clearest expression. The emphasis on "being in action" and lack of pretense is expressed in songs such as "Take Me Just As I Am" and "Tell It Like It Is." Perseverance in the face of oppression is the theme of "Just Keep Holding On" and "Keep Pushing." The battle of the sexes provides the subject matter for "I Loved and I Lost" and "Yes It Hurts, Doesn't It." Even "soul food" is celebrated in occasional songs such as "Grits and Cornbread" and "Chitterling Salad."[18] Nor is it merely the titles and lyrics of songs that express "soul." Each performer has his or her own personal style, a style expressive of their unique and personal interpretations of the shared experiences. The frenzied sexuality of Ike and Tina Turner and the seductiveness of The Supremes and Temptations are themselves expressions of "soul." In fact, the black singer or musician is perhaps evaluated more for his capacity to express "soul" than for his musical ability.

"Soul music"—blues, progressive jazz, or rock—ties together and unifies the many facets of "soul." It affirms by celebration the positive value of the black experience. It gives public expression to a body of shared understandings and intensely personal and private emotions. In doing this, "soul music" loses its exclusive character as an art form and becomes nearly an ideology that at once depicts, interprets, and affirms the value of a way of life.[19]

Nationalism

Black nationalism in one form or another has existed in the United States from the earliest days of slavery. Until the past decade, however, the dominant thrust of black protest reflected an acceptance of American values and was directed at the incorporation of blacks into the mainstream of American life on the basis of full equality. However, violent resistance to non-violent protest, the failure of the government to meet black expectations, the war in Viet Nam, and successful anti-colonial movements in Africa and Asia combined in the 1960s to shift the direction of black protest toward a rejection of American values and to bring black nationalism to the fore of the black movement. Today there are two variants of black nationalism: cultural nationalism and revolutionary nationalism. Cultural nationalism is concerned mainly with the development, elaboration, and perpetuation of an African cultural heritage. Revolutionary nationalism is concerned mainly with the promotion of an effective revolution to alter existing power arrangements between white people and people of color around the world.[20]

Cultural Nationalism . Until recently most black Americans viewed Africa as a vast tropical jungle and native Africans as naked, spear-wielding savages. Holding such misconceptions, most black Americans wanted nothing to do with Africa or the study of Africans. In the mid-1950s, when the readers of *Ebony* magazine were polled on which topics they wished to read about, Africa placed tenth in a list of ten topics.[21] Since that time black American perspectives on Africa have undergone a dramatic metamorphosis. Today, many if not the majority of black Americans of all ages and socio-economic levels have come to regard Africa as the "beloved motherland," and to support programs designed to enhance racial pride through the elaboration of an Afro-American heritage.[22]

This dramatic change in perspective is attributable to the success of anti-colonial movements in Africa. Coincident with the first stirrings of the non-violent civil rights movement in this country was the bloody and successful Mau Mau revolt in Kenya. As school integration was being coercively enforced in Little Rock, Ghana became the first new independent state in Africa. The independence of Ghana was followed by the rapid establishment of other new states in Africa. It was this headlong rush to freedom in Africa juxtaposed to the slow pace of non-violent integration in the United States that altered the thinking of black Americans about Africa.

By 1960, "the partial liberation of Africa had augmented the black American's frustration and caused him to fuse his own struggle to that taking place in Africa."[23] As black Americans have come to redefine themselves and reassess their relations to Africa, there has occurred an African cultural renaissance in America.

The manifestations of cultural nationalism are many and varied, informing public and private discourse, political and personal action, art and literature. "Negro" has come to be seen as a slave name foisted upon the black man in an effort to deny him a heritage. "Black" or "Afro-American" is now the preferred racial/ethnic designation. The adoption of African names has become fashionable as has the wearing of African clothing and jewelry and the acquisition of African art objects. Most noticeable has been the adoption of natural or "Afro" hairstyles. And on college campuses and in public schools Afro-American cultural associations have been established, and battles waged and won to introduce Afro-American studies including Swahili into curricula.

Critics of cultural nationalism are quick to point out that much of the African renaissance is based upon misconception and bears no relation to the actual heritage of black Americans. "Afro" hairstyles, for example, are nowhere to be found in Africa. Swahili is the *lingua franca* of East Africa, and could hardly have been spoken by the ancestors of black Americans who were drawn largely from West Africa. Proponents of cultural nationalism argue that such criticisms are irrelevant. Conceding that the adopted hairstyles are not African in origin, they claim they are nonetheless "a manifestation of the Afro-Americans' effort to cast off imperialist oppression from his make-up, from his mind and from his body."[24] Regarding Swahili, Mulana Ron Karenga has commented that it was chosen precisely because it is not the language of one tribe and thus facilitates the identification of Afro-Americans with all Africans. [25]

Assertions such as the above suggest that the objectives of cultural nationalism are expressive rather than instrumental. Cultural nationalism is a means of improving the damaged self-image of black Americans, and of providing them with a bulwark of identity in the face of the anxieties accompanying mobility in American society. To paraphrase the words of Grier and Cobbs, cultural nationalism is for most black Americans a "psychological redemption."[26]

Revolutionary Nationalism. Contemporaneous with the emergence of black cultural nationalism has been the emergence of black revolutionary nationalism. While black pride is a pivotal element in both movements, the relationship between them is somewhat ambivalent. Revolutionary nationalists have been openly critical of the goals of cultural nationalism. Eldridge Cleaver, for example, has taken cultural nationalists to task for making a fetish of black pride and thereby distracting attention frcm the hard facts of racism. [27] In the mind of Cleaver and other revolutionary leaders, the goals of cultural nationalism should be seen as a means to an end rather than as ends in themselves; cultural nationalism is only a transitional stage in the revolutionary process. Julius Lester, an articulate spokesman for revolutionary nationalism, has stated this view quite succinctly:

A man cannot begin to be involved in the revolutionary process until he looks at himself, and thereby others, with new feelings and new ideas. The cultural revolution has been a dominant factor in this. At the same time, however, it has to be realized that the cultural revolution can serve only as part of the foundation upon which the revolution will be built. . . . It's not possible to beat "the man" to death with your dashiki. [28]

The revolutionary movement is splintered into a number of groups with somewhat differing goals and programs. A recent essay by S. E. Anderson,[29] editor of *Black Dialogue, New Africa,* and *Mojo* provides a good summary of the shared tenets of the movement, however. Anderson writes that "America as it exists today must be completely destroyed and then rebuilt. . . ."[30] The first step in this process is an understanding on the part of each and every black American of the "psychological profundity of white racism within us" so as to be able to control "the segment of our existence where we are most vulnerable to the bestiality of white racism," namely in personal behavior and family life.[31] A second step is the use of white American facilities for the following purposes: (1) to gather useful technical, political, and military information, (2) to develop skills necessary for the revolution and thereafter, and (3) to make contact with Third World people.[32] A third step is the development of a national black political party directed at the election of black mayors and municipal leaders and the control of municipal services such as schools and police. Areas and institutions controlled by blacks are to be used as experimental social laboratories to produce politically conscious and socially sensitive black people and as an internal power base for the revolutionary struggle.[33] A fourth step is the development and institutionalization of cultural similarities with the Pan-African world, and political alliances both with Third World nations and revolutionary groups among American Indians, Mexican-Americans, and Puerto Ricans.[34] Cultural similarities and political alliances, it is argued, will provide black Americans with the leadership, solidarity, and international power necessary for a successful revolution.

Soul and Nationalism. "Soul" and nationalism are distinct ideological currents in black America today. Each provides a basis for group solidarity. Yet, just as there is an incompatibility between cultural and revolutionary nationalism, so also is there a conflict between the perspectives of "soul" and those of nationalism.[35] "Soul" is a product of the American experience. It is a celebration of perseverance in the face of oppression and an acceptance of a life over which one has little control. The "soul" movement is a collective involvement with personal emotions as opposed to a personal involvement with collective problems. Thus, it is difficult to envision how "soul" could provide the solidarity necessary either for collective mobility in a reformed American social structure as is the aim of cultural nationalism or for a worldwide revolutionary movement as is the aim of revolutionary nationalism. Nationalist leaders recognize this inherent weakness of "soul" as a basis for group mobilization, and seek to substitute heroic images of an African past and visions of future greatness for the perspectives of "soul." There is, then, a tension within the black movement between prospective leaders and prospective followers, between the converted and those to be converted. This tension, along with the perspectives that give rise to it, is imported into the prison and shapes the collective adaptations made by black prisoners.

Social Types Among the Blacks

As will become apparent, ideological conflict such as that just described played a major role in both intra-group and inter-group relations in the prison during the time of this study. However, this conflict was apparent only within the Afro-America Society. Outside the organization the black prisoners identified themselves and acted with respect to each other as "brothers" and "partners."

Brothers and Partners

Brothers. For some black inmates a "brother" must be a black, but for most a "brother" is a member of any minority group who displays an awareness of white oppression and a rebellion against it. The following conversation between three black prisoners concerning the composition of a soccer team indicates the ambiguity surrounding the criteria by which one is judged to be a "brother":

'I see they got one brother at least', Sam observed. 'Who's that?' Carl asked. 'Wally Hernandez'. Carl objected. 'He ain't no brother. He's Italian.' Sam replied, 'No, he's a brother. He came up to the meetings for a while. He's Spanish or Mexican or something.' Leroy, who had been quiet, agreed with Sam. 'That's right. He's a Mexican.' Carl sat up in his chair and concluded, 'He might be one of them

Latins but that don't make him a brother does it?' Sam and Leroy looked uncomfortable but didn't answer.

In practice at ECI a black inmate becomes a "brother" through his membership in the Afro-American Society. The organization thus has something of the character of a family. The relationship between "brothers," however, need not be a deeply personal one. One need not know or even like another black inmate to consider him a "brother." One may even be suspicious and mistrustful of a "brother." Here is one of the perspectives of "soul," namely that life is a game and people often seek to corrupt contexts and relationships for personal profit. So, for example, one of the obligations of brotherhood is to acquaint a new "brother" with the institution. Unlike the whites who, as we have seen, avoid new inmates, the blacks seek them out both to "sound" on them and to "run it down" to them. But if one is "cool," he is careful in accepting such interpretations.

As soon as I got here, I didn't know none of these dudes, you know, but when I come in they started comin' around sounding on me to see where I was at. Then they hepped me to the different hacks, which ones was creeps and which ones was all right, you know, and all the things ya gotta know like how to get seconds in the dining hall or where ya can get coffee and toast, what the good jobs were, things like that. Same thing with the inmates. They be tellin' me who's a rat and who's okay. 'Course I didn't make no judgment right then. I keep all these things in my mind and I be careful, but I don't make no final judgment right then, not till I see for myself. Ya can't go by what ya hear 'cause ya don't know but what the dude that's running it down to ya might have some motive, ya know.

The essence of brotherhood, then, is not personal knowledge, liking or even trust. Brotherhood is based on the recognition of a shared fate at the hands of a common oppressor, and the essence of the relationship is mutual aid in the face of oppression. As in the above quote, "brothers" share information so as to protect each other and to make life easier. In the same vein they share material goods. Again, however, this is not an automatic or personal sharing of all that one possesses. If one has a radio, and a "brother" asks to use it, the owner is obliged to loan it. But the owner of a radio is not expected to offer it to a "brother" without one. Much of the sharing of material comforts is institutionalized in the Afro-American Society. Money collected from dues and fines is used to purchase records, books, and musical instruments for the use of all members. On several occasions, the membership voted to loan money to members for some purpose. Many inmates arrive without necessities such as toothbrushes, toothpaste, towels, and razors, and without the means to purchase these from the Inmate Store. Through an "Uptight Program" the Afro-American Society maintains a supply of such items for newly arrived black inmates in these circumstances.

Above and beyond all else, brotherhood implies an obligation of aid in the fact of conflict.

As long as a man's a 'brother' you ain't gonna let nothing happen to him. If he's got a beef then it's your beef. If you got a beef, then it's his.

A "beef," from the standpoint of the "brother" is any conflict with a "non-brother." This may include staff, white inmates, or those black inmates defined as "Toms." In any conflict or crisis situation, a "brother" is obliged to "go down" with his "brothers." Again, in this context, however, there is the element of personal mistrust. A "beef" may in fact be a "game" in which a "brother" seeks to manipulate other "brothers" so as to utilize their collective power for his personal advantage. A "brother" may claim an officer took his radio, and demand that the organization secure its return. An investigation might reveal, however, that in fact the officer had only taken the radio after repeatedly warning the inmate to turn it down as it was after 10.30 p.m. A "beef" of this sort is defined as a "bullshit beef" to which the obligations of brotherhood do not apply. The obligations of brotherhood apply only to "legitimate beefs" in which the "brother" has been wronged.

The brotherhood relation, then, is essentially a symbiotic relation pertaining to mutual aid in time of need. Grounded in the recognition of common oppression, it lacks any essential elements of personal knowledge and intimacy and is subject to several restrictions. Beneath this relationship, buttressing and supporting it, are the relations between "partners."

Partners. "Partners" are black inmates who are "up tight" with each other, who share common interests, who know each other well, who can "rap" easily with each other, and are thus intimate. The relationship between "partners" is diffuse and not subject to restriction. "Partners" automatically share whatever they have without being asked. A black inmate who receives an extra store order from a visit offers part of it to his "partner." Black inmates going to minimum security where they must live in a dormitory give to their "partners" televisions and other items not permitted in the dormitory setting. If a man's "partner" has a "beef," it is his "beef" as well, regardless of whether it is "legitimate" or "illegitimate," or with a "brother" or "non-brother." A "partner" is someone you go all the way with, no questions asked. "Partners" protect each other. They seek to live in cells near one another and to provide a buffer between their "partner" and the eyes of others be they staff, inmates, or white researchers.

"Partners" are of different types and any one black inmate may have several. A basic distinction is made between "street partners" and "jail house partners." "Street partners" are inmates who were "up tight" with each other and "ran" together prior to confinement. Also included in this category are one's actual biological relations. "Jail house partners" are friends to whom one has become related during one's current sentence. "Jail house partners" form a clique or primary group that may or may not include "street partners." For example, several black inmates related by kinship tended not to have the same "jail house partners." But while one may not "hang" with his "street partner" during confinement, the obligations of "partnership" remain. One black inmate clearly explained this relation in an interview.

Q: But if you're 'partners' like you say and you'd lay down your life for them, why don't you hang out together?

A: . . . Let's see. How can I explain that? . . . Me and another dude is 'street partners,' see, but he gets busted 'fore I do. When he comes in he's gonna get with some other dudes—'jail house partners,' you dig. Then I show, but he's already hooked up with three or four other dudes and they's swingin' out together. So I hook up with some others and swing out with them. That don't mean I ain't tight with him no more. We still be tight. I know he's there and he knows I'm over here. Then if he's got a beef I'm automatically involved and the three or four dudes I'm hanging with is involved too and the three or four dudes he be hanging with is involved.

From an adaptive and protective point of view then, it is a sound tactic not to hang with "street partners," but to develop a separate set of "jail house partners." As a result nearly the total black population is bound together by an interlocking structure of diffuse relationships that facilitates rapid mobilization in times of crisis and that provides most black inmates with aid and assistance of a routine nature. This structure of solidarity also serves to obscure a deep ideological division among "brothers" and "partners," a division reflecting the conflict between the perspectives of "soul" and the perspectives of revolutionary nationalism.

Revolutionaries and Half-Steppers[a]

It is probably no accident that revolutionary leaders such as Malcolm X, Eldridge Cleaver, and George Jackson developed in prison. The ideology of black revolution would appear to have immediate relevance for the black convict. Subjected to a series of pains, deprivations, and debasements that

[a]Unlike other labels I have used, the terms "revolutionary" and "half-stepper" are not consensual labels employed by the black prisoners themselves. Nonetheless they are indicative of distinct prison adaptive styles. As noted in the introduction to the previous chapter, the absence of consensual labels for this difference may be attributable to the character of the Afro-American Society, the need to maintain solidarity in the presence of white oppressors and to recruit and socialize new members. The term "half-stepping" is used by black prisoners to refer to verbal behavior in which one is not quite truthful.

destroy their sense of self, all inmates face the problem of constructing a new identity. For many prisoners, black and white, the only alternative in the past has been that of "convict." From the perspective of the convict, inmates are able to preserve their self-esteem by "rejecting their rejectors" and on this basis to develop a form of negative solidarity by means of which other deprivations are neutralized or alleviated. Today, however, black revolutionary nationalism offers to black inmates a more inclusive and positive identity than that of the convict. By viewing themselves from the perspectives of nationalism, black prisoners are able to integrate their role as a prisoner with their role as a black man in a way which places them in the vanguard of a worldwide movement against colonial oppression.

With models such as Cleaver and Jackson, and through their interaction in the Afro-American Society, the black inmates at ECI have developed a collective definition of themselves as political prisoners. Regardless of the nature of their crime, by adopting a revolutionary perspective they are able to interpret it as a political act. Homicide, Robbery, Larceny, and Burglary involving white victims are justified as acts of revolution or, at least, as a means of obtaining what is one's due. Few of their offenses are of this nature, however. In most cases the victims are black, and, in the case of drug offenses, themselves. But the revolutionary perspective is broad enough to include these as well. Such crimes, while not revolutionary acts, are the result of white racism. They are the means by which the white population maintains its dominance over the black. By pitting black against black, by supplying them drugs, whites inhibit the development of racial unity and revolutionary consciousness. As the following excerpt from an interview shows, even the rape of a black woman may be seen as the result of white racism:

Q: Do you feel guilty about anything you've done?

A: Guilty! For What? Them B & E's was 'cause I was on drugs. If I wasn't on drugs I wouldn't have done nothing, and I wouldn't be on drugs if you whites didn't put 'em in my community. You people put 'em there and keep 'em there. It's a round robin is what it is. It always comes back to white society. You're the ones that's guilty, not me.

Q: Is there any crime a black man might be guilty of?

A: What kind of crime?

Q: Say raping a black woman?

A: Ya can't tell, man. You read that book *Black Rage*. . . . Then you can see there ain't no telling why a black man's doing something. Even raping a black woman's probably 'cause of the brainwashing white society done on him.

Similar sentiments are expressed by nearly all the black inmates with whom I had contact. Except for a few, labeled "toms" by the majority, virtually all "talk the talk" of revolution. But "talking the talk" is quite distinct from "walking the walk." This is to say that while nearly all espoused revolution; and defined themselves as "revolutionaries," few fashion their prison behavior in terms of this perspective. The behavior of the majority reflects an orientation to the perspectives of "soul" rather than to the perspectives of revolution.

Revolutionaries. George Jackson provides a model of the committed black revolutionary doing time. He stated:

I've trained myself not to be disorganized by any measure they take against me. I exercise in the yard, and pursue my studies. Since I know that I am the original man and will soon inherit this earth, I am content to just prepare myself and wait, nothing can stop me now.[36]

No more than six or seven black inmates acted in accord with such an orientation. For these few, whom we may identify as "revolutionaries," the significant reference group is not the black inmate population but revolutionary groups beyond the walls. Their orientation is not to the present but to the future. As they see it, it is the historic and obligatory duty of black prisoners, those who are surrounded by the ultimate symbols of white oppression, to utilize their time in preparation for the eventual revolution. Part of their preparation entails an effort to free themselves of attachments to material things, to purify themselves of any dependence upon the materialism of western white culture, and to steel themselves for the adversities to be encountered during the revolution. Their prison existence is stoic. Their cells remain unadorned and contain only necessities such as a bed, desk, typewriter, radio, and books concerned with revolution. Their clothing is, for the most part, only what the institution provides—khaki or green trousers, a khaki or white shirt, and a black wool jacket. They remain uninvolved in the exchange systems by which inmates seek to alleviate material deprivations. The desire for sandwiches or pies from the kitchen is seen as a sign of weakness. The most significant marks of weakness, however, are not pies and sandwiches but drugs and homosexual behavior.

I seen what drugs done to the dudes down around 125th Street in New York. Drugs is genocide, man. It's the way the white system keeps the black man down. As long as his mind's frozen, he's defeated. The way I see it a man can't be black and be shooting drugs. You gotta be strong to be black and shooting drugs is weak. And I definitely can't see it in here. There ain't no reason to use it in here. There ain't enough of it in here for 'em to stay addicted but they keep going back for it.
. . . .
Any man who hits someone in the seat is weak as far as I'm concerned. He's a "fag" just like the one he's hitting.

A second aspect of the prison style of the "revolutionary" is intense involvement in programs directed at self-improvement. To be a "revolutionary" one must rehabilitate oneself. He must rid himself of the "negative images" white society establishes for him. He must abandon any commitment to or identification with the life of the pimp, the hustler, or the dope fiend, as these are the most powerful and insidious weapons of white oppression. Attachment to these lifestyles must be extinguished, and can only be extinguished through "getting in touch with one's blackness" by intense involvement in the cultural and educational programs of the Afro-American Society. Beyond involvement in these programs, most of the "revolutionaries" are engaged in self-designed reading programs, the content of which ranges from Marx and Engels through Mao Tse-tung, Franz Fanon, and Che Guevara to peers such as Cleaver and Jackson. While remaining deeply suspicious of any programs offered by the prison administration, they are nonetheless quick to involve themselves in those in which they can perceive some benefit. So, for example, all are active in the MDTA Vocational Training Program. Partly this is a gambit for earlier parole, partly an effort to prepare for a job after release, but it is also related to their desire to learn skills necessary in the event of the formation of a black state.

The almost complete immersion of the "revolutionary" in self-improvement activities leaves him little time for socializing or participation in recreational pursuits. They seldom go to movies on Friday nights, preferring to stay in their cells and read. Playing cards or pool, watching television, or, worse, just "hanging out" in the wings is "idling" and avoided. Most of their interpersonal relations are structured within the activities of the Afro-American Society, and they hold themselves aloof from the majority of the black population, whom they regard with some disdain.

I don't consider most of the blacks in here to be 'brothers.' They must be jiving with all that loyalty and revolutionary rhetoric . . . if they was serious they'd be getting their heads together in them programs we got going.

Half-Steppers. For want of a better term we may identify the vast majority of the black inmates as "half-steppers." "Half-steppers" "talk the talk" of revolution, but do not "walk the walk." Their public behavior manifests an intense commitment to revolution. Their cells are decorated with portraits of revolutionary heroes and posters proclaiming "Power to the People," "The Revolution is Now," "Burn, Baby, Burn," and "Off the Pigs." Many wear buttons of a political nature—green buttons with a black outline of Africa, and others with slogans such as "Free Angela," "Free Huey," and "Dump Nixon." Their conversations in the yard and wings are frequently punctuated with loud comments denouncing the racist "pigs" and advocating revolution.

The very public and external nature of these affirmations, however, reveals them as self-conscious attempts to collectively claim and support an identity to which they in fact are not fully committed. The prison style of the "half-stepper," their actual behavior and private conversations, reflect an importation and enactment of the perspectives of "soul" within the prison. Where the orientation of the "revolutionary" is to the outside and the future, the orientation of the "half-stepper" is to the present and to opportunities for self-expression within the prison. As they see it, life in the prison is not so terribly different from life in the ghetto.

I'm doing time all my life, man. Don't make much difference if I do it here or out there. It's still time.

Sharing this perspective, "half-steppers" support each other in efforts to collapse time to the immediate present. Even to mention one's case or to work on appeals, activities common among the whites and "revolutionaries," is cause for group sanctions in the form of "sounding," "signifying," or perhaps exclusion. One "half-stepper," for example, was denied parole solely because he had failed to clear up several minor additional charges in the court. To clear the charges would have meant an appearance in court, a guilty plea, and the probable acceptance of a sentence concurrent to the one he was serving. Having been notified several times to appear in court, he had requested continuances. After his parole was denied, I asked him why he had failed to appear in court. The only reasons he could offer were that there had been "too much going on" at the time, and that he had not realized his parole date was so close. A similar orientation was expressed by another black inmate in an interview:

Do you think that black and white inmates might have a different outlook on their time?

You got it there, man. Them white dudes be always looking ahead to the end of that ten or 25 and crying and complaining. I don't know any 'brothers' that even know how much time they got left. Take me. I don't think about my time. I know I'm getting short but if you was to ask me how many days I got left, I couldn't tell ya. I count the years, ya know, but not the days. All the 'brothers' take their time day by day and involve themselves with the 'brothers' here. We be used to time so we be immune to it. . . . Because we been slaves for 400 years.

The final comment in this quote suggests the relation of the "half-steppers" view of time to the "soul" perspective. Through a history of oppression and suffering black people have developed a non-standardized and present-oriented sense of time that, in the prison or in the ghetto, enhances their capacity for "making it with dignity." Likewise, involvement with the "brothers," for the "half-stepper," means involvement in a variety of expressive activities. Unlike the "revolutionaries" or most white inmates, the "half-steppers" do not standardize or schedule the time not regulated by the formal system. I discovered this fact in trying to make contact with certain individuals during the study. I had no difficulty locating either whites or black "revolutionaries," as they tended to follow a standardized schedule I was able to learn and they were often engaged in solitary activities. This was not so with the majority of blacks. They tended to gravitate to wherever the action was at the moment, and to be continually involved in peer group activities that made my entrance awkward.

The content of such activities is extremely varied, but virtually all are expressive in nature. Most common is merely "hanging out" and "rapping" with six or seven others in the yard or wings. These conversations are loud, punctuated by peals of laughter, and involving much body movement and slapping of hands.

At one point Bean stepped out from the group, cocked his head to the left, and opened his huge eyes to the fullest extent, and said in a falsetto voice, "Little Boy, you ain't black! You be married!" The others responded with loud laughing and Bean held out both hands, palms up, and KP slapped on them. Little Boy remained quiet and soon left the group.

The above incident is a form of "signifying" or "sounding." Little Boy, a partner in a homosexual marriage was embarrassed and degraded by Bean in a manner to which he could not respond. Bean's status was enhanced by his ability to fashion an indirect verbal taunt, ("You be married," not a fag), and to express it with the appropriate body style and tone to make it effective. His reward was the highly stylized hand slap by KP, a leader of the clique, given only when one has made a significant point in a verbal exchange.

Verbal exchanges of this sort are a continual preoccupation of the "half-stepper," and ability in such repartee is highly valued. But verbal exchanges are only one aspect of their expressive prison style. In direct contrast to the "revolutionary" who remains unconcerned with personal appearance, the "half-stepper" displays an intense concern with clothing. Hats particularly are one means by which they express their being in action. For the old institutional grey cap once required of all inmates, the "half-steppers" substitute a variety of multi-colored knit "bopper caps," Australian army campaign hats, and broad brimmed felt hats, usually brown or white. These are traded back and forth, an individual desiring one or another depending upon his mood or feeling at the moment. Sunglasses and brightly colored turtle neck shirts are used in the same manner and for the same purpose. On one occasion a "half-stepper" requested that I bring him a pair of "shades." He took great pains to draw me an exact sketch of the glasses he desired. Over the next week I brought him three pairs of glasses on separate occasions. He accepted the third pair, but only reluctantly: "They just ain't me, man."

The efforts of the "half-steppers" to express themselves in dress and action are validated by the individual identifications made by the group. Nicknames are uncommon among the whites, and the black "revolutionary" usually adopts an African name. But nearly all the "half-steppers" are identified by a nickname which, in some inexplicable way, summarizes essential qualities of his person. Names such as "Rump," "Cadillac," "Ticky," "Bean," "Little Boy," "Moose," "Harlem Nat," "Frankenstein," and "June Bug" could fit only those to whom they refer. And, tied as they are to the unique personal style of the individual, the frequent usage of these names reinforces the almost primary group cohesion of the "half-steppers."

This cohesion receives its strongest support through the commitment of the "half-steppers" to music. The Music Committee of the Afro-American Society is one of the most active. They maintain a record library of "soul" recordings that is replenished monthly. Members may borrow records for a weekend, and a frequent pastime of "half-steppers" is to gather at the cell of one who has an expensive stereo and "groove" on the latest hits. On Sundays, the organization utilizes the otherwise unused institutional radio station to produce its own "soul program" in which each member is accorded a turn at being the disc jockey. The committee also purchased several instruments for the use of members and the availability of these gives rise to constant jam sessions in the gym or yard.

"Half-steppers," then, have used the increased permeability of the institution and the greater freedom of interaction permitted inmates to elaborate an expressive prison style fashioned by the perspectives of "soul." The expressiveness of the "half-stepper" style is in decided contrast to the stoic existence of the revolutionary. Nowhere is the conflict between the two orientations more evident than their views concerning drugs, homosexuality, and the future. As we have seen, the "revolutionary" regards drugs as a form of genocide, and homosexual activity as a mark of weakness. From the perspective of the "half-stepper," drugs and homosexual behavior are necessities, and educational pursuits a waste of time that could more profitably be used in socializing with the "brothers" or engaging in a "hustle" to secure some desired commodity.

Man, I got seven and a half years ahead of me and I'm gonna do my thing. I gotta escape from this here reality and I'm gonna score dope any time I can. . . . A lotta dudes think you can't be black and be a fag. I don't see that. There's a lotta black writers that's 'fags' and they're out there doing their black thing. I accept 'em for what they are. And in here they're a necessity. Ya need 'em.

"Half-steppers" involve themselves in the present and seldom talk of their future. But when they do, their comments indicate a continued commitment to the life of the pimp, the hustler, and the dope fiend rather than a commitment to revolution. The following conversation between two black inmates occurred in my presence in the yard:

J: I love that life, man. I don't like what it does to ya but I love the women, the hogs, and the fast money. What else is there for dudes like me? I was born to the life.

R: But what about all them commitments you made to the organization?

J: What about 'em? They wasn't real, man. I had to do it so's I could groove with my 'brothers.' I go along with what them dudes is saying but I'm too much into the life to change now. You be the same too, man. If I was to drop a bundle right now you'd break your neck fighting for it.

R: No I wouldn't.

J: You telling me you wouldn't touch it? You're jiving, man.

R: Hell, 'course I'd use it. But that don't mean I love it. I can take it or leave it.

This conversation continued for nearly an hour, during which time J. sought relentlessly to pierce R.'s pretension at non-commitment to the "life," an effort that was successful. It ended with both jokingly agreeing that as soon as they were released they would be "throwing rocks at the penitentiary," i.e., engaging in behavior that would result in future confinement.

Conflict. The disparity between the prison style of the "revolutionary" and the style of the "half-stepper," between the perspectives of "soul" and those of nationalism, between future orientation and present orientation, between identification with external revolutionary groups and the black inmate population, made for strain and conflict within the Afro-American Society. The organization was established by the "revolutionaries." In their mind it was a vehicle by which they would be able to proselytize and convert the "half-steppers" to,—in the words of George Jackson—"transform the black criminal mentality into a revolutionary mentality."[37] They were able to secure two classrooms for the sole use of the organization, and they decorated these rooms with maps and flags of African states and posters of Angela Davis, Huey Newton, and Muhammed Ali. Every evening from 5 p.m. to 8:30 p.m. they scheduled a number of activities aimed at the goal of conversion. These activities ranged from courses in African cultures and history, through a high school equivalency program utilizing Afro-American materials, to frequent "rap sessions" dealing with problems surrounding the "brainwashing" perpetrated upon black people by white society.

The first President and Board of Directors were self-appointed and revolutionary in their orientation. The by-laws accorded them the power to make and enforce rules as they deemed necessary for the welfare of the organization and its members. Through a set of "Presidential Policies" they attempted to extend their control into the members' extra-organizational behavior. To be admitted to the organization, prospective members had to pledge that they would refrain from drug usage and homosexual activity. All members were required to attend classes. There was to be no "idling" in the wings, and no fighting or arguing outside of organizational meetings. Cells were to be thoroughly cleaned each day. There were to be no infractions of institutional rules. A committee was established to enforce these policies, and the President and Board of Directors sat weekly to dispose of infractions. Penalties imposed ranged from fines of $.50 to $10.00 or more through suspension of membership for varying periods of time. Members were forbidden to communicate or interact in any way with suspended members, an infraction itself punishable by suspension.

Such programs and policies were completely at odds with the interests of most members. For the "half-steppers," the prime purpose of the organization was to make time easier. It was the social activities—the frequent jam sessions, the occasional banquets, the opportunities to meet girls from the street, to rap with each other free from the surveillance of the administration, and similar activities—that were their prime interest. Further, membership in the organization provided them with a sense of security. As one put it, "The main purpose behind the organization is to keep them whiteys off our backs."

As noted above, the obligations of brotherhood extend only to "legitimate beefs" in which a "brother" has been wronged. However, the legitimacy or illegitimacy of a grievance is often difficult to establish. One of the basic conflicts between "revolutionaries" and "half-steppers" was their viewpoint on this matter. Oriented to the outside and the future and placing a high priority on the cultural and educational aspects of the organization, the "revolutionaries" inclined toward a restrictive view and were reluctant to take any action on a grievance until a thorough investigation had been completed. "Half-steppers," with their greater orientation to the present and interest in the prison world itself, inclined toward a more diffuse view of the obligations of mutual aid. From their perspective, virtually any grievance was legitimate and demanding of supportive action.

The lack of consensus between "revolutionaries" and "half-steppers" on such matters as drugs and mutual aid in time of crisis generated considerable antagonism between them. Far from being seen as charismatic leaders, the "revolutionaries" came to be viewed as dictators. As one member put it, "It's like having two sets of hacks." After one meeting in which 22 of the 37 members present were fined for drug usage, one "half-stepper" gave expression to several of the disagreements between "revolutionaries" and "half-steppers," denying that "revolutionaries" were true "brothers":

Ya know what I think. I think they ain't 'brothers' at all. They be weasels, sitting up there playin' them silly games in their rap sessions and classes and preachin' 'bout dope. There ain't but ten of 'em would go down on anything. If they be serious about revolution they be going down on every beef a 'brother' has 'stead giving him that jive that it ain't a legitimate beef. After all them whiteys done to us there ain't no beef that ain't legitimate.

Despite the rather sharp ideological conflict between the "revolutionaries" and "half-steppers," for several reasons the organization did not become dichotomized and dissolve. First, the revolutionary element saw themselves in the role of missionaries seeking to convert sinners. Deviations were to be expected, and while punished, they were forgiven. Second, the nature of the meetings and rap sessions were open and members were encouraged to express opposed viewpoints and vent their emotions. To some extent, then, the meetings served as a safety valve in which issues were dealt with as they arose.[38] Third, and perhaps most importantly, the "revolutionaries" composed only a small number of the membership and remained aloof from primary group relationships with the majority. As several of them were released, other members whose attitudes were more consistent with the majority were elected to their positions. Thus, the organization underwent a gradual change away from the perspectives of nationalism.

In August 1971, a "half-stepper," who had been a well-known pimp and drug dealer prior to his confinement, and who had been excluded from the organization for that reason, was admitted to membership and elected President on the next day. His rapid rise within the organization was due to his immersion in the network of partnerships. Immensely popular and a participant in several cliques, he was able to mobilize their support for his election. In his acceptance speech, he gave expression to a new and creative definition of the situation that neutralized the conflict between the opposed perspectives of nationalism and "soul":

There's just a coupla things I wanna say about some things I been hearing. The first thing is dope. Now I ask you what's the answer to that? Most everybody in this room been into dope at one time or another. All the 'brothers' know how hard it is to stop using it. And how much we using anyway? Nobody here's strung out are they? I don't see nobody nodding. So what's the harm if a man scores a little dope in here now and then. He's still black ain't he? He can still be working for the revolution can't he? Everybody knows ya have to do things in jail you don't do on the street. You gonna tell a man that's got a life bid he can't use no pills once in a while. You can't do that. Every man's gotta get away from here once in a while. He can still think black, he can still act black, and he can still be there when the shit goes down. And that's what counts, 'brothers.'

Thus, by conceptualizing the prison as an exceptional situation, by dissociating prison behavior from "street" behavior, and by restricting the definition of a revolutionary to one who can be counted upon in a crisis, the new President presented the membership with a definition of the situation that allowed them to retain an idealized image of themselves as revolutionaries while continuing to fashion their behavior according to the ghetto perspectives of "soul."

Toms

Terms such as "stand-up guy," "wise guy," "administration man," "fag," and "rat," by which white inmates are labeled and identified are known and used by blacks as well. But among the blacks such labels are subordinate to the distinction between "brothers" and "toms." One might think the designation "tom" is an equivalent term for the pejorative roles identified by the whites. This is not the case. There is some overlapping, to be sure. One cannot be an "administration man" or "rat" and be a "brother." But many "brothers" are drug users or "dope fiends," and some are "fags." This lack of equivalence throws into relief the defining criterion of a "tom." A "tom" is any black inmate who displays accomodative behavior toward whites. Blacks who provide the staff with information or who accept a position of supervision over other inmates are not reproved because they are inmates violating an inmate code, but because they are blacks who reject the ideal of black unity. A "fag" may still be a "brother" if he confines his sexual activities to other blacks. But a "fag" who performs sexual services for whites is a "tom," as is the occasional black inmate who, while playing the active role in a homosexual relation, develops an emotional attachment for a white "fag" or "kid."

Of the approximately 46 black inmates, no more than eight were identified as "toms." Three of these were older "lifers" who had adopted the "administration man" role. One was a proof reader in the print shop, another the foreman of the upholstery shop, and the third was the institutional maintenance man. A fourth was a young "fag" who refused to change his behavior and entered freely into sexual liaisons with any inmate regardless of color. Three others were long-timers who played the active role in a homosexual marriage with white "kids." One other was a 51-year old man on a short sentence who openly engaged in fawning behavior with respect to the staff.

In no way are the "toms" a group or a clique. Except for the four engaged in homosexual activity, they are loners, scorned by the staff, excluded by the whites and hated by the "brothers." No class of individuals is more despised by a group than renegades, potential members who deny the values most affirmed by the group. "Toms" are renegades. Their behavior rejects and denies the very basis of black unity, and their existence is a constant threat to racial solidarity. Further, in the eyes of the "brothers," the behavior of the "tom" makes their time more difficult. As they see it, "toms" confirm the stereotypes held by the white officers concerning the proper role of a black man. The result is a definition of black behavior by the officers, behavior which in the eyes of the black prisoners is merely "being a man," as militant and threatening, and therefore more likely to be penalized. For all of these reasons the "toms" are regarded with utter hatred and disdain.

"Toms" are subject to continual harassment by the "brothers" ranging from verbal insults to occasional assaults. Again, however, such behavior is more typical of the "half-stepper" than the "revolutionary." The "revolutionary" opposes any conflict between blacks that is visible to whites. He avoids the "toms." But for the "half-stepper," caught as he is in a situation in which his behavior is at variance with an identity he claims for himself, verbal and physical aggression against "toms" is a means of proving to himself and others that he is in fact a black revolutionary. Thus, the existence of "toms" and their rejection of the value of racial unity reinforces that unity for a significant number of the black inmates.[39]

Summary and Conclusion

In this chapter we have seen that, unlike the white prisoners, the majority of black prisoners are united in a solidary group. The racial solidarity of the blacks is grounded in two ideological perspectives, "soul" and black nationalism, both of which have their origins in social movements outside the prison and are imported into the prison primarily through the Afro-American Society. While both "soul" and black nationalism provide bases for group solidarity, there is an inherent contradiction between them. "Soul" celebrates an historic black American culture; it affirms the value of perseverance and acceptance. Black nationalism, in contrast, celebrates past African glories, and presents visions of possible future greatness by means of a global revolution against the forces of racism, colonialism, and imperialism. This tension, along with the ideological perspectives which give rise to it, is imported into the prison and shapes the collective adaptations made by black prisoners.

Black prisoners recognize the argot labels used by the white inmates, but the focal concerns connoted by these terms are not the primary axes of life for the blacks. The primary axis of life for most black inmates is racial identification. They identify and act with respect to each other as "brothers," "partners" and "toms." Brotherhood is based upon the recognition of a shared fate at the hands of a common oppressor, and the essence of the relationship is mutual aid in the face of oppression. Underlying the relation between "brothers" and reinforcing it is the relation between "partners." Where the relation between "brothers" does not necessitate personal knowledge, liking, or even trust, these properties are at the heart of the relationship between "partners." The typical black inmate has one or more "jail house partners" and perhaps a "street partner." As a result, nearly the entire black population is bound together in an interlocking structure of diffuse relationships. Standing apart from this structure, and functioning as a negative reference group for the "brothers," is a small number of older "toms," so defined because they display what is regarded as accommodating behavior toward either the staff or white inmates.

From the perspective of an outsider, the majority of black prisoners seemingly are possessed of a single mind. There is, nonetheless, a deep ideological division within the Afro-American Society, a division that reflects the contradiction between "soul" and black nationalism. Black prisoners do not differentiate between prison adaptive styles embodying these perspectives by applying consensual labels to them, but I have labeled them "revolutionaries" and "half-steppers." "Revolutionaries" lead a stoic prison existence designed to prepare them for active participation in the black movement after release. In contrast, "half-steppers," while verbalizing revolutionary sentiments, retain an attachment to the life of the dope fiend or pimp and seek to make the most of their present existence by immersing themselves in the underlife of the institution. The contradiction between these orientations was apparent in disagreements concerning the goals and purposes of the Afro-American Society. The organization was established by the "revolutionaries" as a means of institutionalizing self-improvement programs and converting the "half-steppers." For the "half-steppers," the primary goals of the organization were social and protective. As a result of the restrictive policies of the "revolutionaries" concerning drugs, homosexuality, and relations with staff, they came to be seen as dictators and were displaced from the leadership of the organization near the end of the study period.

6

Hacks, Blacks, and Cons: Discipline

Where the preceding chapters set forth the physical and social context of race relations at ECI, this chapter shifts our concern to the analysis of race relations. Race relations at ECI have both a vertical and a horizontal dimension. The vertical dimension is the significance of race for staff-inmate relations; the horizontal dimension is the significance of race for the relations among inmates. The concern of this chapter is with the vertical dimension. Succeeding chapters will treat race relations among inmates and the interrelationship of these two dimensions.

Custodians and prisoners interact in many contexts, but the essential aspect of the relationship remains the same: discipline. Despite the ambiguities contained in the role definition of the correctional officers at ECI, it remains clear that their primary responsibility is the maintenance of order and control. And despite the many reforms at the institution, the principal resources at the disposal of the custodians remain coercive in nature. While formal rewards such as parole, custody grading and work assignments may be partially dependent upon the recommendations of officers, they are administered by special boards and not by the custodians themselves. As a result, their value to the custodian in securing routine compliance with his directives is minimized. Similarly, the incentive value of other rewards is neutralized in various ways. For example, each inmate is awarded two days off his sentence for each month of work. As long as an inmate is listed as employed, however, he receives these two days through routine administrative action. Thus, the only way an officer can use "industrial time," as it is called, to secure compliance is to threaten its loss through disciplinary action. A reward thus becomes a punishment. A similar process of conversion occurs with respect to "good time." Each inmate is awarded a number of days off his sentence for each month of good behavior, the number of days being dependent upon the length of his sentence. To facilitate administration, however, this time is deducted from his sentence upon his entry into the institution. Here again, then, the officer may avail himself of the resource only by threatening its loss by disciplinary action. Again a reward becomes a punishment.[1] Thus, the actual or potential imposition of coercive sanctions lies at the heart of staff-inmate relations, and for this reason is the focus of this chapter.

There is yet another reason to focus on the disciplinary process. It is the perspective of the black inmates. It is the almost universal view of the black prisoners at ECI that they are the object of racial discrimination in every area of institutional life. As they see it, the fact of their race condemns them to the most undesirable jobs, limits their access to the more desirable cells, and makes the attainment of work release and parole more difficult. The area about which they verbalize the strongest feelings of discrimination, however, is that of discipline:

We're third class citizens in a second class society. It's as simple as that. . . . We get screwed in everything—parole, work release, everything. The worst thing, though is the double standard them hacks got. In booking (reporting) ya. . . . Like just a while ago there was this white guy started throwing his chair around in the dining hall. He was all worked up about something. Took three hacks to get him outta there but they didn't book him or nothin'. The next week a 'brother's' goin' through the line and throws his tray on the floor, 'cause he didn't like the food. Boom! They put him back in BCU (Segregation) for a week. It's shit like that, stuff that goes on every day, that's the biggest thing.

What follows in this chapter, then, is an analysis of racial differences as a factor in the staff-inmate relationship with primary attention given to the area of discipline. First, I shall present statistical data relating to racial differences in the number and type of infractions reported, and to the dispositions made by officers and the Disciplinary Board. Following this presentation, these data will be interpreted in terms of two sets of conditions: (1) the racial bias of the custodians and the pattern of surveillance to which it gives rise, and (2) the differential resources available to black and white inmates to counter the power of the staff.

Racial Differences in Disciplinary Dispositions

As noted previously, there are no written regulations regarding inmate behavior at ECI. Nonetheless, it is understood that prisoners are not to be permitted to engage in any behavior that would threaten the order and/or the security of the institution. Such behaviors range from excessive noise and horseplay to fighting and assaults upon inmates and threatening or assaulting officers. Moreover, all prisoners are required to work and to obey all directives of the correctional officers. Thus, despite the absence of detailed written regulations, there are a variety of behaviors for which an inmate may be punished, and there is a prescribed process by which punishment is to be administered.

The Disciplinary Process

According to established procedures at ECI, officers should handle offenses regarded as minor by firm warnings and counseling. If such actions are not sufficient, the officer, with the approval of his immediate superior, may discipline a prisoner by a one or two night lockup in his cell. In such instances, however, the inmate may refuse the lockup and request a Disciplinary Board. To ensure that in instances of brief lockups, the inmate has been informed of his right to a hearing, he is required to sign a form that waives his right to a hearing and indicates his acceptance of the lockup. Copies of this form are then forwarded to the office of the Deputy Warden and to the Classification Department, where they are placed in the inmate's file.

In cases of infractions judged to be serious, or when the inmate demands a hearing, the officer must prepare a formal written charge. The charge must contain the time, date, place, names of witnesses, and all other pertinent details concerning the alleged violation. As soon as possible after the alleged violation the officer must submit the charge to his superior officer. The superior officer must then conduct a preliminary investigation of the incident. At a minimum, the investigation of the superior officer must include interviews with the reporting officer, with the inmate charged, and with any other officers or inmates indicated as witnesses. Upon completion of his investigation, the superior officer must prepare his own summary of the incident and submit a full report to the Deputy Warden. The Deputy Warden then sets a time and place for a hearing by the Disciplinary Board.

The Disciplinary Board consists of the Deputy Warden and two other members, one each from the custody and treatment sections. In conducting the hearing, the Board must read the charge in full to the inmate and allow him to admit or deny the charges. They may then interrogate the inmate and others as necessary, and the inmate may present information available to himself and others in his own defense. After completing the hearing the Board must make a decision based upon "substantial evidence" and immediately inform the inmate of their decision and rationale. The actions which the Board may take include: (1) dismissal of charge, (2) reprimand, (3) loss of specified privileges for a period not to exceed thirty days, (4) confinement to cell for a period not to exceed thirty days, (5) one to thirty days placement in punitive segregation, (6) loss of good time, and (7) any combination of (3) through (6) above and/or suspended action on any or all of (3) through (6) above.

Infractions and Dispositions

The data presented in this section represent all infractions cited by officers either in the form of lockups or disciplinary reports during the period from July 1, 1971 through October 30, 1971. Infractions were classified as major or minor depending upon the dispositions made by the officers in all incidents of that type. An infraction was classified as major if 50 percent or more of the total incidents of that type were referred to the Disciplinary Board for action. If less than 50 percent were so referred, the infraction was classified as minor. The classification of an infraction as major or minor, then, is dependent upon the aggregated actions of the officers with respect to all infractions of a similar nature and thus represents their judgements rather than those of the observer. As might be expected behavior regarded as major infractions by the officers was behavior involving either an affront to their authority or a direct threat to internal order. Major offenses included insolence or threat to an officer, refusing an order, creating a disturbance, fighting and assault, articles in cell doors, and the possession of contraband items such as money, drugs, or weapons. Minor offenses included being out of place or late for count, horseplay, noise after lights out, the possession of contraband items such as pornography or food from the kitchen, and so forth.

Reported Infractions. As shown in Table 6-1, the officers reported 210 infractions between July 1 and October 30, 1971. Of this number, 32.9 percent (69) were infractions by black inmates. Further, of the 118 major infractions reported by the officers, 37.3 percent (44) involved black prisoners. Given the fact that during this period black prisoners comprised only some 22 percent of the prisoner population, it is unlikely that these figures are the result of chance.[a] For whatever reasons black inmates were cited for disciplinary infractions more than their number in the population would warrant, and this was particularly so for infractions regarded as major by reporting officers. Further, a slight extrapolation from the figures in Table 6-1 reveals that of the 69 reported infractions involving black inmates, 63.8 percent were major infractions. This figure compares with 52.4 percent of the reported infractions involving white inmates. Thus, not only are black prisoners disproportionately reported for major infractions, but also a somewhat higher percentage of infractions involving blacks, as compared to those involving whites, are major infractions.

Dispositions by Officers. As noted above, the first step in the disciplinary process is the decision of the officer to punish an inmate by a brief lockup or to submit a report which will result in a hearing by the Disciplinary Board.

Table 6-2 presents data concerning these decisions by officers and

[a] A two-tailed difference of proportions test reveals that given the fact that black inmates constitute 22 percent of the prison population, the probability that 32.9 percent of all infractions reported would involve black inmates by chance equals .015 and that 37.3 percent of the major infractions would involve black inmates by chance equals .006.

Table 6-1
Reported Infractions by Race and Seriousness in Percentages

Race	Seriousness of Infraction		
	Major (N=118)	Minor (N=92)	Total (N=210)
White	62.7%	72.8%	67.1%
Black	37.3	27.2	32.9
Total	100.0%	100.0%	100.0%

Table 6-2
Percent of Infractions Reported by Officers to the Disciplinary Board by Race and Seriousness

Race	Seriousness of Infraction		
	Major[a]	Minor[b]	Total[c]
Black	97.2% (44)*	8.0% (25)	65.2% (69)
White	93.2% (74)	35.8% (67)	66.0% (141)

[a]$p < .30$
[b]$p < .01$
[c]$p < .99$
*( ) = Base N for the percentage

classified by the race of the prisoner and the seriousness of the offense. An analysis by chi-square of racial differences within each of the infraction categories reveals that there is no significant racial difference in the dispositions made by officers with respect to either total infractions or major infractions. The data on minor infractions, however, reveal a substantial and statistically significant difference by race in the dispositions made by officers. Where only 8 percent of the minor infractions by black prisoners were reported to the Board, more than one-third (35.8 percent) of the minor infractions by white inmates were reported. These differences suggest that in making their dispositions the officers are more careful to distinguish between major and minor infractions in the case of black prisoners than in the case of white prisoners. Whereas virtually all major infractions by prisoners of both races are referred to the Disciplinary Board for action, over one-third of the minor infractions by whites but less than one-tenth of the minor infractions by blacks are referred to the Board.

Table 6-3

Major Infractions Reported to Disciplinary Board by Race in Percentages

Reported Infractions	White (N=69)	Black (N=43)	Total (N=112)
Insolence or Threat to an Officer	34.8%	25.6%	31.3%
Refusal of an Order	24.6	37.3	29.5
Fighting and Assault	8.7	20.9	13.4
Creating a Disturbance	2.9	2.3	2.7
Major Contraband	23.2	11.6	18.6
Articles in Cell Door	5.8	2.3	4.5
Total	100.0%	100.0%	100.0%

(Race of Inmate)

Dispositions by Disciplinary Board. Table 6-3 presents a distribution by race of the major infractions referred to the Disciplinary Board by reporting officers. These data show some differences between black and white prisoners in the infractions for which they were reported. For instance, 34.8 percent of the infractions by whites as compared to 25.6 percent of those by blacks were for insolence or threatening an officer. Thirty-seven percent of the infractions by blacks were for refusing an order and 20.9 percent were for fighting and assault. The comparable figures for infractions of these types by whites were 24.6 percent and 8.7 percent respectively. If the existence of a direct, physical threat to order, security, or the authority of the officers is taken as a criterion of the seriousness of an infraction, then overall the infractions of the black prisoners appear to be of a more serious nature than those of the whites. Fully 86 percent of the infractions by blacks referred to the Disciplinary Board were for actions which constitute such a threat—insolence, threatening an officer, refusing an order, fighting, assault, and creating a disturbance. In comparison 71 percent of the reported infractions by whites were of this type.[b]

Despite the apparently more serious nature of the major infractions of the black prisoners which were referred to the Disciplinary Board, they receive somewhat less severe penalties. Data on the disposition of major offenses by the Disciplinary Board classified by race are presented in Table 6-4. A chi-square analysis of this data reveals a substantial and significant difference by race in the dispositions of the Board. Where 37.7 percent of the infractions by white prisoners resulted in the imposition of the most severe sanctions—segregation and/or loss of good time [c] or confinement in

[b]As determined by a two-tailed difference of proportions test, the probability of this difference occurring by chance is .069.

[c]Loss of good time is seldom imposed as penalty apart from segregation. In only one incident in these data was this the case.

Table 6-4

Dispositions of Major Infractions by the Disciplinary Board by Race in Percentages

Disposition by Board	Race[a]		
	White (N=69)	Black (N=43)	Total (N=112)
Segregation and/or Loss of Good Time	16.2%	19.6%	21.8%
Confinement to Cell	15.9	4.7	11.6
Loss of Privileges	15.9	48.8	28.6
Reprimand or Suspended Sentence	39.2	20.9	32.1
Not Guilty	1.4	2.3	1.8
Other[b]	5.8	7.0	6.3
Total	100.0%	100.0%	100.0%

[a]$p < .001$. Because of the small numbers in this and the following table it was necessary to combine categories in computing chi-square. The categories were combined as follows: (1) segregation and confinement to cell, (2) loss of privileges, and (3) reprimand, suspended sentence, not guilty and other.
[b]Two white inmates and one black inmate were released before Board action. One white inmate and 2 black inmates received job transfers and 1 white inmate was fined $0.50.

cell—only 20.9 percent of the infractions by black inmates were so handled. However, it is also to be noted that 39.2 percent of the infractions by whites, as compared to 20.9 percent of the infractions by blacks, received the least severe penalty, a reprimand, or suspended sentence. Thus, major infractions by black prisoners in comparison to those of whites resulted in both proportionately fewer of the most severe and least severe penalties. Almost one-half (48.8 percent) of the black infractions, as compared to only 15.9 percent of the white infractions, were sanctioned by an intermediate punishment, loss of privileges for a specified period of time, usually not more than seven days. It would appear, then, that the Disciplinary Board has a standard almost uniform response to infractions by black inmates.

One factor that may affect the dispositions made by the Disciplinary Board is the inmate's past disciplinary record. Controlling for this variable (Table 6-5) points up the fact that racial differences in dispositions by the Disciplinary Board occur mainly among those prisoners with no disciplinary reports in the previous six months. While none of the 14 black prisoners with no reports in the previous six months received the more severe penalties of segregation, loss of good time or confinement to cell, 34.3 percent of the white inmates in this category received this penalty. Conversely, only 18.7 percent of the white prisoners with no prior reports received a loss of privileges as a punishment, while the vast majority (78.6

Table 6-5

Dispositions of Major Infractions by the Disciplinary Board by Disciplinary Record and Race in Percentages

Disposition by Board	No Reports in Prior 6 mos.[a]			Reports in Prior 6 mos.[b]		
	White (N=32)	Black (N=14)	Total (N=46)	White (N=37)	Black (N=29)	Total (N=66)
Segregation and/or Loss of Good Time	21.8%	—	15.2%	21.6%	24.1%	22.7%
Confinement to Cell	12.5	—	8.7	18.9	6.9	13.6
Loss of Privileges	18.7	78.6%	36.9	13.5	34.5	22.7
Reprimand or Suspended Sentence	37.5	21.4	32.6	40.0	20.7	31.8
Not Guilty	3.1	—	2.2	—	3.4	1.5
Other	6.3	—	4.3	5.5	10.3	7.6
Total	99.9%	100.0%	99.9%	100.0%	99.9%	99.9%

[a] < .001. Categories combined as in Table 6-4
[b] < .20

percent) of the black prisoners with no reports were so sanctioned. These differences remain among those prisoners with one or more reports, but are reduced considerably. Thirty-one percent of the black inmates with prior reports received the more severe penalties, compared to 40.5 percent of the white prisoners. Similarly, 34.5 percent of the blacks received a loss of privileges, as compared to 13.5 percent of the whites. Thus, it is apparent that the tendency for the Disciplinary Board to adopt an almost standard response to infractions by black prisoners as compared to white prisoners, sanctioning them with an intermediate punishment, is concentrated among those prisoners with no disciplinary reports in the six months previous to the current infraction.

Summary

In this section, I have examined differences by race in both reported infractions and dispositions made by correctional officers and the Disciplinary Board. Several significant differences were noted. First, black prisoners, in comparison to their number in the population, are over-reported for disciplinary infractions, especially for violations regarded as major. Second, in making their dispositions, correctional officers appear to be more careful to distinguish between major and minor infractions in the case of black prisoners than in the case of white prisoners. This is particularly apparent with respect to minor infractions. Less than 10 percent of the minor infractions by black prisoners, as compared to more than one-third of those committed by white prisoners, are referred to the Disciplinary Board for action. Third, and finally, although infractions by black inmates referred to the Disciplinary Board are more serious than those by white prisoners, black prisoners are not punished more severely. In fact, the Disciplinary Board appears to have an almost standard response to infractions by black inmates, as nearly 50 percent of such infractions are punished by an intermediate penalty, loss of privileges. This tendency toward a uniform response on the part of the Disciplinary Board is most apparent among those prisoners with no disciplinary reports in the previous six months.

I have presented these data with no attempt at interpretation. The interpretation of the differences summarized above is the concern of the remainder of this chapter. As will be shown, each of these differences is the result of a set of interrelated conditions. For purposes of analysis, I shall deal with each condition separately. As noted previously, these conditions are (1) the racial biases of the custodians and the behavior to which this bias gives rise, and (2) the differential resources available to black and white prisoners in coping with the power of the staff.

Racial Bias of the Custodians

At ECI prisoners receive their visitors in the dining hall, an area in which there are no physical barriers to separate the prisoner from his visitor. As a substitute for physical separation there are several "understandings" concerning the conduct of prisoners in relation to their visitors, especially female visitors. One such understanding, is a proscription against frequent or extended kissing and fondling. In general, a prisoner is permitted to kiss briefly a female visitor upon her arrival and departure. Physical contact during the visit is not to extend beyond hand-holding. This rule is difficult to enforce for several obvious reasons: first, is the difficulty in establishing what constitutes an extended kiss; second, the enforcement of the rule is likely to prove embarrassing to the officer; third, to enforce rules in the presence of large numbers of prisoners and visitors is to run the risk of provoking a serious disturbance. As a result, the rule is seldom enforced and the behavior in corners of the visiting room frequently is similar to that which might be observed in the darkened corners of a gymnasium during a high school dance.

On only one occasion did I observe an officer terminate a visit because of an alleged violation of this rule. A newly arrived black inmate received a visit from a white female. Meeting at the door they promptly engaged in a long, passionate embrace with the prisoner running his hands over her back and sides. The reaction of the officer was instantaneous: he ran across the room, grabbed the prisoner, pulled him away from the girl, informed them in a loud voice that the visit was terminated, and escorted the prisoner to the Deputy Warden's office to place him on report.

In taking this action, the officer was well within the scope of his authority. But the fact that similar behavior between prisoners and females of the same race seldom if ever elicits this response from the same officer strongly suggests that his reaction was prompted less by the violation of institutional rules than by the violation of what "ought to be" in terms of his conception of racial etiquette. In principle, of course, racial differences should have no meaning within the context of the prison. Officers are officers, and inmates are inmates. In fact this is not so. In previous chapters it was shown that the racial identities of inmates are related to differences in the perception of and definition accorded the prison situation, and to how prisoners organize to cope with its exigencies. In similar fashion the officers, who are overwhelmingly white, import into the prison cultural meanings associated with race in white society. In prison, these meanings are given a more specific content through their interaction with black inmates.

Sources of Prejudice

External Sources. Correctional officers at ECI earn between $6000 and $10,000 per year. They are, then, members of the American middle class, and this most certainly is their subjective class identification. The following characterization, made by the President of the Fraternal Order of Correctional Officers, is typical of the attributions the officers make to themselves:

The average correctional officer is a morally decent person. . . . They're average middle class men. They have a family. Their kids are in school and they wanna see 'em go to college. Most of 'em own their own homes. So they have a lot of bills to pay. I'd say maybe half of them have wives that work, but they're the initial breadwinners in the family. And I don't have to tell you, 'cause you been around long enough to know, they work damn hard for what little they get.

Research in American communities indicates that interracial contact is infrequent and that racial prejudice is prevalent in the segment of the white population from which the officers are drawn and with which they identify.[2] Not one of the white officers with whom I had contact admitted to having social contacts with blacks, including their fellow officers, off the job. For several, their contacts with blacks on the job are the first and only interracial contacts of their lives, and virtually all of them verbalize stereotypical conceptions of blacks as being innately lazy, ignorant, crude, and hypersexual. Such conversations usually arise in the aftermath of some incident such as the one noted above. So, for instance, a young officer who expressed some surprise when an attractive white girl picked up a black prisoner upon his release, was told by a captain, "You know how them niggers are. He's probably over-sized and over-sexed."

The traditional view of race prejudice is that it consists in a set of conceptions, emotions, and action-orientations lodged in individuals. Blumer has challenged this perspective, arguing that prejudice may best be conceived as inherent in a sense of group position.[3] From his perspective, a sense of group position transcends the individual feelings of dominant group members. It involves a feeling of superiority, a belief that the subordinate group is different and alien, a claim to certain areas of privilege and advantage, and fears concerning the intentions of members of the subordinate group.[4] The sense of position is a sense of what "ought to be" in the relations between groups. When the relations are as they should be, unequal and unchallenged, prejudice may take the form of sympathy or paternalism. But when the position of the dominant group is threatened, prejudice is most likely to manifest itself in a defensive reaction of hostility.[5]

It is this sense of threat to group position that lies at the base of the officers' feelings toward blacks. Both of the incidents cited above, for example, involved hostile verbalizations and actions elicited by a perceived erosion of the traditional racial etiquette surrounding relations between sexes. However, the sexual threat is only one dimension of the threat experienced by the white officers as a result of the changes in race relations. The custodians grant no legitimacy to contemporary black militancy or to the governmental responses to black demands. Both are threats to the self-esteem and socio-economic position of the white officers, and they react to them with an admixture of hostility and righteous indignation. The sense of many of their conversations may be summarized in two ubiquitous questions: "I ain't done anything to them so why take it out on me?," and "Why can't they get theirs the same way I'm trying to get mine?" At one point during the study the black students at one of the state colleges occupied the administration building and made demands for more black faculty, black studies programs, and black students. One senior officer whose daughter attended the university expressed his resentment while having coffee with several of his peers:

Cpt: What the hell they got to protest about? I'm bustin' my back to send my kid there and you know what them niggers get? A free ride!. . . No shit! The state gives 'em free tuition, books, board and ten bucks a week. What have they got to bitch about?

Off: It don't make no difference what ya give 'em. The more they get the more they want. They're out for revolution, that's what.

Cpt: Well, if that's what they want, I'm ready. And the sooner the better 'cause when it's over there'll be a damn sight fewer niggers around.

Internal Sources. Definitions of the situation of this type, presented by figures in authority, are crucial in the formation and maintenance of racial attitudes.[6] Not only does this statement legitimize the sentiments of the officers, it also serves to draw together two independent sources of threat experienced by them: the threat to their position as whites posed by black militancy and the threat to their position as custodians posed by prison reforms. In Chapter 3 the situation of the officers was described as anomic as a result of the reform emphasis at ECI. The reforms have occurred gradually since 1956. In the eyes of the custodians, however, the incursions upon their powers and status occurred dramatically in the aftermath of the disturbances in 1968-1969. It will be recalled that the first two disturbances involved primarily black inmates against the staff. In Gouldner's terms, these disturbances have become "paradigmatic experiences" for the custodians, i.e., specific, shared past experiences "that constitute a frame of reference in terms of which men perceive, judge, and react to current situations."[7] Although the majority of the disturbances at ECI in 1968-69 were either racially mixed or precipitated by whites, and although the court decrees were brought about by the action of 24 white inmates after an all-white sit-down strike, the memories of the officers have been blurred. As they see it now, the disturbances were caused by the blacks and "the whites didn't want any part of it, but when the coloreds started it they had to get involved because the lines were drawn." The memory of these disturbances evokes quite specific emotions among the staff, giving rise to expectations concerning the future. Two senior officials, for example, recounted their reactions in the following terms:

You know what them niggers did to the New Building when they had that riot? . . . They broke every pane of glass in the building. Every book in the library was ripped to pieces. All the furniture was busted. Just talking about it gives me the chills. My skin crawls every time I see one of them niggers.

. . . .

We had control of the joint till them niggers started the riots a couple of years ago. That's when we lost control. This group's no different from the other one. It's just a front for the Panthers. They ain't interested in improving themselves. They want control of the joint, complete freedom. They should never have allowed it. They're all Panthers, they're militant as hell, and it's gonna blow up in our face.

In brief, the white custodians regard the black inmates with a mixture of hostility and fear derived from several sources. As members of the white middle class, they share many of the traditional stereotypes of blacks and see their status threatened by the current wave of black militancy. As correctional officers in a reform-oriented institution, many of their powers and much of their status has been eroded, and this threat—coincident during the latter part of the study period with incidents such as the Attica tragedy—is interpreted to a large extent in racial terms. Thus, on the one hand, the officers see the black prisoners as lazy, ignorant, crude, and hypersexual; on the other hand, they view them as dangerous, conspiring revolutionaries whose intentions are not only to challenge the authority of the custodians but quite possibly to seek control of the institution by means of open rebellion.

Such conceptions differ markedly from those the custodians have of the white inmates. To be sure, the officers harbor negative conceptions of the white prisoners: "Just by virtue of the fact they've committed a crime makes them the enemy." But, unlike the blacks, the whites are not seen as enemies who are likely to precipitate open warfare. They are immoral, lazy, greedy individuals who are virtually incapable of rehabilitation, but basically accommodating. Their fighting and mutual exploitation is to be expected, is what the officers are prepared to handle, and is not viewed as a threat to the authority of the staff. The white prisoners challenge the authority of the officer by manipulation on a personal basis, a challenge not physically threatening. Moreover, in spite of the moral distance between the respectable white guardians and convicted white criminals, they share many subcultural orientations, and thus the behavior of the white convicts is more easily understood by the white staff.

Sure, the whites try to get around you too. But it's different than with the colored guys. The whites are sneaky . . . more cunning. They'll try to con you and take advantage of you by any method possible, but an officer can educate himself to this.

Prejudice and Behavior

Close Surveillance. These differential conceptions of black and white prisoners dispose the officers to be more vigilant in their surveillance of black activities than of white. Two areas in which the greater vigilance of the officers is evident are inmate organizations and visits. Not only do the officers see the Afro-American Society as intent upon fomenting a disturbance within the institution, they also believe that most of the drugs entering the institution are brought in by individuals associated with the organization. Thus, while white visitors to the "Jay Cees" are admitted to the institution without a search, black visitors to the Afro-American Society frequently are subjected to thorough searches. Similarly, black inmates are more likely than white inmates to be searched after receiving a visit and to have gifts from visitors searched before being permitted to bring them into the institution. Several casual observations of inmates leaving the visiting room after visits revealed that about six of every ten black inmates were subjected to at least a superficial search as compared to only about two of every ten whites. On one occasion, a black inmate and a white inmate who lived on the same tier both received several record albums from visitors on the same day. The white inmate was permitted to bring the records back to his cell after only a cursory examination of the album titles. The black inmate, however, was forced to wait two days while his albums were opened and inspected.

A similar pattern of closer surveillance of black prisoners occurs in the wings and yard. Wing officers are expected to search a number of cells each day while the inmates are at work, and to enter the cells searched in a wing log book. A check of the log book in North State Wing for one week revealed that of 27 cells searched, 48.1 percent were occupied by black inmates. During that same week only 26.8 percent of the 56 occupied cells in that wing were occupied by black inmates. If this week is representative, the search activities of officers are disproportionately focused on black prisoners.

From 4 p.m. until 9 p.m. on weekdays and all day Saturday and Sunday, prisoners are free from any duties. But, as we have seen, facilities for recreation are extremely limited. For the most part inmates spend their time "hanging out" in groups around the yard and wings. To the officers, these groups are a major security problem. They, even more than the inmates, believe in "doing your own time." But the degree to which a group is perceived as threatening is related to its color. Any congregation of black inmates numbering more than five or six is liable to draw the attention of an officer. One evening, for example, I was sitting on a bench with seven black inmates when an officer came by and told us to "break it up." Not more than ten feet away was a group of six whites whom the officer did not even seem to notice.

Another facet of this pattern of closer surveillance pertains to movement about the institution. It has been noted previously that officers are willing to give passes and to allow inmates into unauthorized areas if the inmate is not a "troublemaker." Blacks more than whites are viewed as troublemakers and are less likely to receive passes than are whites. In the Print Shop one day I observed a white inmate receive a pass from an officer to go to his cell to get cigarettes, not a legitimate reason. Not more than five minutes later a black inmate requested a pass to the barber shop to get a haircut. He was refused with the explanation that workers in the Print Shop are allowed to get haircuts only on Wednesdays. On another occasion I observed two black prisoners refused admittance to South State Wing.

After they had left a white prisoner entered the wing, walking directly past the officer who had refused entry to the blacks. Still a similar incident occurred in a wing one evening when two white inmates came down from a cell block tier with coffee cups in their hands at the same time that an officer was denying a black inmate permission to go up on the tier to get a cup of coffee.

Relation to Discipline. Each of these incidents is one aspect of a pattern of closer control of black inmates than whites. To the officers, given their preconceptions, it does not represent discrimination but sound custodial control. Nonetheless, the pattern of closer surveillance is likely to result in more black infractions, and, as was noted in Table 6-1, black inmates are in fact reported for infractions more than their number in the population warrants. Moreover, it is to be expected that the infractions for which black prisoners are reported would be of a type directly related to the closer control exerted upon them. The pattern of closer surveillance places the officer in a position of issuing proportionately more orders to blacks: to submit to a search, to return to work, not to go up on the tier, etc. Such orders, given the extension of these privileges to at least some whites, must necessarily appear arbitrary and capricious and are thus likely to provoke a refusal or a hostile response. Thus, as noted in Table 6-3, 37.3 percent of the major black violations as compared to 24.6 percent of the white violations were for refusing orders. Moreover, 72.7 percent of the eleven black violations for insolence or threat were related to refusing orders. That is, the original infraction was refusing an order but was compounded by the reaction of the inmate to being reported. By comparison only 37.5 percent of the 24 white infractions of this nature were related to another offense, and less than half of these other offenses were refusing an order. Thus, it seems that the closer surveillance of black inmates by officers is to some extent a cause of the higher incidence of major black infractions, in particular refusing orders and insolence or threat.

The racial preconceptions of the officers may also influence their perception of the seriousness of an infraction. As noted in Table 6-1 black inmates were reported disproportionately for major infractions. In this respect, it is noteworthy that 20.9 percent of the major black violations as compared to only 8.7 percent of the major white violations, as shown in Table 6-3, were for fighting and assault. In contrast, only 8.7 percent of the 23 black violations compared to 25 percent of the 48 white violations handled by brief lockups were for horseplay. In many cases, the distinction between horseplay and fighting, as the following incident shows, is difficult to make and depends largely upon the perception and judgment of the officer:

Coming back into the wing we stopped at the Snack Bar. A young inmate went running past us with a mop handle and someone said "a fight between them two oughta be something." As we rounded the tier we came upon a scuffle between Ralph Cohen and the kid. The kid had his head down into Cohen's stomach and was holding Cohen with his hands. Cohen was sort of pushing him around with his body—like a dance. As I struggled to get around them the kid kicked for Cohen's groin and missed. Then Cohen placed a well aimed kick in the kid's crotch. The kid began yelling "kick me in the balls you bastard, I'll get ya" and went at Cohen with both hands flailing, like a madman screaming and yelling all the time. Finally Price, an officer who was nearby, took notice of the incident and ran over between them. He told Cohen to walk down the block and grabbed hold of the kid who kept squirming, punching, and yelling.

This incident involved two white inmates. In my estimation it was clearly a fight and not merely horseplay. The action of the officer however, was to give the young inmate a two night lockup for horseplay in the wings. I have no comparable data on similar black infractions. But the fact that proportionately more blacks than whites are reported for fighting, and that proportionately fewer are cited for horseplay suggests that if this incident had involved black inmates it may well have resulted in a report for fighting rather than a lockup for horseplay.

In sum, it is likely that the higher incidence of major black violations of certain types is due to the racial preconceptions and the resultant behavior of the white officers. Viewing black inmates as the major threat to order and control, white officers exert a somewhat more vigilant surveillance of their activities. This pattern of closer surveillance places the officer in the position of issuing more orders to black inmates, orders that are likely to be viewed as arbitrary and capricious and thus refused. Further, in refusing the order, black prisoners may compound the infraction by reacting in a hostile and aggressive manner. Finally, the preconceptions held by the officers may affect their perceptions of certain infractions, causing them to see black infractions as more serious than comparable white infractions.

Black Resources

The conceptions of black inmates that are held by the correctional officers and the closer pattern of surveillance to which these conceptions give rise is only one condition that affects outcomes of the disciplinary process. Another condition is the collective adaptations of the prisoners. It is well known that the lower level participants in complex organizations, such as prisoners, may achieve considerable informal power and may use this power to protect themselves from the authority of higher ranking participants. As noted by Mechanic,[8] some of the common sources of power of lower level participants are the following: (1) access to knowledge of the organization, its procedures and techniques, (2) access to persons either within or outside the organization and upon whom the organization is dependent, and (3) access to aspects of the physical structure of the organization or its resources. By obtaining, maintaining and controlling access to information, persons and instrumentalities lower level participants make higher ranking participants dependent upon them and may thus manipulate them and circumvent their authority. It is such a pattern of dependence and manipulation between guards and inmates that Sykes termed the "corruption of authority."[9] He noted that although guards may report inmates for disobedience, frequent reports would give prison officials the impression that the guard is unable to command obedience. Guards, therefore, enter into tacit agreements with inmate leaders whereby they overlook violations of certain rules in return for inmate cooperation in maintaining order and meeting the production quotas set for prison industries.[10]

The ability of the black prisoners at ECI to corrupt the authority of the custodians in this manner is limited, however. It is limited not only by the racial biases of the guards, but also by the identity claims of the black prisoners themselves. It will be recalled from Chapter 5 that the majority of black prisoners at ECI form a solidary group who view their imprisonment as a consequence of racial oppression, who define themselves as political prisoners and revolutionaries. For a black to enter a relation of tacit cooperation with the staff is to define himself as a "tom," to place himself from the perspective of the "brothers" in a position analogous to the house servant or overseer on the slave plantation. Thus, the majority of black inmates avoid positions within the institution that would draw them into close and continuous contact with the white custodians and that would thereby facilitate the corruption of authority. Relatively few black prisoners are employed in key work positions. Key work positions are positions providing the incumbents with freedom of movement and/or access to knowledge, persons or resources that may be manipulated to their own advantage. Included in this category are all clerical positions, wing porters, library and hospital workers, cooks, electricians and plumbers. Of the 49 key positions within the institution only six were occupied by black prisoners. Of these six prisoners, five were defined as "toms" and were not members of the Afro-American Society. The sole exception was the President of the Afro-American Society, who worked as a clerk and porter in the New Building. The reputation of this individual and his duties in this position—mainly the administration of the organization and the maintenance of its meeting rooms—placed him beyond reproach. Thus, while the low representation of black prisoners in key positions may result partly from bias by supervisors, the evaluation by their peers of those who occupy such positions suggests that few blacks seek them.

The corruption of custodial authority is only one means of countering the power of the staff, however. If the identity claims of the black prisoners limit their capacities to corrupt authority, they enhance their ability to neutralize it in other ways. Based upon an idealized conception of themselves as black revolutionaries, the black prisoners fashion a line of action in relation to the white staff, an approach that not only counters the authority of the custodians but serves to validate their pronounced identities by evoking in the staff conceptions corresponding to those the black prisoners have of themselves.[11] Rather than attempt to corrupt the authority of the custodians, the black prisoners confront it.

Confrontation

At any given time inmates outnumber the custodians at ECI by ratios of five to one or more. Thus, individual officers continually live with the threat of being overpowered and assaulted, and the entire institution is continually faced with the threat of an inmate rebellion and takeover for however brief a period it may be. Superior numbers alone, however, do not make the threat of physical force an effective source of power. At least as important as superior numbers is the capacity of the group to mobilize its members. This capacity provides the black inmates with a means of countering the authority of the staff. The ideology of the black prisoners and their solidary social organization enable them to mobilize rapidly rather large numbers of inmates to confront individual officers in the process of reporting one of their members. On a higher level, the Afro-American Society provides them with a means of bargaining and negotiating with the administration, a process backed by the implicit threat of a planned and organized disturbance.

These collective capacities of the black prisoners were evident on many occasions. In the following pages I shall present in detail one incident that I observed closely and that illustrates several principles by which the black prisoners organize to confront the staff.

I was interviewing Lotus Rhodes today and was about 45 minutes into the interview when someone called him through the open window of the Chaplain's office, Lotus went to the window and was visibly upset when he returned. He told me he had to go because they were lugging J. D. back to segregation. He rushed out of the door past Officer Gowodski. In the yard he picked up Norm Green who must have been the one at the window. They rushed through the open door into South State and met Nat, Manny, and Tickie at the Rear Hall Door. The Downeys and their clique were not far away, leaning against the wall and watching the action. Lotus began banging his fists against the door shouting 'I want to see the Dep. Tell the Dep. I wanna see him.' A guard came to the door, asked what he wanted, and went into the Deputy's office. He came back and told Lotus to 'put in a pink slip like everybody else.' Lotus exploded. 'What d'ya mean like everybody else? There's plenty of guys goes in to see the Dep whenever they want. They don't need no pink slip. I want satisfaction. I want it now and he's the only one who can give it to me. I ain't puttin' in no pink slip.

You tell him I wanna see him right now.' The guard walked away with Lotus yelling after him. Tickie commented, ''what d'ya expect. We know the bag them racist pigs is comin' outta.'' There was considerable rumbling of this type. All the time Lotus is banging on the door and yelling for the Deputy. . . . A lieutenant came by and Lotus grabbed him by the arm, telling him he wanted to see the Dep. The lieutenant went to the officers' phone and called the Deputy. He returned and told Lotus that the Deputy wasn't going to be explaining his actions to him. This got the others yelling about Gestapo tactics, and why wasn't he man enough to come out and face them. Several minutes later they wandered off down the wing muttering about how they'd have a meeting and there was gonna be trouble. All the time this was going on there were two guards not more than ten feet away who chose to ignore the entire incident. Over the door is a sign ''No Standing Around the Rear Hall Door. To Do So Will Result In Disciplinary Action.''

This incident, occurring over a 20-minute period, illustrates several principles underlying the mobilization of black inmates. First, it is to be noted that there was no apparent knowledge of the reason for which J.D. was reported. Although, as it developed later the participants may well have had some suspicion as to the reason, at this point the reason was unimportant. The first level of mobilization involves the activation of partnership relations. As we noted in the previous chapter, ''partners'' are obliged to support each other in any conflict situation regardless of cause. In this incident J.D., Lotus, Norman, and Nat were ''jail house partners,'' a relationship necessitating their direct and active support of each other. Second, while the Downeys were physically present, they did not participate actively. Their presence and lack of active participation is a further illustration of partnership. Norman and one of the Downeys were ''street partners.'' Thus, the obligations of the Downeys extend directly only to Norman and only indirectly through him to J.D. and Lotus. If the protest had evoked a response from the staff either in the form of physical retaliation or a disciplinary report, the Downey's undoubtedly would have become involved through the activation of their relationship to Norman. There was, however, no action on the part of the staff, and this is the third point. In all, nine black inmates were directly or indirectly involved; all were out of place, and several might well have been reported for threatening or being isolent to officers, creating a disturbance, and standing around the Rear Hall Door. The speed with which the nine black inmates were mobilized, however, neutralized the power of the staff. Only two officers were present, and for them to attempt to impose sanctions on the protestors would have been to place themselves in a dangerous situation. Moreover, it might well have drawn nearly the entire black population into the conflict through the extension of partnership alliances.[12] The custodians thus chose to disregard the infractions of the protestors. As it turned out, only J.D. was reported, and the Afro-American Society did not become involved.

The second level in the mobilization of the black inmate population involves the entry of the Afro-American Society into the conflict. At this level, however, two additional considerations beyond the fact of partnership relations become relevant: (1) the legitimacy of the grievance, and (2) the status of the inmate within the organization. To mobilize the entire organization in the support of one of its members may result in a direct physical confrontation with the entire custodial force, a battle that the leaders know they would lose. Moreover, it might well cause the administration to disband the organization. The leaders of the organization, then, generally conduct their own investigation of the incident before taking action. Their investigation of the incident may involve speaking with the officer and Deputy as well as their own members since they are well aware from prior experience that members may attempt to manipulate them in an effort to gain their support. If after their investigation they are assured that the grievance is legitimate, they will seek redress through meetings with the Warden. They may also enlist the support of various community groups with whom they are allied. While the threat of a disturbance by the entire membership is always present, such disturbances are rare.

Collective disturbances are likely to occur only when the incident involves a high status member of the organization. The higher the status of the member within the organization, the more partnership alliances he is likely to have. Thus, even the immediate confrontation with the staff is likely to involve a substantial portion of the membership in a spontaneous demonstration. Moreover, the higher the status of the member the more pressure there is on other leaders to enlist the organization in his support. To fail to support a member held in high esteem by others may jeopardize the position of the leaders by eroding their base of support.

In the incident involving J.D., no action was taken by the organization. While a member, J.D. had not been an active participant in the organization for several months. Thus, there was little pressure on the leadership to support him. They conducted an investigation of the incident, and it was the decision of the Board of Directors that J.D.'s grievance was not legitimate. Several days after the incident related above, the President gave the following report at a general membership meeting of the organization:

The first thing I wanna talk about tonight is the incident with J.D. When I learned he was locked up I held a meeting of the Board and then I went to the Deputy. I went in there just like this. I'm tellin ya exactly what I said. I told him "I wanna know why you got J.D. locked up." He came back outta that same bag, you know. "He's okay. He's got his books and everything. Nobody touched him. You can go see for yourself." "That ain't what I asked you," I said. "I asked you what you got him locked up for?" You know what he told me? "We found dope in his cell" and outta his desk he pulled a set works and two nickel bags. Right then I told him "Sign my pass so I can get outta here." I'm telling you this so there won't be no misunderstanding of what we did. I know a lot of you "brothers" is friends with J.D. but as far as I'm concerned he ain't a member of the family. Lately he ain't been to no meetings and he ain't showed no interest in the organization. Now maybe he still be a "brother" but he ain't part of the family 'specially if he be dealing dope. So the Board don't think we should put the organization on the block for him. We had to use our judgment and that's what we decided. But we're puttin' it to the membership now. If anybody thinks we shoulda acted different stand up and say so.

No questions or objections were raised. However, the rather defensive nature of the report suggests that objections were anticipated. In fact there probably were objections to the decision. At this time the members of the organization were chafing at the opposition of the leaders to drug usage and the seeming reluctance of leaders to commit the organization to direct confrontation tactics. One month after the incident there was an election in which the original leadership of the organization was replaced. As noted before, the new leadership sanctioned drug usage. At the same time confrontations with the staff began to increase. It was several months after the election that the only incident involving nearly the entire membership in a confrontation with the custodial staff occurred.

The President of the organization and another leader were observed assaulting a third black prisoner. On being approached by two officers, they ran. After an extensive search of the institution, they were discovered in the chapel. Ordered to return to their cells, they refused and were reported for disobeying an order. At this point they might have been physically returned to their cells. It was Saturday afternoon, however, and a movie had just ended. The wings were crowded with prisoners and the captain in charge feared a disturbance if he were to attempt action of this sort. Thus, he decided to allow them to remain out of their cells for dinner and then to keep them locked up in their cells after the early evening count. After dinner he received a call from the wing that black inmates refused to enter their cells for the count. Going into the wing he was confronted by approximately 30 black prisoners. Backing him into the corner they demanded that the two inmates be released after the count and that the report be discarded. Under intense pressure of this sort, the captain assented to both of these demands. The incident did not end here, however. In response to this disturbance the correctional officers staged a two-day work stoppage during which they demanded, and were promised, stricter custodial controls. One result of the work stoppage was that the two inmates were given a disciplinary hearing. Even then, in view of the seriousness of the original incident and its consequences, the punishments imposed were relatively minor. Each received five days in segregation.

Relation to Discipline

The use of such direct confrontation tactics by black prisoners affects the outcome of the disciplinary process in several ways. First, it is likely that such tactics are partially responsible for the higher proportion of major infractions by black prisoners. To be sure, the biases of the officers are involved as well. But the shared ideology of the black prisoners and the knowledge that they will be supported by their "partners" is likely to predispose them to refuse custodial orders even in instances where these orders are not arbitrary or capricious. Thus, the proportionately greater number of infractions by blacks for refusing an order (37.3 percent v. 24.6 percent) is likely the result of two conditions: (1) orders seen as arbitrary and capricious because they do not apply equally to whites, and (2) a stronger predisposition on the part of black prisoners to refuse even legitimate custodial directives because such refusals affirm their identity claims and because they can expect support in their refusal.

Also, such tactics appear to be successful in moderating the sanctions imposed upon blacks for infractions. While the officers are predisposed to a pattern of closer surveillance and control of blacks, they are at the same time intimidated by them:

It's a frightening effect. Here you are all alone surrounded by ten or fifteen blacks and it's your problem, you know. Good luck! What are they gonna do to me? Are they gonna drive me into the ground? Or is one gonna come at me with a razor blade and slash my throat? Or are they gonna beat the shit outta me? Believe me, all this is possible. . . . Well whenever possible, I don't book 'em. 'Course that's not always possible. I mean there are some things you can't let go. . . . If I tell one of 'em to do something and he calls me a m.f. I got to book him. If I don't, if I let him get away with that, then I'm dead, you know. They'll walk all over me. But if it's a minor thing, being outta place or something, and there's no shit involved, then I'll give him a lockup. Maybe I should book him, but I can do without that kind of aggravation.

The threat posed by the direct action of the blacks gives rise to a rather contradictory enforcement pattern on the part of the officers. On the one hand, they seek to exert greater control over the blacks. On the other hand, they are more circumspect in their disposition of black infractions. It is these contradictory tendencies that explain the more uniform dispositions of black infractions by reporting officers, which we have noted. To avoid confrontations, the reporting officers are careful not to overreact to minor infractions by submitting a disciplinary report. Minor infractions by blacks are disposed of by the imposition of the minimum possible sanctions by the reporting officer.

As noted, a similar almost uniform response is apparent in the disposition of black infractions by the Disciplinary Board. Nearly half of the infractions by blacks are met with an intermediate punishment—loss of privileges. In arriving at its decision, the Board must consider not only the offense but the effect of its action on both the officers and the inmates. Aware of the hazards faced by officers in reporting infractions by blacks, the Board is under pressure to impose some penalty in order to sustain custodial morale. At the same time, they are equally aware that the imposition of strong punishments upon blacks may provoke a disturbance. The result is a compromise whereby nearly half the blacks receive an intermediate penalty, and proportionately fewer blacks than whites receive either extreme or mild punishments.

Further support is lent this interpretation by the fact the disparity between the dispositions of black and white infractions is greatest among those prisoners with no reports in the previous six months. In this category none of the fourteen black prisoners as compared to one-third of the 32 whites received segregation, loss of good time, or confinement to cell. Such differences, while present among those with prior reports, were not nearly as large. It is likely that this results from the pressures to which the Board is subject. The fact that a black inmate had one or more recent infractions is likely to increase the pressure on the Board to impose a more severe penalty in the interest of custodial morale despite the threat of a disturbance. There is yet another and perhaps more important factor, however. As we have noted, the threat of a disturbance by the blacks increases directly with the status of the inmate. In this regard it is noteworthy that of the fourteen black prisoners who had no prior reports and received minor sanctions, nine were elected leaders of the organization. On the other hand, only two black leaders were punished by segregation, loss of good time, or confinement to their cells. The incidents leading to this disposition were noted above, and, as we saw, the penalties were comparatively mild in light of the seriousness of the infractions. Thus, it would appear that the imposition of intermediate penalties upon black inmates by the Disciplinary Board is, to a large extent, the result of a fear of disturbances by black prisoners if more severe penalties were to be imposed.

In brief, while the direct confrontation tactics of the black inmates may result in a higher proportion of reported major violations by black prisoners, they are also effective in moderating the sanctions imposed. Reporting officers are intimidated by the threat of physical force and utilize minimum sanctions whenever possible. In a similar fashion the Disciplinary Board attempts to balance the need to sustain custodial morale against the threat of a black disturbance. The result is a compromise whereby black offenders are handled in a more or less uniform manner through the imposition of an intermediate punishment.

White Resources

The Corruption of Authority

The ability to corrupt the authority of the custodians is largely a prerogative of the white prisoner. Not all whites have this capacity, however. Rather it is limited to certain members of the white elite upon whom the staff is dependent. The preeminent group in this respect is the small clique known as the "mafia." In Chapter 4, I noted several incidents in which members of this clique came to the aid of the staff in controlling potentially dangerous situations. It will be recalled that they intervened to quell a threatened disturbance at a "Jay Cee" banquet, and on another occasion, they aided the staff in controlling the influx of drugs into the institution. While direct intervention of this nature on their part is rare, occurring only when their interests in "easy time" are threatened, the crisis nature of these situations reflects the staff's dependence upon the "mafia" in their efforts to maintain order. On a less obvious and more routine level, the "mafia" aids the staff by exerting some degree of control over the most disruptive members of the white population, the "wise guys," by virtue of the close relations existing between the two cliques.

In return for their tacit cooperation, the "mafia" themselves are relatively immune from the impositions of custodial controls. For example, all of them work as wing porters. This is a highly valued job because it requires only about one-half hour's labor each day. For the remainder of the day the "mafia" are free to move about the institution as they desire. In their movement about the institution, moreover, they are free to engage in activities for which others would be punished. One clear instance of this immunity is the following incident in which an officer permitted a "mafia" member to pass an item to another prisoner confined to segregation after assaulting an officer with a knife:

I stood in the shop entry after work call. It was threatening to rain and not many were in the area, having gone to work. Al Verrechia was exercising in the bull pen behind the hospital (solitary confinement cells are in the hospital building and there is a fenced-in exercise yard behind the hospital). Tony A. came out of the state wing and went over to the fence to talk with Verrechia and after several minutes of conversation passed an item to Verrechia through the fence. An officer near me noted this and started to move in that direction but changed his mind after one step and came back to the doorway. Tony came towards us, greeted the officer, and went into the Industrial Building. About five minutes later another prisoner approached the fence to talk with Verrechia. The guard immediately ran over and moved him out, threatening to book him if he didn't get to work. Returning to the shop entry he exclaimed to me, "It's a bitch tryin' to keep those guys away from there. But all we need is for one of 'em to give that asshole a shiv." I noted to him that Tony had given something to him. He passed it off with the explanation that "Tony don't want trouble like that. He probably gave him some gum or something. That's the way he is."

Thus, the assistance of the "mafia" to the staff in maintaining order and control gives rise to a conception on the part of the staff that they are trustworthy. They need not be controlled, as they would do nothing to endanger security and control. Moreover, to attempt to control them may result in the loss of their cooperation.

The assistance rendered to the staff by the "mafia" and the high regard with which they are viewed by the custodians enables them to extend their influence beyond personal immunity. A pattern somewhat similar to that of the symbiotic relation between the guards and the "mafia" exists between the "mafia" and the "wise guys." It is in the interests of the "mafia" to control this group, to keep their potentially disruptive activities within bounds, but at the same time to be able to utilize the physical power of the "wise guys" if a situation should demand it. Thus, as we have noted, they maintain close relationships with the "wise guys." From this relation the "wise guys" derive status, material rewards, and perhaps the hope of more secure criminal employment after release. "Wise guys" also secure a degree of immunity from control. The "mafia" at times use their influence with the staff to fix a case for a "wise guy." Thus, for example, one evening an officer noticed Harry Frye, a "wise guy," coming out of a cell of another prisoner. Entering the cell he found the occupant on his bunk with a bleeding nose and a laceration under one of his eyes. The inmate informed the officer that Frye had assaulted him, a story he repeated to the captain investigating the report submitted by the officer. Later that evening, however, one of the "mafia," Rico, talked to the prisoner and convinced him to change his story, assuring him that he would not be assaulted again, but that he could not be responsible for what would happen if the prisoner did not change his story. The next day both met with the captain and the inmate changed his story, claiming that he had fallen against his bunk and that Frye had come to his aid. The captain informed them that he did not believe them and that the report had already been submitted, but that in view of the change in the inmate's charges and the guarantees of Rico, he would see what could be done. At the Board, Frye received a reprimand.[d]

"Wise guys," however, are not solely dependent upon the "mafia" for immunity from custodial controls and sanctions. Several occupy positions on work details whereby they are able to achieve a considerable measure of freedom. These are work details where the supervisors are extremely dependent upon inmate cooperation for the performance of their assigned tasks. The kitchen supervisor, for example, is completely dependent upon inmate labor in the preparation of three meals a day for over 300 people. Supervisors in the plate shop, print shop, and sign shop must meet production quotas set for them by other state agencies, quotas that may vary from week to week. There is thus considerable pressure upon these supervisors to delegate authority to inmates who have the ability to secure the necessary cooperation. To a large extent, these straw bosses are "wise guys."

[d]The details of this incident were related to me in interviews with both the captain and the prisoner who was assaulted.

They do not occupy positions—such as cook, clerk, or proofreader—that formally place them in control of other inmates. Rather, they are likely to occupy rather low status positions with few duties. Their actual function, however, is to secure cooperation from other workers. For this they are paid top wages. Further, they are able to secure considerable freedom of movement throughout the institution by means of passes issued by their supervisors, a freedom essential to their control of illicit activities, and, as in the following case, they are able to exert considerable influence on the selection of inmates for the detail:

I stopped off in the Print Shop for a few minutes to talk with Mike and Dan. While we were talking Officer DeLong came over. New orders are piling up and he needs more help. He asked Mike and Dan who he should ask for. They gave him several names and Mike said he'd have more in the morning.

By consulting the "wise guys" on the selection of new workers, the supervisor to some extent guarantees that problems of order and discipline on his detail will be minimized. For their part, the "wise guys" are able to convert this influence to their own advantage. For example, by offering their protection and a good job, they may secure themselves a "kid." Or they may gain access to drugs by recommending inmates who they suspect have connections, thus placing them under their scrutiny and control. Thus, the work positions occupied by several of the "wise guys" not only offer them disproportionate wages but provide them with a means of controlling and operating illicit activities with a minimal risk of custodial interference.

Two other categories of white inmates also occupy positions providing them with the capacity to corrupt authority. For the most part, the key formal positions within the institution—clerks, cooks, proofreaders, electricians, plumbers, and others—are the province of the "politicians" and "administration men." Work supervisors are dependent upon them for the performance of specialized tasks. To place one of these prisoners in segregation or to confine him to his cell would severely impede the operation of the detail to which he is assigned. Thus, on the rare occasions when one of them is reported, their supervisor commonly makes his dilemma known to the Disciplinary Board. The following dialogue occurred among the members of the board in reaching a decision concerning a cook who had been found guilty of fighting.

Deputy: Well, what do ya think we should give him?

Counselor: Five days in his cell, the same as the other guy.

Lieutenant: We'll have some problems with that. Henderson (kitchen supervisor) will go bullshit if he loses the guy for five days. He can't run the kitchen without him. I say let him off this time. He ain't a troublemaker anyway.

Counselor: How can we do that? We already gave the other guy five days.

Lieutenant: But he's an asshole anyway. The way I see it he probably started the whole thing anyway, and I can't see screwing up the kitchen just because we gave some fuck-off five days. I vote for a reprimand.

Deputy: I think you're right. I'll go for a reprimand too. How about you?

Counselor: I can't buy that. I say five days in his cell.

In most cases prisoners found guilty of the same offense by the same Board receive the same penalty. This accepted principle lay at the heart of the counselor's argument and dissenting vote. Overriding this principle in the minds of the custodians, however, was the fact that the application of the principle in this case would seriously impede the operation of the kitchen. When challenged, this rationale was supported by a second: that the other inmate probably started the fight. In fact, there was no evidence to support this argument. It was the importance of the prisoner to the operation of the kitchen that resulted in the imposition of the more minor sanction. Thus, the occupation of functional positions by "politicians" and "administration men" operates to grant them a measure of immunity from the imposition of the more extreme penalties.

Relation to Discipline

In sum, there exists at ECI a white prisoner elite who are largely immune to custodial controls and sanctions by virtue of the dependence of the custodians upon them. This fact contributes to the observed racial differences in outcomes of the disciplinary process in several ways. First, an unknown number of infractions committed by this white elite go unreported by the officers. Thus, the fact that a disproportionate number of the reported infractions (32.9 percent of all reported infractions and 37.3 percent of the major infractions) involved black inmates is to some extent the result of the underreporting of infractions by members of the white elite. Second, the relative immunity of the white elite is related to racial differences in the penalties imposed upon inmate leaders. We noted in the previous section that black leaders received less severe penalties because of the threat of a disturbance. Still, of the black inmates who appeared before the Disciplinary Board between July 1, 1971 and October 30, 1971, 11 of the 43 (25.6 percent) were black leaders. Of these 11 leaders, two received segregation, seven received loss of privileges, and three received reprimands. In contrast, of the 69 white inmates who appeared before the board during this same period, only three (4.3 percent) were members of the elite discussed in this section. Two of these cases, involving an assault and fight, we have noted above. The third incident involved a "politician" who was found guilty of insolence and profanity to an officer. In each of these three cases, the penalty imposed was a reprimand. Thus, if we compare only the reported infractions and penalties imposed upon inmate leaders, it appears that the capacities of the white leaders to corrupt authority are a more effective resource than the confrontation tactics of blacks in preventing the imposition of coercive controls.

Third, there are two consequences that follow from the above. The first is that the coercive power of the custodians is most effectively employed against rank and file white inmates. The white inmates reported for either major or minor violations are largely those without effective resources to combat the authority of the custodians. Unlike the white elite, they do not occupy either formal or informal positions upon which the custodians depend. Unlike the black prisoners, they are not supported by a network of alliances that may be activated to exert pressure upon the staff in their behalf. Thus, the staff, reporting officers, and Disciplinary Board alike need not be circumspect in dealing with them. In consequence, minor offenses committed by them are more likely to be referred to the Disciplinary Board, and the penalties imposed on them for major infractions are more severe than those on black inmates.

A second consequence of the above concerns is the perceptions of black inmates. At the outset of this chapter, we noted the existence of a consensus among black prisoners at ECI that they are discriminated against in the disciplinary process. In fact, however, the statistical data show no evidence of systematic unequal treatment of black prisoners as compared to white prisoners in this regard. To be sure, black prisoners are disproportionately reported for disciplinary infractions, but at the same time less severe penalties are imposed upon the blacks than upon the whites. It is not all whites with whom the black inmates compare themselves, however. Rather, it is the white inmate elite. In an interview, one black leader made the following pointed observation:

The biggest thing, though, is the double standard they got in the rules, one for the whites and one for the blacks. I shouldn't say all whites. It's only the upper class. The others get screwed as much as the blacks. The thing is though, that the black dudes only be seeing that upper class when they be comparing themselves with the whites. They don't see that the lower class has to follow the rules just like us.

Thus, the perception of discrimination on the part of the black inmates is shaped by the social structure of the institution. The positions occupied by the white elite, their relations with the staff, and the freedom and immunity granted them make them a highly visible reference group for the black inmates.[13] In comparison with this group, which is seldom reported for infractions and which receive reprimands if reported, the black prisoners, whether they be leaders or rank-and-file, are indeed deprived. It is their relative deprivation in comparison with this group that supports their intense and pervasive belief in racial discrimination.[e]

Summary

The purpose of this chapter has been to examine the significance of race for staff-inmate relations at ECI, what I have referred to as the vertical dimension of race relations. More concretely, the focus has been upon the relations between staff and inmates in the disciplinary process. Not only does this relationship lie at the heart of staff-inmate relations in the prison, but, as noted, discipline is an aspect of institutional life in which the black prisoners at ECI strongly believe they are subject to discrimination. The operation of the disciplinary process was sketched and statistical data concerning racial differences in the outcomes of the disciplinary process from July 1, 1971 through October 30, 1971 were presented. While these data do not indicate any clear pattern of unequal treatment of black inmates, several differences in disciplinary outcomes were noted. The remainder of the chapter interpreted these differences in terms of two interrelated conditions that influence disciplinary outcomes: (1) the racial biases of the custodians and the actions to which they give rise, and (2) the differential resources of blacks and whites to combat the power of the staff. In this summary, I shall bring the observations from the statistical data and these two sets of conditions into sharper focus.

First, it was noted that black prisoners are, in comparison to their number in the population, disproportionately reported for disciplinary infractions, especially for those of a serious nature. To some extent this is due to the conceptions of the custodians, who view the black inmates as dangerous and conspiring revolutionaries. These shared conceptions dispose the custodians to a pattern of closer surveillance and control of the black inmates than of the white inmates. Many orders issued by the custodians are likely to be seen as arbitrary and capricious by black prisoners, as they do not apply equally to white prisoners, and thus to provoke a hostile response from the black prisoners. Further, the conceptions and fears of the custodians with reference to the black prisoners are likely to color their perceptions of black infractions, so that minor infractions such as horseplay, for example, may be seen as fighting by the officer.

The conceptions of the officers and their consequent actions are not

[e]The rank-and-file white inmates make comparisons similar to those of the blacks, but cannot of course ascribe their deprivation to racial discrimination. In fact, as one white remarked, "we're the only ones that really get screwed. . . . the big guys, you know, the mafia and them, they got the connections and the hacks is scared to death of the niggers. So it's your average white guy that's getting screwed."

entirely without foundation. In fact, the conceptions of the officers bear a close correspondence to the identity claims of the black prisoners. If the officers view the black inmates as revolutionaries, the black prisoners likewise define themselves as such. The correspondence between the conceptions of the officers and the identity claims of the black prisoners is the result of the line of action fashioned by black prisoners with respect to the white staff. By confronting the authority of the officers, the black prisoners seek to neutralize custodial controls in a manner that validates their claim to being revolutionaries. The interest of the individual black prisoners in this regard, together with the knowledge that they will be supported by a number of other prisoners who are bound to them through partnership alliances, likely increases the incidence of such infractions as disobedience and insolence or threatening officers on the part of black prisoners.

Finally, the disproportionate number of reported infractions involving black prisoners must be viewed in relation to the resources of the white prisoners. There exists at ECI a white inmate elite upon whom the custodians depend because of the formal or informal positions they occupy. Members of this elite are virtually immune to the imposition of custodial controls. Thus, to an unknown extent, the disproportionate number of reported infractions involving black inmates is a consequence of the underreporting by officers of infractions by members of the white elite.

A second observation made from the statistical data was that, in making their dispositions, reporting officers are more careful to distinguish between major and minor infractions by black inmates than in the case of those by whites. This is especially true with respect to minor violations. Here the pressure resources of the blacks are effective. The ability of black inmates to mobilize a number of others in their support intimidates reporting officers. Thus, while disposed to greater surveillance and control of black inmates, officers are nonetheless circumspect in their disposition of infractions by black inmates. Whenever possible, they mete out light punishment. Correlatively, the white prisoners most subject to custodial controls present no direct threat to reporting officers, nor are the officers dependent upon them. As a consequence, a large proportion of apparently minor white infractions result in disciplinary reports and hearings before the Disciplinary Board.

Third, it was noted that the Disciplinary Board disposed of reported major infractions by blacks in a more uniform and less severe manner than those involving whites despite the apparently more serious nature of the black infractions. This pattern was particularly apparent among inmates who had no previous reports in the six months prior to the current report. On the one hand, the Disciplinary Board, like the reporting officers, is faced with the threat of direct physical force on the part of the black inmates. On the other hand, they must sustain the morale of the officers, who are often faced with intimidation in submitting reports on black inmates. As a result of these pressures, the Board is moved toward a compromise solution whereby nearly half of the reported major infractions by blacks result in the imposition of an intermediate penalty, loss of privileges. That this pattern is most evident among those with no recent reports results from the fact that a large proportion of black inmates in this category are black leaders, which thus increases the risk of a disturbance if more severe penalties were imposed. Moreover, the pressure from guards to impose harsh penalties upon black inmates is likely to be greater in cases where there have been additional recent violations.

Here again, however, the racial differences noted are influenced by the capacities of the white leaders as well as of blacks. Far fewer white leaders than blacks appear before the Board, and the penalties imposed upon them are less severe than those imposed upon the black leaders. Thus, the less severe penalties imposed upon the blacks as compared to all whites is affected by the fact that 95 percent of these whites are rank and file inmates with no resources at their disposal. It is not this rank and file, however, with whom the black prisoners compare themselves. Rather, it is the conspicuous white elite who are relatively immune to control that serve as the reference group for blacks in this regard, and it is this unequal treatment that supports the belief of blacks in pervasive discrimination.

7

Blacks and Cons: Routine Activities

We have already seen that the miseries of confinement at ECI do not remove the importance of racial distinctions. Nor apparently do they eradicate the prejudice commonly associated with these differences. The verbalizations of prisoners, both solicited and unsolicited, make it clear that the relations between black and white prisoners are permeated by attitudes of racial prejudice. White prisoners regard black prisoners with ambivalence. Lacking solidarity among themselves, most whites perceive black solidarity as a threat to their physical security, and they respond with fear and hatred. This same black solidarity, however, when viewed from another perspective—that of the inmate as opposed to that of the white male—elicits respect. It is obvious to white and black prisoners alike that the blacks more than the whites live by the inmate code. More so than the whites, black prisoners are ''men''; they ''don't rat''; they are loyal and do not exploit one another. Thus it is that, given the dual perspective of the white prisoner, black solidarity is the object of both fear and respect. In this alloy of fear and respect, however, fear is the stronger emotion and perhaps the majority of white prisoners would prefer total segregation by race. The following quote taken from an interview with a white inmate illustrates these ambivalent emotions and predispositions:

They think they're superior and they push us around all the time. Like in the dining hall. If I was late and tryin' to catch up with a buddy and cut in front of one of them, I'd probably get piped. But they cut in front of white men all the time and nothin' happens. . It's the same in the wings. The tier I'm on used to be all white. Now it's 50-50 and it ain't safe for a white to walk along it. If he does he better walk quick and keep his eyes open. . . . In here I got to hate 'em even more than I did. . . . You gotta respect 'em as men, though. They stand up for what they think is right and they won't back down. They can't be bullied. They ain't afraid to be counted. I hate 'em but I respect 'em, ya know? . . . The only way I can see to make it better is to have two joints, one for them and one for us.

The attitudes of the majority of black inmates with respect to their white peers are not marked by such ambivalence. In the eyes of the blacks most whites are weak, racist, and politically unaware. Moreover, the racial identification between the white prisoners and staff is seen by the blacks as a potentially antagonistic alliance against them. Black solidarity is as much a defense against this perceived threat as it is an attempt to cultivate the indefinable essence of ''blackness.'' Both factors—the perceived threat of an alliance between the white prisoners and staff, and the desire to be "black"—produce a common attitude among black prisoners that extols segregation from white prisoners and from white people generally.

You look at a farm and what do you see? Out in the field all the cows be together in one place, all the sheep be together in another, right? It's a natural thing for animals to stay with their own kind. It's a natural thing for people too. Any place you go out in the street if there be a mass of people, they be all white or all black. It's a natural thing. It should be the same here.

Attitudes such as the above, however, are not necessarily predictive of actual behavior. A considerable body of research conducted in both natural and experimental settings demonstrates that situational variables intervene and modify the direct relation between expressed attitudes and overt behavior.[1] Among these intervening conditions are factors such as the roles into which an individual is cast, group norms and the definitions of the situation provided by leaders, the reference groups with which an individual identifies and the visibility of his behavior to these groups, and the penalties and rewards which may follow upon different courses of action. In short, the brunt of evidence indicates that interracial behavior depends upon the surrounding socio-cultural system at least as much as it does upon individual attitudes.

As the early study by Kohn and Williams[2] indicates, such situational variables are operative in unstructured as well as in structured groups. It seems probable, however, that socio-cultural factors, as opposed to individual attitudes, are of greatest importance in formally organized groups. To the extent that a group is characterized by a hierarchical power structure and stable relationships, decisions need take less account of the desires and attitudes of lower level personnel. Moreover, the specificity of roles and the formality and social distance in relationships characteristic of bureaucratic organization are likely to mitigate interpersonal tensions. And finally, in bureaucratic organizations violations of stated policy are likely to be conspicuous and punished. It is precisely in terms of such characteristics that Moskos explains the ability of the Army to implement a rapid and relatively peaceful policy of racial integration during the early 1950s when in 1951 only 25 percent of the white soldiers favored racial integration and 44 percent opposed it.[3]

In considering race relations among the prisoners at ECI, we must consider not only the expressed attitudes of prisoners but also conditions associated with the organizational structure of the prison that impinge upon relations among prisoners. Three conditions associated with the physical structure and formal organization of ECI are of direct relevance to race relations among the prisoners: (1) the policies of the Warden with respect to racial integration, (2) the degree of control exercised by the staff over various inmate activities, and (3) the limitations of space and facilities.

It will be recalled from Chapter 2 that the Warden was appointed in the aftermath of a prolonged period of racial disturbances. One of the first tasks he faced, then, was the reduction of racial hostility. Largely as the result of his experience as a parole supervisor in a predominantly black area during the 1960s, he had become deeply committed to the goal of racial equality and to integration as the means of achieving this goal. In both public and private statements soon after his appointment he made clear his intolerance of racial segregation or separatism in the prison. Rather than maintain the segregation in the prison that prevailed at his arrival, he began a program of reintegrating black prisoners into the population while conducting biracial meetings with prisoners. In these meetings, ''I let them know I don't intend to run two cans. They're in this together and they're gonna have to learn to live and get along with each other.'' Thus, in the hope of reducing racial conflict and promoting understanding, the Warden sought to implement a policy of managed integration.

At the disposal of the Warden in implementing such a policy is the control exerted by the staff over inmate activities. To varying degrees nearly all prisoners are required to work, they are assigned to work details by the staff, and the work must be performed within designated areas at specified times. Similarly, where a prisoner lives—his cell—is assigned by the staff, and much of the recreation available to prisoners is organized by the staff. Thus, through the use of such controls an integrationist policy as espoused by the Warden can be imposed upon the prisoner population. At the same time, however, integration may be only as extensive as the controls imposed, and avoidance may be the rule in activities not subject to formal control.

A third factor also exerting pressure toward integration is the limitation of space and facilities. Maximum security at ECI encompasses only some 50 acres. Within these 50 acres, bounded by walls and bars, black and white prisoners must work, eat, sleep, play, and carry on all other activities necessary to their existence. Moreover, within this restricted space there is only one dining hall, one gym, barely enough cells to house all prisoners, one baseball field, one basketball court, and so forth. These facts alone necessitate interracial contact to some degree.

In sum, the formal social organization and physical structure of the prison imposes upon prisoner behavior constraints that stand in opposition to the prisoners' own apparent preferences for racial segregation. The concern of this chapter is with patterns of interracial behavior that emerge in response to these cross-pressures. I will describe various contexts in which interracial contact occurs, how this contact is influenced by features of the formal organization of the prison, and the resultant form of behavior in each context. In the chapter these contexts are ordered according to the degree of control exercised over various activities by the staff: (1) work and cell assignments, (2) organized recreation, (3) inmate organizations, and (4) "hustling" and "hanging out," informal activities over which the staff has virtually no control. In analyzing these forms of behavior I will rely upon a typology developed by Molotch[4]. Forms of interracial behavior will be analyzed according to three types: demographic integration, biracial interaction, and interracial cohesion. As defined by Molotch, demographic integration occurs whenever a "setting contains both blacks and whites in some specified proportions." Demographic integration refers then to the physical presence of blacks and whites within a setting. Biracial interaction refers to non-antagonistic forms of social interaction such as exchange and cooperation in which race remains an important defining characteristic. Interracial cohesion refers to intimate and spontaneous expressive interaction between blacks and whites in which race ceases to function as an important defining characteristic or source of cleavage.

It will be noted that this typology makes no reference to interracial conflict or competition. This is by no means to deny the prevalence or importance of such behavior. For analytic purposes, however, I will deal only with non-antagonistic forms of interraction in this chapter and reserve conflict and competition for treatment in later chapters.

Work and Cell Assignments

The two areas of prison life over which the staff exercises the greatest control are work and cell assignments. In these areas the policy of managed integration is most successful.

Work Assignments

The conception of imprisonment as confinement at hard labor has long passed at ECI. Nonetheless, the organization and supervision of prisoner labor remains an important concern of administration. Work is not only a means of occupying the time and energies of prisoners, it is also a means of reducing operating costs through the provision of services and commodities required by ECI or other state agencies. Under the threat of confinement to their cell or to segregation, all able-bodied sentenced prisoners are required to work. In return for their labor prisoners are paid a nominal wage ranging from $ .50 to $4.00 per day, with which they must purchase many necessities such as toilet articles and any permissable luxuries they may desire. In addition to wages, all employed prisoners receive two days off their sentence for each month of labor.

Each prisoner, upon completing his period of orientation, is assigned to a work detail by the Classification Board. Thereafter, he may be reassigned

Table 7-1
Assignment of Prisoners to Work Details by Race

Work Detail	Race		
	White	Black	Total
Wings	17	1	18
North Wing	6	1	7
South Wing	7	0	7
A/O and PCU[a]	4	0	4
Main Building	32	10	42
Rear Hall	2	0	2
Braille Room	4	0	4
Hospital	4	1	5
New Building	7	2	9
Barber Shop	3	3	6
Kitchen	10	3	13
Maintenance	2	1	3
Industrial Building	75	28	103
Machine Shop	2	4	6
Brush Shop	2	1	3
Upholstery Shop	2	2	4
Carpentry Shop	3	0	3
Garment Shop	1	2	3
Plate Shop	10	2	12
Print Shop	16	2	18
Sign Shop	5	0	5
Laundry	18	7	25
MDTA[b]	16	8	24
Yard Gang	5	0	5
Total	129	39	168

[a]Admission/Orientation Wing and Protective Custody Unit.
[b]Manpower Development Training Act Vocational Training Program.

at the annual review of his status by the Board at the request of his work supervisor, or occasionally at his own request. At all times, however, the concern of the administration with meeting institutional needs remains paramount. The cost reduction purpose of prisoner labor is immediately apparent in the distribution of the prisoner labor force as it was on March 19, 1971. These data are presented in Table 7-1. At ECI there is no large class of "idle men," as was found by Sykes at the New Jersey State Prison[5]: of the 186 sentenced men in maximum security on that date, 168 were employed. Fully 85.6 percent of those employed were engaged in activities of direct or indirect economic benefit to the institution. Seventy men were employed in jobs directly related to institutional maintenance: porters, hospital workers, barbers, cooks and kitchen workers, machinists, sewing machine operators, yard workers, electricians, and plumbers. Another 74 men were employed in jobs providing needed commodities to other state agencies: license plates and street signs, stationery and forms, brooms, brushes, furniture, and laundered sheets and linens.

In combination with the integrationist policies of the Warden, the assignment of prisoners to work details on the basis of institutional needs produces a substantial degree of demographic integration in work settings. As can be seen in Table 7-1, black prisoners are employed on 14 of the 22 work details and white prisoners are employed on all 22. Thus, every employed black prisoner works in a setting in which the opportunity exists for on-the-job interaction with whites, and 77.5 percent of the employed white inmates work in settings providing the opportunity for interaction with blacks. In all, 82.7 percent of the employed prisoners at ECI work on details providing the opportunity for interaction with prisoners of the other race.

Repeated observations, however, show that for the most part interracial interaction in work settings is sporadic and superficial. Usually it is limited to what is necessary to accomplish a specific task. Thus, for example, one of the whites in the upholstery shop continually requests the aid of a more experienced black in covering chairs. In the MDTA printing program, it is not uncommon to see black trainees receiving instruction in the photo reduction process from a more experienced white or to see a racially mixed group of trainees working together on math and English assignments.[a] More common, however, are incidents of the following type, where a black prisoner in the laundry worked in close proximity to several white prisoners without any exchange of verbal communication:

In the front east corner near the shirt and pants presses were "Detroit" and five whites, DiDonato and Mangiacomo among them. Two of the whites were working on the middle of the three presses with the three others sitting on a table behind them, talking and joking. "Detroit" was working the two presses on either side of the one used by the whites. He would put a pair of pants in one press, turn it on, move through the group of whites to the other press, wait until whatever was in there was done, take it out and put something else in, thread his way back through the group of whites and then repeat the process. I watched for nearly 30 minutes. At no time did a word pass between "Detroit" and any of the whites. He neither asked for nor received any assistance despite the fact that he was doing twice the work. While waiting, he sat on a table directly in front of one of the presses not more than two feet from the table on which the whites were perched, looking at them or staring out the window. They seemed oblivious of his presence except when they had to step aside to let him pass through, and this procedure was accomplished almost unconsciously, with no words and only an occasional hand gesture.

---

[a]Prior to entering the program trainees are given scholastic aptitude tests, and there is a pre-vocational program designed to overcome deficiencies.

A good portion of the prisoners' time on the job is spent in pastime activities. As suggested by the incident above, informal groups engaged in these activities are clearly segregated, and in many shops this segregation has clearly defined spatial boundaries. A black prisoner who works on the mangle in the laundry has equipped the northwest corner of that shop with a coffee pot, card table, a chess set, and dominos. Black workers in the laundry congregate in this corner during their breaks. White workers have appropriated the clothing room in the front of the shop and similarly equipped it. The print shop and the MDTA program occupy the second floor of the Industrial Building. Between these two shops is a small coffee break area. For the most part this area is used by the blacks from both shops. White prisoners prefer the private office of *The Beacon* located at the rear of the print shop. Thus, while the high degree of demographic integration characteristic of work settings provides opportunities for biracial interaction among the prisoners, this interaction is limited and instrumental in nature. Spontaneous and expressive interaction associated with informal peer group activity is clearly segregated, usually accompanied by the withdrawal of small groups into areas of the shops they have appropriated as their own space.

Cell Assignments

A similar pattern of voluntary avoidance within a context of demographic integration occurs with respect to cell assignments. Prisoners in maximum security are locked in their cells from 9 p.m. until 7 a.m. and for one-half hour at lunch and dinner. Prisoners in maximum security thus spend at least 50 percent of their time there under lock and key. This alone makes cell assignments a matter of concern to inmates, a concern intensified by the differences in cell amenities. Some cells are considerably larger than others. Some cells have faucets; others have only spigots. Some command a view of the street; others only of a blank wall. In some cells a prisoner is continually disturbed by traffic in the wings and resulting requests for coffee and cigarettes; in others he could be dead for several hours before it would be noticed.

As cells offer varying degrees of comfort and privacy, they are an object of competition among prisoners. To avert possible conflict arising out of this competition, the administration regulates cell assignments. When a cell becomes vacant, it is allowed to remain vacant for two days. During this time prisoners may bid for it by submitting request slips to the senior captain. On the third day the senior captain awards the vacant cell to one of those requesting it on the basis of two criteria: (1) length of sentence, and (2) time served on current sentence. The administration, then, seeks to avert conflict by awarding cells, particularly the more desirable cells, on the basis of universalistic criteria.

It is in the inmates' interest, however, that cells be awarded on the basis of more particularistic criteria. Not only is it important that a prisoner live in a desirable cell, but it is also important that he live next to prisoners with whom he is friendly or at least trusts. The loneliness of hours spent in the cell can be eased somewhat by living next to a friend with whom one can talk, share items, and play cards, checkers, or chess through the bars. A prisoner in a cell, moreover, is in a rather helpless position. The presence of friends or trusted others in nearby cells offers him some insurance against physical attack by other prisoners or staff.[b]

Prisoners therefore attempt to undermine the formal process of cell assignments in a variety of ways. One tactic is for a prisoner about to be realeased to arrange with the captain to exchange cells with a friend in a less desirable cell. In this way, many of the more desirable cells never become vacant. Vacant cells, moreover, are not advertised. Notice of vacancies or impending vacancies is spread by word of mouth. It is thus possible for a group of inmates to restrict such information to a select few, who then request the cell as soon as it becomes vacant. If all else fails, and it appears that a cell may be awarded to an undesirable, prisoners in nearby cells may purchase the services of a longtimer who will then remain in the cell only briefly until more secure arrangements can be made.

Such tactics on the part of prisoners are motivated by the desire to cell next to friends and trusted others. As the bounds of friendship and trust seldom cross racial lines, however, these tactics exert a pressure toward racial segregation in cell assignments.[6] As a counter to this pressure, the assignment of cells according to universalistic criteria promotes demographic integration. The result of these cross-pressures is a pattern of racial segregation within a larger context of integration.

Table 7-2 presents the distribution of cell assignments by race as it was on March 19, 1971, excluding the hospital and segregation units. Black prisoners, it can be seen, live on fifteen of the eighteen tiers, and white prisoners live on seventeen of the eighteen. Of the 37 black prisoners, 30 or 81.1 percent live on tiers with whites. Of the 126 white prisoners, 103 or 81.7 percent live on tiers also occupied by blacks. In all, 81.5 percent of the 163 prisoners reside on tiers placing them near at least one member of the other race.

It is to be noted that, in contrast with the other cell blocks, the tiers in the lower South State Block are rather highly segregated. All three of the all-white tiers are in this one cell block, as is the one all-black tier. The greater degree of segregation in this block is explained by the greater

[b]Shortly before this section was written, an inmate in a nearby state prison was killed in his cell when it was set afire. The inmate in the cell next to him has been charged with the murder.

Table 7-2
Assignment of Prisoners to Cells by Race

Cell Block and Tier	Race		
	White	Black	Total
Lower South State	34	10	44
G1-8	8	0	8
G9-16	5	2	7
H1-8	7	0	7
H9-16	8	0	8
I1-8	6	1	7
I9-16	0	7	7
Upper South State	51	12	63
J1-13	11	1	12
J14-26	10	3	13
K1-13	9	3	12
K14-26	11	2	13
L1-13	3	1	4
L14-26	7	2	9
North State	41	15	56
M1-13	6	4	10
M14-26	6	3	9
N1-13	6	4	10
N14-26	8	1	9
O1-13	9	1	10
O14-26	6	2	8
Total	126	37	163

discretionary powers in cell selection of its occupants. This block contains the most desirable cells and houses a large proportion of those serving long sentences as well as large percentage of the inmate leaders. Where the median sentence for all prisoners in maximum security is 7.3 years and the mean time served on the current sentence is 21.6 months, the comparable figures of those housed in Lower South State is 11.4 years and 29.6 months. Thus, as a result of the seniority of its occupants and the informal leadership positions of many of them, the pressures toward racial avoidance and segregation are greater in this block than in the others.

Racial segregation in all cell blocks is greater than the figures in Table 7-2 reveal, however. Each tier contains from eight to sixteen cells. The primary interest of prisoners is in who lives next to them rather than in who lives at the far end of the tier. Black and white prisoners are not distributed randomly along each tier. To the contrary, on nearly every tier there is a small island of two or three cells occupied by blacks. Of the 37 black prisoners, 29 or 78.4 percent live in cells next to another black prisoner. Thus, while black prisoners reside in every cell block and on 83 percent of the tiers, there is nonetheless an evident pattern of racial segregation and avoidance within this larger integrated context.

With respect to work and cell assignments, then, the cross-pressure created by an administrative policy of racial integration and a high degree of formal control on the one hand, and inmate preferences for racial avoidance on the other hand results in a pattern of micro-segregation within a larger context of demographic integration. While the vast majority of black and white prisoners work and live close to one another, there occurs little biracial interaction in these contexts beyond that necessary to satisfy instrumental concerns.

Organized Recreation

Recreational activities sponsored by the prison provide prisoners with another opportunity for interracial contact and interaction. Unlike work and cell assignments, however, these activities are subject to only a moderate degree of control by the staff. Participation by prisoners is voluntary, and thus recreational activities tend to be less integrated than work and cell assignments.

Sports

Each summer the institution sponsors both a softball and a basketball league, with four teams in each league. The purpose of the program is twofold: to provide entertainment for the population during their hours in the yard, and to provide an outlet for the energies of the players. To sustain interest over the entire summer, the amount of talent on each team must be balanced. Thus, while team captains are permitted some discretion in the selection of players and subsequent trades, the Recreation Director maintains a veto power in both of these processes. A second purpose of his regulatory power is to promote racial integration. One belief of the Warden is that interracial contact in sports may promote interracial understanding. Correspondingly, one fear of the administration is that "salt and pepper games," involving all-white and all-black teams, may generate racial antagonism and, with the majority of the population in the yard during games, result in a race riot.[7]

Despite this concern of the administration to maintain a racial balance in the sports program, a decided racial imbalance exists. We have noted previously that black prisoners more than white prisoners immerse themselves in the life of the prison. Nowhere is this difference more obvious than in their participation in sports. Twenty-four of the 43 (55.8 percent) prisoners requesting to play softball and 28 of the 38 (73.7 percent) desiring to play basketball were black.[c] Thus, at the beginning of the program in May all teams were integrated with between 50 percent and 75 percent of the players on each team black when only 22 percent of the prisoner population was black. This imbalance became even more pronounced as the season progressed, largely as a result of the number of white players who quit. The softball team was disbanded in July for this reason. And by the end of the season, 21 of the 26 (80.8 percent) remaining basketball players were black, and two of the four teams were all black.

Opportunities for biracial interaction in organized sports, then, are more limited than for work and cell assignments. Moreover, the biracial interaction that does occur tends to be confined to the: necessary to the game and to be bounded by the playing area itself. Due to the greater degree of racial balance and the periodic movement of entire teams on and off the playing field, the limited nature of biracial interaction is more evident in softball than in basketball. The following incident is typical:

As the teams changed positions it was obvious that the playing field delineated the arena of black-white interaction. The teams did not sit together as groups but mixed with the spectators as they came off the field. Black and white players engaged in mutual chatter and encouragement on the field and in conversation coming off, but would split at the foul line. For example, "June Bug" (a black) was pitching to a white catcher, Randy P. Frequently they would meet halfway between the mound and home plate to discuss strategy and after every inning they walked off the field together. At the foul line they might pause for a moment but would soon split and sit with their own groups.

Movement on and off the playing field is a movement from one type of activity to another, and the changing pattern of biracial interaction occurs in the context of a collective effort oriented to a shared goal, winning a game. In contrast the behavior of spectators on the sidelines is a form of informal peer group activity. Spectators are drawn to the playing field less from their interest in the outcome of the competition than from the opportunity it provides for the sharing of individual performances, both on and off the field, that lie at the heart of informal peer group activity. As players leave the field, then, they leave a public arena and enter a net of private peer relations. Correspondingly, the character of interracial behavior changes from cooperation to avoidance.

The net of peer relations extends onto the playing field and frequently transforms the nature of the action which occurs there as well. The interest of the spectators is primarily in the performances of individual players and is structured more along the axis of race than of team. This is perhaps more

---

[c]There is no restriction on prisoner participation in both leagues. Several inmates play on both a softball and a basketball team. Thus there is no contradiction in the fact that there were more black participants than the total number of black prisoners.

true of the black prisoners, as the fashioning of a unique style of play is indicative of "soul". Basketball more than softball is conducive to individual performances of this sort, and basketball games frequently become personal duels between players rather than contests between teams:

During the first half the focus of attention was the duel between "Tickie" and "June Bug." Every time "Tickie" got the ball he drove on "June Bug" usually behind his back. Scoring, he would start up the court, yelling to "June Bug." "Caused you to quit. Caused you to quit. Play so good," or when he missed a shot he might yell, "Just funning. Just funning. We ahead so much we don't need it." All the time there were constant shouts from the spectators—virtually all black— "Looking cool, Tickie, I see ya." . . . Late in the second half, "Cadillac" came strolling by, checked the score and decided to play. Immediately "June Bug's" team called time out and replaced "June Bug" with "Cadillac" who came onto the court with his hands clenched above his head admist loud cheers from the sidelines. For the last four or five minutes of the game the tenor of play changed. All the cheering was for "Cadillac" as he put on a display of driving and shooting around "Tickie" while "Tickie" gave up shooting in favor of passing off.[8]

As the majority of players and spectators are black, the frequency with which games become arenas for the display of individual style serves to isolate the white participants. In the game above, for example, the other three black members of "Tickie's" team willingly supported his performance. The one white, on the other hand, seldom touched the ball, did not join the team during time-outs or half-time, and by the end of the game was not even moving into the forecourt on offense. Thus, despite the fact that he is 6'5" tall and one of the better players in the prison, he scored only two of his team's 94 points. After the game, on his way into the wings, he angrily denounced his team to a group of friends and stated "I ain't gonna play with them niggers no more." He did not quit the team, but he played only irregularly for the rest of the season. This incident suggests that one factor possibly contributing to the increased racial imbalance of the sports program during the season was the alienation of white players through the frequent absence of biracial cooperation in team play.

The Gym

Where there is a rather well-developed program of organized recreation during the summer months, during the winter months there is not. From October through May, the only recreational facilities available to the prisoners are the gym and the movies on Friday evenings. The gym is a small box-like room in the basement of the New Building. The fact that the ceiling is only eight feet from the floor prevents its use for team sports; the only facilities available are two pool tables, a ping-pong table, several card tables, an undersized handball court, and a set of weights.

As a result of the greater degree of spatial confinement of these activities and the virtual absence of formal controls over inmate participation, the pattern of racial avoidance and segregation noted above is cast into sharper relief in the winter than it is in the summer. Figure 7-1 is a sketch of the racial distribution of activity in the gym on a typical evening. Although the population of the gym changes continually during the course of an evening, the basic pattern of voluntary racial segregation in activities remains constant. Black inmates concentrate in the lower left corner of the gym around a pool table used almost exclusively by them. White prisoners congregate in the upper right corner and around the handball court, an activity engaged in only by a few whites. The result is the creation of a diagonal line dividing the gym into black and white sections.

The only appreciable biracial interaction in the gym occurs around the ping-pong and pool tables, which are located along this boundary line. There is only one ping-pong table in the gym, and as all games are played on a round-robin basis with a prisoner playing until he loses, the games alternate in racial composition—two whites, two blacks, and a white and black in nearly equal proportions. A slightly different situation, but with the same result, occurs with respect to pool. There are two pool tables. One is occupied almost exclusively by blacks and is old and in poor condition; the other is new. Because of the large number of prisoners desiring to play on the new table, the officer in the gym maintains a list of those wishing to play and prisoners play in the listed order. Again, this control results in about one-third of the games played on the new table being interracial.

Like basketball, pool provides players with an opportunity to develop and to display unique individual styles. Games of pool also frequently take on the character of expressive performances. The nature of these games as performances may be gleaned from the following account of a game between two blacks, in which the status of one is enhanced as much by his shrewdness as by his victory:

The game between "Milwaukee" and "Rump" was played with style. "Rump," cigarette from the corner of his mouth, the ever-present shades and Afro, eased his way around the table hustler style, crouched over and each stem involving a sharp heel to toe movement. "Milwaukee" countered this show by manipulating the cue with a flourish, often spinning it like a Queen Anne's salute. Each shot was followed by chatter. "Ain't no way you can beat me, Milwaukee." "All you do out there is drink beer and be cool." . . . The game was close, "Milwaukee" keeping a slight lead. As he tried to sink the eight ball, "Rump" leaned against the table. "Milwaukee" missed and remonstrated "I oughta take that shot over but I'll give you a chance, you so bad you gotta cheat." "Rump" sank the next shot but as he tried for the eight ball, Milwaukee gave a slight tap on the end of the stick as he brought it back. After eight or ten incidents like this, each drawing an angry response from "Rump." Milwaukee let him shoot and he missed. "Got you, got you, you gonna lose now. See how I got you psyched. "Milwaukee" grabbed the stick and sank an easy shot.

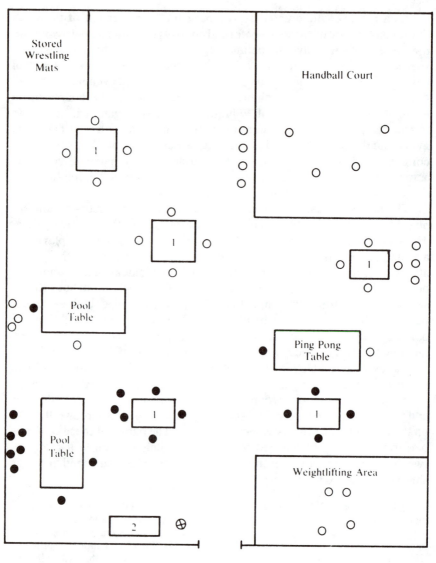

Key

○ White prisoners
● Black prisoners
⊗ Guards
1 Card Tables
2 Guard Desk

Figure 7-1. Racial Segregation of Prisoners in the Gym

Games involving white participants, though more subdued, are often of a similar character. In contrast, as the following description makes clear, interracial games are usually perfunctory matters involving little of the expressive behavioral styles and verbal exchanges that characterize all-black or all-white games.

When I arrived in the gym a pool game was on between "Tickie" (a black with a reputation for style) and Kennedy. The game lasted only a short time and there was virtually no communication between the participants except to indicate, by pointing with the stick, which pocket one was shooting for. On two occasions Kennedy mumbled a comment about a shot he was about to make but there was no indication from "Tickie" that he had even heard the remark. Awaiting their turns, both would move back against the wall paying more attention to what was going on in other parts of the gym than to the game they were playing. About three-quarters of the way through the game two blacks came over to watch. "Tickie" missed a shot, handed the stick to the white, and joined the two, bumming a cigarette from one. His back was to the game and Kennedy had to call him when it was his turn. Nonchalantly, and to the cheers of the two observers, he ran off a string of four sinking the eight ball on the last shot. Rather than taking on the next player, however, he moved off with the two observers to the other table.

The only exception to the rather muted nature of interracial pool games are the occasional encounters between black and white players of exceptional skill. Such players are regarded by others as champions of their race, and games between them draw large groups of spectators not only because they are highly skilled performances but also, and perhaps more importantly, because they are a form of symbolic aggression. Unlike most games, contests of this type are played on a best-of-three basis. The action at the table is accomplished with the style and flourish of all-black games, and is accompanied by shouts of advice and encouragement to each participant from his supporters and by frequent interracial betting and occasional encounters.

Matches such as these occur only once a week at best, however. For the most part, activities in the gym give rise to biracial interaction of only a cursory and highly constrained nature.

The Movies

Even more limited than the biracial interaction in the gym is that which occurs at the movies. At the movies, prisoners are permitted to sit wherever they desire, the result being near complete racial segregation as shown in Figure 7-2. The first four rows on the left side of the auditorium are used exclusively by blacks. The remaining seats always are occupied by whites,

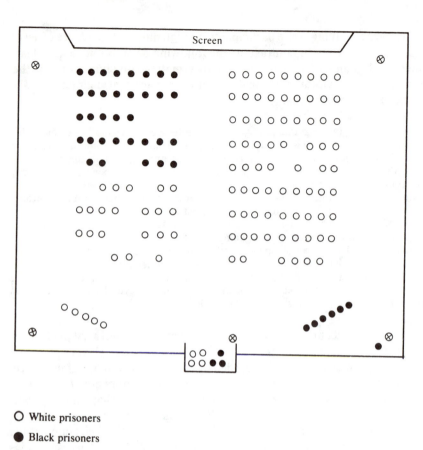

O White prisoners

● Black prisoners

⊗ Guards

Figure 7-2. Racial Segregation of Prisoners at the Movies

the only exception being some six or seven seats near the rear exit, which are usually occupied by "toms."[d]

This high degree of segregation in seating as well as the passive nature of movie entertainment itself precludes any sustained biracial interaction in this context. Natural needs and the desire to smoke, however, make some interracial contact inevitable in the single restroom at the rear of the hall.

[d] A similar pattern of segregation occurs in the dining hall. At every meal the blacks occupy some fifteen tables in the southeast corner of the room. The vast majority of whites sit on the north side with a few in the southwest corner.

Nonetheless, contact in the room is minimized by a pattern of temporal segregation in occupancy. Movements to and from the room typically occur in racially segregated groups of from four to eight prisoners who are seated together. As the room is small—a maximum of seven can stand in it and still watch the movie—the entrance of one group precipitates the exit of the previous occupants. The contact between black and white prisoners in this area then tends to be limited to physical contact involved in passing each other going to and from their seats.

Inmate Organizations

As was noted in Chapter 2, in an attempt to articulate community resources with inmate needs and interests, the administration at ECI has permitted the development of a variety of semi-autonomous inmate voluntary organizations. The three largest and most durable of these are the "Jay Cees." the Afro-American Society, and *The Beacon*. In keeping with the policy of granting considerable autonomy to these organizations, there is no administrative control over their membership policies or elections, beyond the stipulation that no prisoner be excluded from membership or office on the basis of race, religion, or national origin. One result of this policy is nearly complete racial segregation in these organizations. There are no blacks on the staff of the *Beacon;* and of the 67 members of the "Jay Cees" in May 1971, only six were black. Of the 38 members of the Afro-American Society at that time, only one was white.

Both the six blacks who belong to the "Jay Cees" and the one white member of the Afro-American Society are marginal men.[9] The black members of the "Jay Cees" are either inactive members of the Afro-American Society or "toms." Moreover, with one exception to be noted below, neither are they active in the "Jay Cees." In neither organization are they members of the elected leadership or committee members, nor do they attend meetings regularly. The main interest of the blacks is to maximize their opportunities to attend the parties and banquets sponsored by each organization. At the banquets, these individuals sit at out-of-the-way tables. Four of the six have either white girl friends or wives, a fact which suggests that their marginality within the prison is a product of their pre-prison experience and that the issue is race rather than identification or lack of identification with a criminal subculture.

The one exception to the non-involvement of these marginal blacks is a prisoner named Stephen Joseph. In several ways, Joseph is an atypical prisoner at ECI. First, at age 34 he is older than the majority of prisoners; second, he is a first offender on a life sentence for murder; third, he has two years of college education and was employed for several years in a junior administrative position. Perhaps as a result of these differences from other inmates, his mode of adaptation to prison is one of withdrawal and non-involvement. Nonetheless, he possesses skills that are in short supply among prisoners, and that are of considerable value to both the "Jay Cees" and the Afro-American Society. Thus, while at first he is seldom appointed to committees in either organization, he is frequently called upon to chair committees whose work is floundering. So, for example, when the Mental Health Committee of the "Jay Cees" had failed to make the necessary arrangements for an arts and crafts program for mentally retarded children, Joseph was appointed chairman of the committee two weeks prior to the date on which the program was to begin. Taking the work of the entire committee upon himself, he successfully organized the program. On another occasion he succeeded the chairman of the "Jay Cee" Youth Guidance Committee under similar circumstances and organized a program to provide counseling to residents of a nearby state training school for youth. Likewise, he was called upon at the last minute to assist in the preparation for the annual banquets of both the "Jay Cees" and the Afro-American Society.

Despite the services Joseph provided to these organizations during the year, he received no recognition. So little known was he by the officers of the "Jay Cees," for example, that without exception they reversed his name, calling him "Joseph Stephens." At the annual banquet of the "Jay Cees," awards are given to all committee chairmen whose committees have successfully completed their projects during the year. At the banquet, Joseph's name was never mentioned, and the awards for the Mental Health and Youth Guidance Committees were presented to the chairmen he replaced. Joseph's relationship with the "Jay Cees," then, is one of exploitation. While his skills and talents are used by the leaders of the organization, he is denied recognition for the services he performs.

A similar relationship obtains between the one white member of the Afro-American Society and the leadership of that organization. Like Joseph, this inmate, Tom Matthews, is an atypical prisoner. At age 23 he is younger than the average prisoner. He also is a first offender serving a life sentence for murder. Similarly, he has one year of college education and leads a solitary existence within the prison. Matthews, however, has a fanatical commitment to the goals and purposes of the Afro-American Society. He was a member of the original group that was disbanded in 1969. In the ensuing disturbances he was beaten severely on several occasions by white prisoners and was nearly killed when his cell was set afire. Nonetheless, when the current organization was established in 1970, he consented to assist the members in drafting the by-laws and was subsequently appointed Executive Advisor to the President. In this capacity he acted as a policy advisor to the President and as his aide in supervising and coordinating the work of the more important committees. Still the position of Matthews within the Afro-American Society remains essentially similar to that of Joseph in the "Jay Cees." Despite his dedication to the purposes of the organization and the prominence of his position within it, the members shun any personal involvement with him outside the organization. He is not considered a "brother," nor does he identify himself as such. Moreover, the very importance of his role within the organization is a source of embarrassment to most members. This was made clear after the annual Legislative Forum at which Matthews was introduced by the Warden as the Executive Advisor to the President of the Afro-American Society. Many members believed that this incident made it appear to outsiders that the organization had a white overseer, and at the next meeting Matthews was forced to resign.

Administrative policies to the contrary, then, race acts as a barrier to participation in the inmate organizations. For the most part these organizations are segregated by race, and the few prisoners who are members of an organization dominated by prisoners of the other race are a marginal group, being non-active members in either the "Jay Cees" or the Afro-American Society. The two exceptions are both atypical prisoners whose skills are used by the leaders of the organizations, but who are denied full acceptance and formal recognition for their services.

Hustling and Hanging Out

In the first section of this chapter we considered the degree of intergration and biracial interaction in work and cell assignments. Closely tied to these formal activities and partially structured by them are two informal activities of central importance in the underlife of the institution: "hustling" and "hanging out." These are activities over which the staff exerts virtually no control and in which prisoner preferences for avoidance result in near complete segregation by race.

Hustling

The formally organized work assignments are not the central economic activity of prisoners, which is rather "hustling" or "wheeling and dealing." Jobs are valued less for the formal rewards they offer than for the access they provide to goods that may be exchanged for other items or services. As virtually every job affords access to some exchangeable item or service, the work details are the center of a vast network of informal economic activity. Prisoners in the laundry do private laundry. Those in the garment shop tailor clothing. Kitchen workers supply meat sandwiches, pies, and cakes. The print shop is the source of personalized stationery. Belt buckles, bracelets, and knives are manufactured in both the machine shop and the plate shop. Tapestries, upholstered foot stools, shadow boxes, and picture frames may be acquired from the upholstery and carpenter shops. Painting may be done in the sign shop; hairstyling in the barber shop.

The way this array of goods and services is distributed among the prisoners is varied and complex, depending as much upon the non-economic relationships existing between the parties as upon the commodity being exchanged. In general, however, there are three forms of economic exchange: sharing, trading, and selling. By sharing is meant the voluntary giving of a service or of some material good without any expectation of immediate reciprocity or usually any agreed upon form of reciprocity, although future reciprocation is expected. One prisoner, for example, may provide another with a television or radio with only the expectation that he will receive some good or service of equivalent value in the future. Sharing, then, may be viewed as a form of gift-giving divested of its mythical and ceremonial trappings.[10] This form of exchange is most common among black "partners," and as noted previously it creates bonds of obligation and alliance that reinforce black solidarity. Trading, by comparison, is the provision of goods and services with the expectation of immediate reciprocation in the form of an equivalent item or service. A kitchen worker, for example, supplies sandwiches to a number of prisoners with whom he is on friendly terms. In return his laundry is done each week, he receives a supply of stationery from the print shop, and he is able to decorate his cell with items from the carpenter shop. Trading is the most common form of exchange among prisoners, occurring among blacks who are not "partners" and being the usual form of exchange among members of white cliques. Cliques, however, are seldom large enough to supply an individual with all of his wants. Moreover, there are commodities that—because of their limited supply or danger to the provider, e.g., blank checks or knives—exceed the bounds of reciprocity even among clique members. While selling is prohibited by the bonds of brotherhood among blacks, among whites transactions involving the prisoner with others not in his clique or that are for scarce or dangerous items require payment, usually in advance, in the form of cash or cigarettes, which are legal tender in the prison. As most prisoners must enter sales transactions at least occasionally, nearly all try to strike a balance between trading commodities to members of their clique and selling the same commodities to non-clique members. As a result, selling is as common as trading.

Biracial economic exchanges of any type are infrequent. The diffuse nature of sharing necessitates a closeness and trust among the parties that is absent in the relations between black and white prisoners and creates bonds of obligation that are not desired by either group. Biracial trading is not necessary for the satisfaction of normal and recurring needs. The demographic integration of work assignments insures that both blacks and whites have access to the most commonly exchanged commodities. Thus, the integration of work details imposed by the formal organization contributes to the existence of a racially segregated informal economic system. It is only when the desire for a particular commodity cannot be satisfied by a transaction within one's own racial group that biracial economic exchanges occur, and these are on a cash basis.[e] Beyond infrequent transactions of this sort, however, normal "hustling" or "wheeling and dealing" for routine items occurs within the confines of boundaries established by race.

Hanging Out

A large portion of the prisoners' time, especially in the winter, is spent engaged in informal peer group activity of an expressive nature, "hanging out." From the perspective of an outsider and from that of the staff as well—"hanging out" may appear to be mere idle behavior. Yet it has considerable importance for the maintenance of a prisoner subculture and hence for the self-esteem of prisoners. Through lengthy individual narratives concerning their experiences with women, alcohol, drugs, crime and the criminal justice system prisoners are able to develop a more or less shared and coherent view of the world and their place within it.[11] Moreover, the form of the interaction permits each participant to present himself as a model of the very standards that are being sustained and thus to secure from others favorable responses essential to the maintenance of his self-esteem. The following excerpt, while not capturing the full dialogue, nonetheless communicates the nature and form of the interaction involved in "hanging out":

Sullivan and I were tripping the wing when he suggested that we join Tom Smalley, Jim Ryun and another character I don't know but who looks like Satan dragged through a sewer. "Satan" and Smalley got off on their joint escapades, each jumping up from the floor to give his part, the other sitting down. They were telling about the night Smalley was 'plexed up' (high on pills) and assaulted a cop. "Satan," at one point, jumped up. 'I pulled him outta the bar and we went to a diner to get some coffee. There was these two (looks around, cups his mouth and lowers his voice) big niggers in there with some white tail. He just goes for 'em — two of 'em, big bastards. He was outta his mind. I says 'oh no, not again; but what could I do? So I got in it too and we chased them two niggers outta there. Then we took the

---

[e]As noted before, this is the case with drugs. Because of the importance of drugs and the lack of direct association of buying and selling drugs with job assignments, we will treat race relations surrounding drugs in the next chapter.

broads and went over to my joint and fed 'em pills. I swear them chicks was somethin' else. They couldn't get enough. We musta fucked for three days.''

The conversation turned to a description of ''Satan's'' joint. He and Smalley described it and its activities in great detail. According to ''Satan'' he ran it for fun not profit. He had his phone in a coffin, the signs on the rest rooms were reversed as were the handles on all the doors. Every night about twelve he'd put Spanish flies in all the drinks and close at one. Everyone would take off their clothes and have an orgy. He handled the cops by letting them in.

Performances such as this constitute the core activity of ''hanging out.'' They are representations of fanciful accounts in support of an idealized image of oneself. To be successful, they require an audience that is receptive and supportive of one's claim. The non-mutuality of experience associated with race and the atmosphere of mistrust and suspicion which permeates black-white relations preclude any significant degree of biracial ''hanging out.''

Further, the physical structure of the cell blocks and the moderate degree of racial segregation in cell assignments contribute to the rigid racial segregation in ''hanging out.'' From October to May prisoners ''hang out'' in the wings, and as prisoners are not permitted to loiter on the upper tiers, ''hanging out'' is confined to the ground floor tiers. The one all-black tier noted in Table 7-2 is a ground floor tier located, as one views Figure 7-3, on the left side of Lower South State block. As depicted in Figure 7-3, due to architectural arrangements this area is somewhat isolated from the rest of the wing. Termed ''Soul City,'' it is used exclusively by black prisoners for purposes of ''hanging out.'' White prisoners ''hang out'' in more dispersed groupings throughout the remainder of South State wing and all of North State wing.

''Hanging out'' is not confined to the wings, of course. During the summer months, this activity moves into the yard. In the yard it is also characterized by racial avoidance and segregation, but, unlike the wings, there are no clearly defined black or white areas. An area which is occupied by blacks on one evening may be occupied by whites on another. Despite this difference, however, the basic pattern of segregation in this activity remains unchanged.

''Hustling'' and ''hanging out'' are informal activities standing at the center of institutional underlife. They are relatively free from the routine control of the staff. Thus, the integrationist policies of the Warden have little effect upon interaction in these activities, and the preferences for racial avoidance on the part of prisoners result in a pattern of near complete racial segregation.

Summary

Imprisonment at ECI does not abolish the importance of racial distinctions,

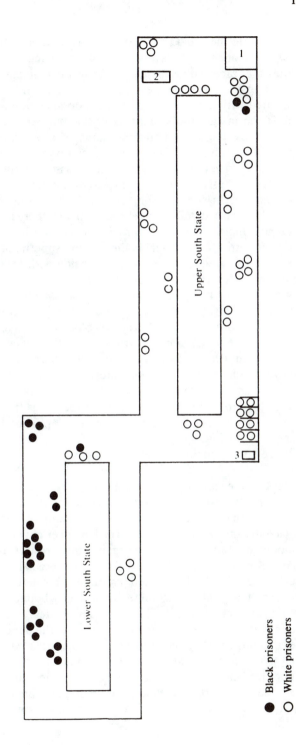

Figure 7-3. Racial Segregation in Informal Groupings in South State Wing

nor apparently does it eradicate the prejudice commonly associated with them. Both black and white prisoners express mistrust, suspicion, fear, and hatred of prisoners of the other race and predispositions toward avoidance of interracial contact. In opposition to these predispositions, however, are several conditions associated with the physical and social organization of the prison. These include the integrationist policies of the Warden, the control of inmate activities by the staff, and limitations of space and facilities. In this chapter I have analyzed forms of association between black and white prisoners that arise in response to these cross-pressures.

The pattern that emerges is basically one of demographic integration and limited biracial interaction. In settings subject to a high degree of administrative control, such as work details and cell assignments, there is a substantial degree of demographic integration. Biracial interaction in activities taking place in these settings, however, is limited and superficial. Thus, black and white prisoners frequently work side by side with little communication beyond that required to accomplish a specific task. Moreover, the high degree of demographic integration in work assignments makes possible the existence of a segregated informal economic system. Similarly, while black prisoners are to be found in all cell blocks and on all three of the 18 tiers, they are not randomly distributed on these tiers. Rather, nearly every tier has an island of two or three cells occupied by black prisoners who turn to each other for sociable interaction during the long hours spent under lock and key. The existence of one all-black tier gives the black prisoners claim to a rather isolated area of the wings they have termed "Soul City." This area is used exclusively by black prisoners for purposes of "hanging out"' an intimate and expressive form of interaction of central importance to the maintenance of group solidarity and individual self-esteem.

Activities and settings that are less subject to administrative control are also less integrated. Participation in organized recreation, for example, is voluntary. As a result, despite an attempt to balance the racial composition of teams, a decided racial imbalance exists due to the small number of white participants. The autonomy granted to the inmate organizations results in virtually complete segregation in this activity as well. Again, biracial interaction in these voluntary activities is limited and instrumental in nature. Biracial interaction on the softball and basketball teams is clearly bounded by the confines of the playing field or court. Even this limited degree of interracial cooperation in team sports is frequently disrupted as the net of informal peer group ties extends onto the playing area and transforms team contests into individual performances and duels between players of the same race. The handful of prisoners who are members of an organization dominated by the other race are, for the most part, marginal men who are inactive participants. The two exceptions are clearly atypical prisoners who possess skills used by the leaders of the organizations, but who are denied recognition for their services and full accreditation as members.

The close proximity of prisoners and the necessity to share facilities does not alter appreciably the basic patterns noted above. Rather, the limitations of space and facilities throw into sharp relief the patterns of avoidance and segregation prevailing in routine activities. In the wings, we have noted, there is an area termed "Soul City." Racial territories such as this are to be found in the shop, in the dining hall, in the gym, and at the movies. Where spatial segregation is not possible, as in the smoking area at the rear of the auditorium on movie nights, a pattern of temporal segregation may be substituted. And where the limited facilities impose biracial interaction, such as in playing pool or ping-pong, the activity is typically carried out in a perfunctory manner.

In brief, while the conditions associated with the physical structure and formal social organization of the prison produce a substantial degree of demographic integration in some settings, this integration results in no more than limited and superficial biracial interaction. In most routine activities in the prison, there is clearly a discernable color bar.

8

Blacks and Cons: Focal Concerns

Given the existing relations between staff members and prisoners, the pressures toward racial integration and cooperation among prisoners that are exerted through the formal organization of the prison are not strong, positive supports for such behavior. Hence, as we have seen, while prisoners accept demographic integration in settings subject to administrative control, there is only limited biracial interaction in these settings. However, other pressures contravene prisoner predispositions toward racial avoidance. Unlike the pressures exerted through the formal organization, these pressures have their origin within the informal social organization of the prison, deriving from objects and activities that are of a salient interest to large segments of the prisoner population: drugs, sex, keeping the peace and meeting the public. These objects and activities constitute focal concerns of the inmate subculture. To some extent they function as superordinate goals, "goals which are compelling and highly appealing to members of two or more groups in conflict but which cannot be attained by the resources and energies of the groups separately."[1] drawing black and white prisoners into relations of exchange and cooperation. Contact does not always lead to harmonious relations, however. The scarcity of drugs, the symbolic meaning of sex, and differing interests with respect to the staff and the public introduce elements of interracial competition and conflict into the relationships that develop around these objects and activities. Whatever the form of interaction involved, however, each of these concerns draws differing segments of the black and white prisoners into contact, and thus they provide links across the color bar described in the preceding chapter.

Drugs

"Dope fiends are color blind." "When it comes to drugs, color don't make no difference." Statements such as these summarize the unanimous view of the prisoners at ECI. In their eyes, race is not a bar to exchange and cooperation in the network of relationships that surround traffic in drugs. While this view is not entirely accurate, the high demand for drugs amid a limited supply secured at considerable risk does in fact minimize the significance of race. In no other activity is biracial interaction so extensive.

Five distinct activities underlie the web of relations arising from drug usage: "connecting," "stashing," "dealing," "scoring," and "fixing." For drugs to enter the prison economy, a connection with an outside source must be established and the drugs must be carried into the prison. Once inside the walls, the drugs must be "stashed" in a secure place or with a secure prisoner not immediately associated with the owner but to whom he has ready access. If profit is to be realized the drugs must be advertised and numerous transactions executed. These transactions comprise "dealing." "Connecting," "stashing," and "dealing," then refer to the procurement and distribution of drugs; "scoring" and "fixing" are consumer activities. "Scoring" refers to the purchase of a supply from a dealer, and less directly to a number of ancillary activities such as raising the necessary money and securing a set of "works," paraphernalia with which to use the drugs. "Fixing" denotes the actual consumption of drugs.

Connecting and Stashing

Connecting. It is a common belief that a major conduit for drugs into a prison is the custodial force. While this may be true at other institutions, there was no evidence to suggest it at ECI. In fact, prisoners claimed that due to lax security it was so easy to secure drugs through visitors that it was not worth the risk or the price to bribe a guard. Most typically, the connections developed by prisoners at ECI are regular visitors with whom they were associated prior to their confinement. As few inmates have interracial friendships outside the prison, this fact alone makes for segregation in "connecting." There is an additional reason, however. The best connection is one that is inconspicuous. For this reason female connections are preferred. In an institution with no matrons to search female visitors, female connections run less risk of detection than do male. Moreover, the intimacy expected and permitted between prisoners and their female visitors provides ample opportunity for the drugs to be passed successfully. Nothing, however, draws the attention of the officers more quickly than does an interracial visit with a female. Thus, the combination of racial and sexual identities operates to make the most reliable connection one between prisoners and females of the same race, and the most unreliable one between prisoners and females of different races.

The successful acquisition of drugs from a visitor is only the first step in "connecting." The second step is the transportation of the supply from the visiting room into the prison itself. Official policy calls for all prisoners to be searched thoroughly before leaving the visiting room. The sheer number of those receiving visits, however, permits a careful search of only a few.

For the majority of those making a connection, then, the transportation of the supply into the prison is not a great problem. They are able to conceal the drugs on their person in such a manner as to transport them successfully without assistance. Those known or suspected of using drugs, however, run a higher risk of search. This problem is circumvented by means of prior arrangements with a prisoner who is not a user or at least not known to the officers as one. Being careful to leave the visiting room at the same time, the prisoner making the connection passes the supply to his "front man."[a] On occasion, this form of collaboration may involve a black and a white; most commonly, it does not. Again, a requisite of a successful connection is inconspicuousness. As we have seen in the previous chapter, communication between blacks and whites is uncommon. Even a fleeting contact in a public area such as the visiting room is thus liable to draw the suspicious attention of an officer. Thus, the extensive segregation characteristic of routine activities impedes biracial cooperation in at least this one illicit activity.

Stashing. Transporting drugs into the prison shades into the second activity, "stashing." A prisoner in possession of drugs is in a highly vulnerable position. Not only must he conceal them from the staff, he must also conceal them from other prisoners who might hijack his supply. Drugs, then, must be "stashed." Prisoners with only a small supply intended only for their personal use may conceal the drugs in an area near their cell or work assignment. Those with a larger supply intended for sale prefer a more secure "stash." In return for a share of the profit, "dealers" frequently hire non-users to hold their supplies. In the case of known or suspected "dealers," this arrangement is often an extension of the "front man" collaboration. Where such collaboration is not necessary, it is an arrangement independent of the transportation of drugs into the prison. In neither instance, however, does "stashing" entail extensive biracial cooperation. As a "stash" has control of the supply, he must be trusted not to "deal" himself. Trust is no more characteristic of black-white relations in the prison than it is in the surrounding community, and this absence of trust precludes extensive biracial collaboration in this activity.[b]

Dealing

The difficulties associated with "connecting" and with raising the neces-

[a]This term possibly has its origins in the subculture of professional or organized crime where a "front" is a legitimate enterprise utilized to cover illegal activities.

[b]One black dealer, however, commented that he always uses a white prisoner for a "stash." His reason is that he believes all blacks are users and would try to steal some of his supply. Descriptions of dealing by other blacks suggest that he is an exception.

sary money place severe limits on the amount of drugs any one prisoner is able to acquire. Moreover, large-scale "dealing" is likely to be curtailed by inmate leaders if not by the staff. The white "mafia" view drug use as a potential threat to their interest in tranquillity; the black "revolutionaries" see it as genocide. For the most part, "dealing" remains a small-time but pervasive activity engaged in by "dope fiends" and "half-steppers." The consuming interest of "dope fiends"—black and white—compels them to "deal" despite the risks involved. "Dope fiends" must sell a portion of their supply to raise the cash necessary to maintain their connection. Moreover, if they should lose their connection or consume their supply in the period between visits, the cash on hand from "dealing" enables them to score from another "dealer." Thus, while the incumbents of distributive and consumptive roles are largely the same individuals, there is a continual movement from one role to the other.

The high risks entailed by "dealing" make the sale of supplies an urgent matter. To avoid detection by the staff or hijacking by other inmates, the "dealer" must dispose of his supply as quickly as possible. One limit on his ability to sell is the difficulty prisoners face in raising money. Because of this obstacle "dealers" must sell to the largest possible market. To enlarge the potential market and at the same time to protect themselves and their supply, "dealers" hire "runners." The function of the "runner" is to spread the word that drugs are available, to collect the cash and return it to the "dealer," and to distribute the drugs. "Runners," however, are never in control of the drug supply and usually are not informed of its location. The relation between a "runner" and a "dealer" does not involve the degree of trust between a "dealer" and a "stash." As few prisoners have close associations with inmates of the other race, and being under pressure to sell quickly, it is expedient for both black and white "dealers" to use "runners" of the other race. It is at the point of distribution and sales that black and white prisoners are drawn into exchange relations in drug-related activities.

When the word gets out there's some dope in here you be seein' black dudes and white dudes together all over the place, tryin' to get them enough bread to buy a bundle. All discrimination just leaves, man. They be puttin' their cash together and buyin' a bundle. Then they all be crowdin' 'round for their turn at the needle. It's somethin' else.

Scoring and Fixing

Scoring. As this comment suggests, the quality of biracial interaction in "scoring" and "fixing" differs from that involved in "dealing." In "dealing," the relations are strictly on an exchange basis, such as those between a buyer and seller or an employer or employee. By contrast, "scoring" and "fixing" draw black and white users into cooperative relations.[2] Two conditions account for this biracial cooperation. First is the price of drugs. The dangers associated with "connecting" and "dealing," and the consequent proliferation of middle-men, greatly inflate the price of drugs in the prison. Heroin selling for five dollars on the outside brings twenty dollars on the inside. Few prisoners have this amount of cash at their disposal. Thus, they are forced into collaborative relations, and their knowledge of the "dealer's" interest in a quick sale combined with their own overwhelming desire to "score" draws them into collaboration with others who have the cash regardless of race. A second pressure toward cooperation is the scarcity of "works." Prisoners in a position to "score" may lack the implements necessary to use the drugs. Quite often, therefore, a user with a good set of "works" is brought into the confederation. Again, greater importance attaches to his having the necessary paraphernalia than to his race. Economic and instrumental concerns induce a measure of biracial cooperation in "scoring."

At the same time, however, the high valuation accorded drugs and their scarcity in the prison produces both intra- and interracial conflict and competition. Both "dealers" and users are in highly vulnerable positions. Despite the precautions taken by the "dealers," other prisoners may be able to trace the path to the supply and "beat" the "dealer" out of drugs and possibly his profits. Conversely, "dealers" and "runners" may conspire to "beat" users by refusing to deliver the drugs after collecting the money, perhaps claiming that they themselves have been beaten. As the term "beat" connotes, the buying and selling of drugs is viewed as a competitive game, one norm of which is "never trust a junkie." An inmate enters the game with the expectation that others will attempt to "beat" him and takes whatever precautions he can to protect himself. If he is "beat," however, he has little recourse other than to suffer the loss. He cannot take his case to the custodians, nor can he usually gain the support of the most influential inmate leaders, as they themselves are opposed to drug use. And, as those who are "beat" are usually low-status or newly-arrived prisoners having few friends or allies, physical retribution is often not an alternative. Still, the frequent thievery associated with the drug traffic does give rise to occassional encounters between small groups of black and white prisoners, and is a continual threat to the harmonious coexistence of the two groups.

Fixing. Notwithstanding the factors of compulsion and suspicion that underlie biracial cooperation in "scoring" and "fixing," such cooperation at times leads to more spontaneous and intimate forms of interracial behavior.

There are not enough drugs in the prison for any prisoner to maintain a physical addiction. Unlike addicts on the street, users in the prison are "fixing" to "get high" rather than to ward off the pains of withdrawal. "Fixing" is a festive occasion, and the period of time between "scoring" and "fixing," a time during which the confederates share a mutual excitement at the prospect of "getting off," may be characterized by biracial joking, horseplay, and other gestures of intimacy:

B.J. (black) looked at his watch and said to "Street Cat" (black), "It's 'bout time to go see that friend of yours ain't it?" "Street Cat" nodded and communicated his desire that I not accompany them by saying "We got some business to take care of." I watched as they walked across the grass and sat on one of the benches. Several minutes later Bob E. (white) came up to them. "Street Cat" and B.J. jumped off the bench and all three exchanged hand slaps with B.J. and "Street Cat" exclaiming, "You're my man! You're my man!" For several minutes they engaged in a highly animated conversation accompanied by backslapping and laughter. When the buzzer rang to clear the yard, the three went into South State together, "Street Cat" with his arm draped around Bob's shoulder. . . . After lockup I walked past "Street Cat" and B.J.'s cells. Both were "spaced out."

As the activities surrounding drugs in the prison come closer to the actual consumption of drugs, the significance of race as a barrier to interaction decreases. Where "connecting" and "stashing" are largely segregated, "dealing" entails biracial exchange relations, "scoring" draws blacks and whites into collaboration, and in "fixing" there is some semblance of interracial cohesion. It is only in the moments preceding "fixing," however, that black and white users interact freely and without any apparent awareness of race. Having "fixed," users retreat to their cells and in their cells they retreat into their own inner worlds. The next day the quest for drugs may find them aligned in an entirely different combination, and perhaps attempting to "beat" the very same individual with whom they were so intimate.

Homosexual Behavior

In Chapter 4 I noted that to judge by inmate verbalizations the deprivation of heterosexual contact and means of sexual satisfaction are the most severe deprivations experienced by prisoners at ECI. In response to this felt deprivation, there exists among the prisoners a variety of homosexual relationships analogous in form to heterosexual relationships in the free community: marriage, prostitution, rape, and seduction. These relationships have both intra- and interracial aspects. Here, however, I am concerned with their interracial dimension.

Marriage and Prostitution.

Marriage. Studies of prisons for women have found homosexual marriages to be the basic unit of the informal inmate social structure.[3] In contrast, discussions of homosexuality in prisons for men have emphasized its largely physical and occasionally violent nature.[4] The structure of sexual relationships at ECI is consistent with the findings of this prior research. Homosexual marriages are rare. During the period of study, I became aware of only six such unions. Three of these were intraracial involving white "fags" and "wise guys,"[5] and three were interracial, being liaisons between older black prisoners in an active role and young white "punks." These few interracial marriages appeared more similar to the dyadic relations found among female prisoners than to the intraracial marriages among the whites. Unlike the marriages among the whites, the interracial marriages seemed to be of long duration. All three lasted throughout the study period, two having been formed prior to the study and one commencing after I had been in the prison about five months. In one case, the black partner refused a raise to minimum custody presumably to maintain the marriage. Also, unlike the marriages among whites, the partners are publicly as well as privately intimate. I observed no instance in which one degraded or demeaned the other and public displays of concern and affection were relatively common.

That three of the six known homosexual marriages were interracial with blacks in the active role may be explicable, at least partially, in terms of the psychological process of projection. Psychologically oriented studies of race relations have made extended comment upon cross-racial sexual attraction.[7] Presumably, the internalization of white standards of beauty, the deprecation of blackness, and the power and prestige of whites relative to blacks combine to make whites attractive sexual objects to blacks of the opposite sex. Conversely the caste patterning of sex makes sexual relations with blacks a forbidden fruit for whites. Presumably, whites project onto blacks many of their repressed sexual desires and fantasies, coming to view blacks as more animal than human and possessed of vigorous, insatiable appetites for sex. Given this line of reasoning, it is at least plausible that the deprivation of heterosexual contact and the inability of older black prisoners to establish close associations with other blacks predisposes them to transfer their attraction to white females onto white males who have been collectively defined as "female." By providing the white partner with affection, material comforts, and some degree of protection from abuse, older black prisoners are able to establish intimate relations with partners whom, by virtue of projection and transference, they value highly.

However, one not need resort to psychodynamic explanations of this sort to explain the attraction of the white partner to the relationship. After having been abused sexually, facing the prospect of either future abuse or extended isolation in segregation, and being deprived of friendship, the rewards offered by a marriage relation must be appealing to many white "punks." Abuse does not end with the establishment of the relationship, however. Other inmates, both black and white, view such marriages negatively. Where the black "revolutionaries" and "half-steppers" are in conflict on the question of liaisons with black "fags," they agree on the question of marriage to a white "fag." Any black who becomes so attached to a white is a "tom," and each of three blacks in homosexual unions with whites were excluded from the Afro-American Society, ostracized from black peer group activities, and subjected to continual assault and verbal taunts from other blacks. In similar fashion, the white partner is the object of verbal taunts from other whites, ostracized, and occasionally assaulted sexually. These common external pressures to which both partners to the marriage are subject may in fact be a force sustaining their cohesion. Interracial marriages, to a large extent, appear to be intimate bonds grounded in adversity, relations of support and consolation between individuals who collectively constitute a disaffiliated and abused segment of the prisoner population.

Prostitution. The most common form of sexual relationship at ECI is prostitution. For the most part, however, this relation is an intraracial one. Nonetheless, the following two excerpts, the first from an interview with a white "fag" and the second from an interview with a white "stand-up guy," suggest that "fags" of both races are attracted to sexual relations with active partners of the other race and at least occasionally sell their sexual favors across the color line.

I'm a homosexual and I don't care if the guy I'm with is white or colored. The only thing with me is he's gotta be a man. I won't go with no weaklings. . . . I been with colored guys on the outside and I liked it. Most of the time it's better than it is with whites. . . . I can't explain it really. It's just better, more exciting or something. . . . In here I never gone with no colored guys. I'd like to. I think most of us would. . . . It's like I said before, it's just better. And they respect ya more. They treat you better than white guys do. . . . I'm scared. If I left Frankie for a colored guy he and the others might kill me. I get together with one or two now and then but I always keep it behind closed doors.

. . . .

I was walking through the wing the other day when one of them black fags, the one that calls herself 'Ellen,' called me into the corner. She asked if I wanted a hand job. Now I ain't one to pass up an opportunity like that! So I let her do it. She's a real pro! It was the best job I ever had. She didn't ask for nothin' but I gave her a carton and figgered that was it. Yesterday I'm in the yard with Joe H. and she comes and sits on the bench beside me and starts rubbin' her hand up my leg. Then she says, 'Tony, I'd like to marry you.' I damn near fell off the bench. At first I thought she was just screwing around but than I seen she was serious and I told her to bug off. . . . None of them black fags appeal to me. I ain't seen one I'd like to lay. Havin' a fag or a kid in here is like havin' a broad on the street. You like to show her off, ya know? It might be a big thing for a black guy to have a white kid, I don't know. But it sure as hell ain't no big thing for a white guy to have a black kid. Especially when there's so many nice white kids running around.

Presumably, the attraction of "fags" to active partners of the opposite race is explicable in terms of projection as noted above in the case of the attraction of black "toms" to white "punks." Standing in opposition to the attraction of the "fags," however, is a combination of strong social disapproval and a lack of attraction to the relationship, at least on the part of potential white partners. Unlike "punks," white "fags" are highly valued by other white prisoners. Their disaffection from a relationship with a "wise guy" in favor of a relation with a black is thus likely to result in open conflict in which the "fag" would probably be the ultimate victim. In similar fashion, the rationale behind admitting black "fags" to membership in the Afro-American Society, at least in part, is to prevent them from embarassing other blacks by establishing open relations with whites. The involvement of the black "fags" in both the formal and informal activities of the Afro-American Society operates to keep their activities under close surveillance in much the same manner as do the pseudo-marriages between "wise guys" and "fags" among the whites. Finally, there is apparently little attraction to such relationships by potential white partners. As seen by them, a marriage or a relation with a "kid" should enhance one's status. But a marriage to a black "fag" would reduce one's status rather than enhance it.[c] For these reasons, then, prostitution of a biracial nature is relatively uncommon at ECI, occurring only in the form of secretive and fleeting acts.

Rape and Seduction

Certainly not the least of many gains that have accrued to white males by virtue of their dominance over blacks in this country has been in the area of sex. From the beginning of slavery white males have been accorded access to black as well as to white females. At the same time, reciprocal access to

[c]This may not be true if the black "fag" were a true "drag queen." Both black and white prisoners frankly admitted their desire for a black "queen" who had been released just prior to the study. Unlike the "fags" present during the study, this "fag" apparently had had silicone injections to simulate female breasts, wore female undergarments and long hair. Both black and white prisoners competed and fought for his (her) attentions.

white females has been denied to black males by the not infrequent use of crude violence and the atmosphere of fear thus created. This caste patterning of sexual relations has had implications for black males beyond the asymmetrical access to females. More importantly, it has degraded the black male through repeated demonstration of his inability to protect black women.[8] Indeed, the issue of the sexual dominance of white males has been so salient in the history of race relations in this country that some writers have suggested that racial conflict may well have its roots in mutual lust and jealousy.[9]

One need not subscribe to such a view to recognize that culturally patterned sexual tensions are of considerable importance to the understanding of race relations in the prison. In the prison, where the significance of sex is intensified by the deprivation of heterosexual contact and where black and white males live close together, the role of sex in racial conflict is thrown into sharp relief. In the confines of the prison, the rage of black males at their psychological emasculation is vented against white males.

Rape. An analysis of prison disciplinary records and interviews with informants places the number of sexual assaults at ECI at 40 to 50 per year. More striking than the number of sexual attacks is the extent to which they are interracial. Each of my 21 informants—black and white prisoners and staff members alike — estimated that 75 percent or more of the sexual assaults involve black aggressors and white victims.[10] The following case study, condensed from an interview with one white victim, is illustrative of the process of sexual assault, the motives of the aggressors, and the career of the victim.

Alan entered ECI in April, 1970 to serve an 18-month sentence for Breaking and Entering. He is 5'6" tall and weighs about 135 lbs. At the time he entered ECI he was twenty years old, had graduated from high school, and had never been confined previously. By his own admission he was "scared to death" at the prospect of sexual assault.

Soon after he arrived black inmates began to harass him, calling him "white trash," a "white whore," and threatening "to make a little girl out of (him)." When two black inmates cornered him in his cell one evening before lockup and threatened to throw acid over him—it turned out to be orange juice—he submitted to them, allowing them to commit buggery. Terrified, he requested protective custody.

After one month in protective custody, however, the strain of being locked in a cell for 23 hours a day and never being allowed out of the wing proved to be too much, and he requested return to the population. Soon after his return to the population he was approached by Willie, a large and powerful black inmate. Willie told him that he didn't approve of what the others had done, felt sorry for Alan, and would take care of him. He gave Alan a carton of cigarettes and signed over a five dollar store order to him. Over the next several weeks the relationship developed into what Alan considered a real friendship. He was no longer harassed and his fears abated. One evening Willie told Alan to "get off" with him. Alan accepted, but when he arrived at the back side of the third tier in the lower South State block, he found himself confronted with five or six other blacks. Willie demanded that he "take care of us." "I been taking care of you, now you gotta take care of me and my friends." Alan refused and tried to struggle free but was overpowered. Willie held him down by the head and shoulders while the others took turns committing buggery upon him.

Then he was forced to commit fellatio upon Willie. As Alan remembers it, during all of this time he was repeatedly called a "white punk," a "white bitch," and asked questions such as "How does it feel to have a black prick in you, white boy?" He was warned that if he told the guards, they would kill him.

"If I was to go back to PCU (protective custody) they'd want to know why and I couldn't tell 'em. Besides I couldn't stand it back there anyway. So I decided to stay out and give it up if I had to." Over the next several months Alan was subjected to repeated assaults of a similar nature by a large number of black inmates. Then, in September, a well-known white inmate asked him to be his "kid." Alan entered a relationship with this prisoner and several of his friends. They provide him with cigarettes and store orders, and since entering the relation he has not been assaulted.

Interviews with other informants confirmed the essential details of Alan's story and indicated that with minor variations his experience is typical of those white prisoners who come to be labeled as "punks" or "kids." Invariably, the victims are considerably younger than other inmates and physically underdeveloped for their age, have completed more years of formal education than the average prisoner, are on their first sentence, and often have long hair. In short they possess many characteristics that might be symbolic of feminity in an all male population. Frequently, as in the case of Alan, the prospective victim is subjected to a period of harassment and threat. Such verbal abuse probably increases the excitement of the aggression, but it serves more practical purposes as well. First, it is a means of discovering if the victim has friends who may come to his assistance. If he has ties with any inmates who are able to mobilize any significant number in his defense, then the attack will be stopped. Second, as happened to Alan, verbal aggression is a means of manipulating the victim into a position of trust and dependence upon an inmate who may in fact be the prime mover in the plot against him. Such manipulation facilitates an undetected assault. On occasion, such tactics of intimidation and manipulation are unnecessary, however. Some young white prisoners, by virtue of their political identifications, are predisposed to friendship with blacks. By reason of their overtures of friendship, however, they may find themselves ensnared in a situation that culminates in sexual assault.

At ECI sexual assaults are termed "train jobs," indicating the group nature of the attack. While all interracial assaults involve several blacks attacking a white victim, the composition of the attacking group changes as more and more black prisoners become involved. The one exception is the "ripper." The "ripper" is that prisoner who plans and initiates the attack. After the initial assault, usually undertaken with several of his closest associates, the "ripper" commonly makes his "punk" available to others in subsequent attacks. As the victim becomes less resistant to particular acts, these later attacks may force him into more degrading acts, for example buggery to fellatio. At some point—either when the victim has become completely submissive or a new victim is being manipulated or perhaps when all those interested have been involved—the attacks cease. At this point, white inmates may come forward to offer the victim protection in return for his services.

Sexual assaults of this type are acts of open, direct, and violent aggression, which from a psychological perspective are closely akin to homicide. Given the nature of the act, it is obvious that the largely black-onto-white character of these assaults is not explicable solely in terms of conditions immediately associated with confinement. Factors such as the deprivation of heterosexual contact, the proximity of black and white males, the prison definitions of homosexual behavior, and the greater solidarity of the blacks make such assaults possible. But the motive force behind them has its roots deep within the entire socio-historical context of black-white relations in this country. The prison is merely an arena within which blacks may direct aggression developed through 300 years of oppression against individuals perceived to be representatives of the oppressors.

According to frustration-aggression theory, the instigation to aggression is greatest when a strong drive is repeatedly frustrated in a nearly total manner.[11] Historically, such has been the condition of the black male in relation to one of his strongest drives, the affirmation of his masculinity. In American society masculinity traditionally has been affirmed by qualities such as assertiveness, self-determination, power over others, and the ability to provide for and protect a wife and family. It is precisely such attributes that have been denied black males, first by slavery and more recently by the legacy of racism. One consequence of the structure of race relations in this country has been the development among black males of an image of themselves as emasculated and dependent beings, and a rage at white males as the perpetrators of their condition.[12] In the prison, the subservience of black males to the authority of white-dominated institutions is immediately visible and other means of self-affirmation are denied them. Under such conditions, black rage undoubtedly increases. Such an anger is articulated by black prisoners when speaking of the motives behind their sexual aggression against whites:

Every can I been in that's the way it is. . . . It's gettin' even I guess. . . . You guys been cuttin' our balls off ever since we been in this country. Now we're just gettin' even.

. . . .

To general way of thinking it's "cause they're confined and they got hard rocks. But that ain't it at all. It's a way for the black man to get back at the white man. It's one way he can assert his manhood. Anything white, even a defenseless punk, is part of what the black man hates. It's part of what he's had to fight all his life just to survive, just to have a hole to sleep in and some garbage to eat. . . . It's a new ego thing. He can show he's a man by making a white guy into a girl.

. . . .

The black man's just waking up to what's been going on. Now that he's awake, he's gonna be mean. He's been raped—politically, economically, morally raped. He sees this now, but his mind's still small so he's getting back this way. But it's just a beginning.

Any internalized inhibitions black prisoners may have regarding such attacks are neutralized by several conditions.[13] First, the very prevalence of anti-white sentiments provides strong group support and approval for the assaults. While two or three black prisoners have a reputation as "rippers," black informants agree that virtually all black prisoners play the role at some time in their prison career. Generally, this occurs soon after their arrival as they seek the support and acceptance of other "brothers." The instigation of a sexual assault, then, is to some extent an initiation rite by which black prisoners demonstrate their manhood and blackness to their peers.

A second condition that may neutralize inhibitions against the act is contained in the rationales offered above. It is an act of revenge. It is a retaliation in kind for the violent attacks of white males against black people. It is thus justifiable and even moral in a sense.

Finally, there is the definition accorded homosexual behavior by the prisoner subculture. Inmate definitions resolve any threats to the participants' masculine self-images by defining only the behavior of the passive participant as homosexual. Not only do such definitions alleviate anxiety concerning masculinity, they also function to make the act an assertion of manhood. In a population in which normal male-female comparisons are lacking, a greater stress is placed upon physical toughness as an indicator of masculinity. The ability to force another male into a degrading sexual act is thus a symbol of manhood. In short, there exist within the black prisoner subculture several rationalizations for the sexual assault of white males.

From the perspective of the theory of frustration-aggression, the characteristics of the victims of these attacks take on added significance. The strongest aggressive responses evoked by frustration are directed against the source of the frustration, and may be generalized to other objects to the degree that these objects are perceived as similar to the frustrating object and exempt the aggressor from retaliatory responses.[14] Seen in this light, the assault of young and isolated white males may be interpreted as aggression that is displaced from the primary objects of frustration—the white custodians, and the class they represent—out of fear of their retaliatory power. A similar consideration of power potential is probably operative with respect to the more dominant white male prisoners. Here, however, there is an additional consideration. The dominant white male prisoners may not be perceived by the blacks as representatives of the oppressive class. They share with the black prisoners a criminal identity; they also have been rejected and labeled as outcasts by those in power and react to them with bitter hostility. Given this consideration, there appear to be several reasons for the selection of victims. First, their youth and physical underdevelopment are suggestive of femininity in an all-male world. Second, their isolation precludes retaliatory responses. Third, their lack of a criminal identity and their higher than average education may lead black prisoners to perceive them as members of the white middle class, which they regard as their prime oppressor.

Seduction. There is one final question to be treated. When the rape of white females by black males traditionally draws such a violent response from the white population, and when even consensual relations between white women and black men are subject to strong social disapproval, why is it that the homosexual rape of white males at ECI does not arouse the racial consciousness of the white prisoner population and precipitate a retaliatory response? The answer to this question lies in the fact that the white inmate leaders are the direct beneficiaries of these assaults. While they may lack the intense anger involved in these attacks, they also need to affirm their masculinity, and these assaults create and maintain a class of inmates upon whom the white leaders depend for the satisfaction of that need. In response to my questioning, one white leader was quite candid about the tacit biracial cooperation in this regard:

Sometimes if I really need a "kid" and I see one that looks real good, then I might slip the word over to the spooks that he's really gay. Most of the time though I just sit back and watch the action. I wait till it looks like they're done with him then I come on like a knight in shining armor, see. I take him under my wing and start doing things for him and promise to keep the others away. After what he's been through it ain't nothing for him to take care of me and a coupla others. He's glad to do it.

Rather than oppose these assaults, white inmates use the fear generated in the victims to seduce them into more permanent roles as "punks" and "kids." Thus, what from the perspective of particular individuals is a situation of brutal, physical conflict is—from the broader perspective of group relations—a form of symbiotic cooperation.

Summary

We have seen that the interest in sexual activity gives rise to a variety of biracial social relationships ranging from brutal conflict to interracial cohesion. In contrast to evidence from womens' prisons, biracial interaction in consensual sex is infrequent at ECI. It occurs mainly in the form of secretive acts of prostitution initiated by "fags" of both races. While "fags" may be attracted to more permanent relations with active partners of the opposite race, such marriages are precluded by the strong social disapproval accorded them. The only semblance of interracial cohesion emerging from sexual activity are three marriages between black "toms" and white "punks." The fact that both partners in these unions are ostracized and subjected to continual abuse is evidence of the disapproval accorded such relations.

The most common and open form of coerced homosexual behavior is the rape of young white inmates by groups of blacks. These acts may be seen as acts of violent aggression against individuals perceived to be representatives of the class primarily responsible for the psychological emasculation of the black male. These violent encounters, however, seldom if ever precipitate large-scale racial conflict. One reason for this is that the ultimate beneficiaries of these assaults are white inmates who are provided with a class of "punks" and "kids" to satisfy their own needs. Thus, brutal racial conflict on one level creates a bond of tacit racial cooperation on another level.

Keeping The Peace

The preceding discussion in this chapter as well as in Chapter 6 suggests that at ECI there is a high potential for widespread racial conflict both among inmates and between staff and inmates. Large-scale racial conflict, however, is contrary to the interests of both the revolution-oriented black leaders and segments of the white leadership, particularly the "mafia" and the "politicians." Thus, a focal concern drawing these three groups into cooperative relations of a biracial nature is their interest in keeping the peace both among inmates and between inmates and the staff.

Among Inmates

The racial violence of the period from 1969 through 1970 remains etched in the memories of most inmate leaders. The knowledge of the rapidity with which interracial conflict can erupt in an atmosphere permeated by rejection, frustration, and prejudice, and a fear of future conflict of this nature form the foundation for conflict resolution. After the black prisoners had been reintegrated into the general population during the summer of 1970, several meetings were held between the future Directors of the Afro-

American Society and members of the white elite. Out of these meetings there developed a consensus on several matters. First, it was agreed that most of the previous conflict had been instigated by the staff who had spread malicious rumors concerning the intentions of one group to members of the other. So, for example, the whites explained that they had attacked the blacks in segregation because of the stories they had heard from guards about blacks shouting obscenities at white female visitors. The blacks denied that they had shouted obscenities. (Several blacks who were in segregation at the time, however, admitted to me privately that such remarks had been made on one or two occasions.) Second, they agreed that the officers have an interest in promoting racial conflict among the prisoners and that such conflict, whether or not instigated by the guards, could only benefit the custodians and harm inmates. In the inmates' view, the guards had instigated the past conflicts in an effort to gain public support for their campaign to secure higher pay and pension benefits.[d] They believed that any future conflict would be used by the custodians to obtain more stringent regulations and the revocation of many of the privileges the prisoners now enjoyed. Third, both the "mafia" and the black leaders assured each other that their own wishes were for peaceful coexistence, the "mafia" wanting to do their time as quickly as possible with a minimum of trouble and revolution-oriented blacks wanting to use the time to educate themselves and the membership of their organization.

On the basis of this consensus they developed an arrangement to contain future racial conflict. A black leader described this arrangement to me in the following terms:

It was a beautiful thing, man. For the first time blacks and whites was getting together and talking as equals, man to man. . . . We decided all beefs would be individual. If any blacks was running around trying to stir up shit with whites, they'd (the mafia) come to us and we'd deal with them (the troublemakers). If it was the other way we'd go to them and they'd take care of it and report back to us what they did. If it was just a thing between two dudes and we couldn't work it out, you know push come to shove, then we'd bring 'em together and let 'em fight it out themselves. . . . It's worked out good. Since then we ain't had no real trouble. There's been beefs but they ain't spread into wars.

On several occasions during the study, potential group conflicts were averted by this arrangement. In the cavernous confines of the wings, noise is a constant irritant among the prisoners. At one point during the winter months, the continual noise generated by the stereos and electric guitars of

---

[d]As I pointed out in Chapter 3, the guards did in fact use these disturbances to dramatize their demands. One need not subscribe to the view that they instigated the conflicts to recognize how they utilized them to advance their own interests, however. Still, the idea that some staff members instigate racial conflict cannot be dismissed lightly. Many officers and members of the administration believe this to be so. I was never able to corroborate their contentions, however.

the blacks living on the bottom tier (Soul City) of lower South State block threatened to provoke a disturbance with the older, long-term whites living on the tiers above them. The intercession of the "mafia" resulted in a proclamation by the President of the Afro-American Society to the effect that no stereos or guitars were to be played after 9 p.m., and that there was to be no "idling in the wings."

Another common feature of prison life with the potential to disrupt the coexistence of black and white prisoners is the "rip off." Small groups of prisoners, usually young inmates with short sentences, burglarize cells that are left open. Most commonly the victims like the offenders are recent arrivals with no close ties with other inmates. On occasion, however, the cell of a prisoner with some status may be burglarized or the activities of a group may become so widespread as to be generally disruptive. On at least two occasions, the cooperation between the black "revolutionaries" and the "mafia" prevented conflicts of this type from developing into group confrontations. One incident involved the alleged theft of a gold watch from the cell of one of the Directors of the Afro-American Society. Having seen the watch on a "kid" associated with several "wise guys," he brought the matter to a member of the "mafia," demanding the return of the watch. The "kid," however, maintained that it was his watch and his contention was supported by his associates. Unable to resolve the issue peacefully, the "mafia" and the black leadership arranged a fight between the two. Rather than fight, the "kid" surrendered the watch.

In another incident, a number of white prisoners accused a black of stealing cigarettes and radios from their cells. After an investigation, the accused prisoner was summoned before the Disciplinary Committee of the Afro-American Society. The Committee ordered him to make restitution to the whites and warned him that he could expect physical reprisals from the organization if his activities continued.

Prior to the outbreak at Attica, the most immediate threat to orderly relations between the black and white prisoners came in the form of racial slurs during a movie. The movie, entitled "The Landlord," contains several explicit scenes of sexual intercourse between a white man and the wife of a militant black leader, and she becomes pregnant. These scenes drew muffled comments and laughter from some whites, which increased in volume until one comment was clearly audible: "That nigger whore's gonna have a white baby." The blacks had been sitting in stony silence but at this remark they stood up as one and began screaming that the officers stop the laughter and comments. The lights went on, and the blacks stormed out of the auditorium in a highly agitated state. With virtually the entire black population milling about in lower South State wing and additional correctional officers being summoned in the event of a disturbance, the Directors of the Afro-American Society met with the "mafia." The blacks demanded a confrontation with whites responsible for the comments, and the "mafia" agreed to produce them. While an investigation was conducted to uncover those responsible for the remarks, the leaders continued their discussion, coming to an agreement that ultimately the administration was responsible for the incident because of the inflammatory nature of the film. To prevent further incidents of this sort, they agreed to form a biracial committee to advise the administration on movies, a proposal to which the Warden later assented. Within a half-hour three white inmates were brought forward and made to apologize to the assembled blacks and the incident ended without violence.

Until upset by internal changes within the Afro-American Society and the outbreak at Attica, this arrangement between black "revolutionaries" and white "mafia" functioned to contain effectively occasional encounters between blacks and whites. The change in this arrangement will be discussed in the next chapter.

With Staff

The formation of a biracial movie committee is illustrative of the second form of conflict resolution. As in any prison, the inmates at ECI have numerous grievances with the staff. Occasionally, there are complaints of brutality. More commonly, grievances center on matters such as food, classification procedures, medical care, conditions of parole, intrusions by the custodians on the autonomy of the inmate organizations, and the like. The Warden looks upon the elected leaders of the inmate organizations as an informal advisory council in such matters and meets with them periodically to discuss these problems.

Almost without exception these meetings are initiated by white "politicians." It is only after a time and place for the meeting has been set that the black leaders are notified and requested to submit items for an agenda. The reason for this lack of symmetry in these arrangements lies in the differing interests of the two groups. Where the "politicians" view themselves as arbiters for all prisoners, the interests of the blacks are more particularistic. As they perceive the situation the basic conflict is between blacks and whites rather than between staff and inmates. Thus, they see their problems as unique to themselves and not amenable to resolution by inclusion within broader grievances such as a demand for clear guidelnes for parole decisions. Nor in presenting their grievances are they entirely comfortable in their role as members of a biracial group. More to their satisfaction are meetings between the white staff and black inmates alone, and such meetings are held, although infrequently. There is, however, one motive that impels black attendance at the white initiated meetings. That motive is their suspicion that their absence would be utilized by the "politicians" to gain an advantage over them in some way. Thus, black attendance at these meetings is prompted as much by a concern to guard their interests against possible subversion by the white inmates as it is by the opportunity to advance their interests or resolve conflicts with the staff.

The watchdog nature of the black role at these meetings is evident in their participation. For the most part the black representatives are observers who interact with the white participants only when a question is directed explicitly at them. On the few occasions when they do initiate interaction, as the following excerpt illustrates, it usually follows some perceived gain of the whites and is directed at evening the balance. Moreover, unlike the conciliatory tone of the white participants, the emotional content of the black communication tends to be openly hostile.

White inmate: We have a bit of a problem with *The Beacon*, Warden. You told us we could work weekends and keep the camera. Now Mr. Spivey says no weekend work and the Deputy wants to lock up the camera when we ain't using it.

Warden: You can keep the camera as long as you use it only for *Beacon* business and don't abuse it. (to Deputy) Can you live with that?

Deputy: (nods in affirmation)

White inmate: We can't put the paper out unless we work weekends. Even then we fall behind. Can we have the weekends?

Deputy: I don't have the men on weekends. Would letting you work two or three nights a week help? I have the men then.

White inmate: I think we could do that.

Warden: It's settled then.

Black inmate: What about our paper?

Warden: What about it?

Black inmate: There ain't gonna be no objections to having our paper printed outside is there?

Warden: There could be. I can't see why you don't take a page or two in *The Beacon*. This is a big, expensive proposition you're getting into and the state won't pay for every group in here to have its own paper.

Black inmate: I already told you and the others the members don't want no part of *The Beacon*. They voted for their own paper and they're gonna pay for it themselves.

Warden: Okay. But you'll have to follow the same guidelines. There'll be no name calling and no partisan politics. We can't allow that in a paper sponsored by the state.

Black inmate: Ours ain't sponsored by the state! That's their paper (points to white inmates) you're talking about. We're paying for ours.

Warden: It's still coming out of ECI under the state emblem so we're responsible for it. If you want to write articles for another paper you can do what you want. But if it's coming out under our emblem then you'll have to follow the same guidelines as *The Beacon*.

Black inmate: I don't know if the members will buy that. What about a camera for us too?

Warden: Why can't you borrow *The Beacon's?*

Black inmate: If we got our own paper we want our own equipment to put it out.

Warden: Put your reasons in writing and I'll consider it. What's next on the agenda?

By virtue of their pursuit of particularistic goals that diverge to some degree from those of the white inmates, and the alienated and antagonistic tone of their communication, the black representatives tend to dominate these meetings. More subtly, their dominance is supported by other verbal and non-verbal behaviors such as entrances and exists, seating arrangements, note-taking, and non-group directed communication. By means of such tactics the blacks displace a considerable portion of the group's attention from the matters being discussed and direct it onto themselves. In effect, they become focal concerns for the other participants. The meeting from which the above excerpt was taken can be used to illustrate these tactics. The meeting was scheduled for 4 p.m. All participants except the black representatives had arrived by 4:15, at which time the blacks were summoned to the meeting over the public address system. Arriving at 4:30, the blacks entered together, offered no explanation or apology, and displaced two whites as they seated themselves around one corner of the table diagonally across from the Warden, who was seated in the center of the opposite side.[15] One of them produced a notebook and for the entire meeting took what appeared to be verbatim notes, the only participant to do so. Except for the excerpt cited above, the other two representatives displayed little attention to the meeting, engaging in extended conversation behind the back of the representative taking notes. So engrossed were they in these conversations that one failed to respond to two queries directed at him by the Warden.

Biracial cooperation between white "politicians" and black leaders to resolve problems with the staff is thus marked by a high degree of competition. After meetings of the sort described above statements such as "them niggers think they can run the joint" and "you can't talk to them, they won't cooperate on anything" are commonly voiced by the "politicians." What are designed to be forums wherein black and white prisoners may coact to resolve common problems with the staff serve, by virtue of the interaction that occurs, to reinforce tensions already existing in the relationship.

Meeting the Public

As a result of the policy of humanitarian reform, ECI is a highly permeable institution. This permeability is most evident in the activities of the inmate voluntary organizations, the purposes of which are to articulate existing community resources with prisoner needs and interests. In pursuit of this objective, there is extensive contact between representatives of community groups and members of the organizations. As the organizations are largely segregated by race, so then are most of the programs with citizens from the community. However, certain functions entail interorganizational coordination. Activities of this nature are of two types: purely social functions such as Christmas parties and banquets, and political functions such as the annual Legislative Forum.

Racial integration of these public affairs is ensured by the regulatory powers of the Warden. While the functions are initiated and coordinated by inmates, administrative approval is required. As the Warden can use these occasions to demonstrate to the public his success in restoring racial harmony to the prison, his approval is dependent upon the attendance of both black and white prisoners.

In fact, the insistence of the Warden upon racial integration meets with little resistance from the prime movers of these events. With the exception of the annual banquet of the Afro-American Society, these affairs are sponsored by the white organizations. The leaders of these organizations, the "politicians," are particularly concerned with the image presented to the public by the prisoner population. Implicitly at least, they accept their rejection by society and seek to impress representatives from the community that prisoners, notably themselves, are capable of rehabilitation. Given the past history of racial conflict within the institution, their concern with their public image extends to race relations. They, as much as the Warden, have an abiding interest in presenting to the public an appearance of racial integration and harmony among the prisoners.

This concern with a public image of racial harmony is not shared by the black leaders. It is to their interest to demonstrate publicly that racial tension does exist within the prison, particularly between themselves and the staff. This interest is most evident in their legislative proposals. Unlike the proposals submitted by the whites, those submitted by the blacks are not of a type to benefit all inmates, but are directed specifically at eliminating perceived racial discrimination. To call for the elimination of discrimination is to proclaim its presence and thereby to undermine to some extent the public image desired by the Warden and the white "politicians." A second concern of the blacks is similarly at odds with the interests of the other parties. This concern is their desire to demonstrate to the black community the solidarity of the black inmates and their autonomy with respect to both the prison administration and the white inmates. Thus, black inmates accept invitations to social functions sponsored by the white organizations reluctantly and seek to avoid reciprocity with respect to their own social affairs.

As a result of this disparity of interests, biracial cooperation in meeting the public is tenuous. On several occasions, the underlying strains threatened to dissolve the relationship. One incident concerned attendance at parties and banquets. The arrangement agreed upon was that each organization sponsoring a banquet or party would invite the directors of the other organizations. A party sponsored by the "Jay Cees" was the scene of a serious disturbance. For security reasons their next banquet in June was limited to 150 people—75 inmates with one visitor each—rather than the usual 300. In consequence they invited only the President and Vice-President of the Afro-American Society, taking care to explain the reason for their action. Despite the explanation, this action was interpreted as an insult by the black leaders. In August, they invited only the President and Vice-President of the "Jay Cees" to their banquet. Seeing this action as illegitimate and not wishing to spend an evening with the blacks and their visitors, these leaders decided to decline the invitation. Threatened with the cancellation of their banquet if the white representatives did not attend, the black leaders eventually consented to invite the Editor and Assistant Editor of *The Beacon*. Nonetheless, the action of the whites in refusing the initial invitation left a residue of resentment among the blacks.

Concessions of this nature are by no means made solely by the blacks. Because of their interdependence on these public occasions, the black leaders are able to exact compromises from the whites as well. An example occurred in conjunction with the Legislative Forum. The black leaders sought to propose a bill to establish three high level policy positions in the Department of Corrections to be filled by blacks who would have discretionary powers to review all parole, classification, and disciplinary decisions involving black inmates. At a meeting to coordinate the forum, this proposal met with resistance from the white leaders. They suggested that the Afro-American Society present a bill that would effect substantial administrative reorganization of the prison with the stipulation that every effort be made to hire blacks for the new positions. This suggestion evoked the following reaction from the Afro-American Society legislative committee:

E.A.: They're a bunch of racist bastards. Anything that says black and white they object to. They say all the bills should be for the whole population. But we're black and we're only concerned with the black man in here, and that's who we're writing for.

S.R.: That's right. I speak from experience. It's just more of the white devil's tricks. If we go with that bill, it'll change everything and won't mean nothing. I say we present our bill the way we got it or we don't present nothing at all.

The recalcitrance of the blacks on this issue forced the white leaders to permit the presentation of the original proposal. It was presented in a strident, defiant manner by the black representative and met with considerable hostility from the largely white legislative group. Later, when for the first time all of the prisoners' proposals were rejected by the legislature, the white leaders placed the blame on the black proposal and the way it was presented.

Despite these backstage tensions, the front stage appearance on public occasions is generally one of racial integration. With the exception of the Afro-American Society banquet, all public affairs are attended by black and white prisoners in numbers proportionate to their numbers in the population. The conviviality of these occasions, moreover, creates an impression of racial harmony, although there is in fact very little biracial interaction. The black representatives and their guests form an enclave sitting at three or four segregated tables in one corner and venture outside this space only to secure food. And this is accomplished in a manner calculated to display black solidarity and disaffection. Food is served cafeteria style. By prearrangement the blacks remain seated until all of the whites have been served and then move as a group through the serving line.

Thus, while black and white leaders cooperate in meetinq representatives of the public, their cooperation is forced and beset with strain due to a disparity of interests. Such occasions present an appearance of racial harmony. In fact, however, they represent only a form of demographic integration, and close inspection provides ample evidence of the racial tension that underlies them.

Summary and Conclusion

It is apparent that the conditions of confinement at ECI do not eliminate the barriers to interaction constructed upon racial differences. Neither their rejection by society, nor their proximity within the prison, nor their common subordination to the authority of the custodians, nor the integrationist policies of the Warden, nor the material deprivations they suffer are sufficient to produce a cross-racial solidarity among prisoners. In all routine, day-to-day activities there is a clear pattern of racial avoidance and segregation. As a consequence of administrative controls black and white prisoners may live, work and play next to each other, but their interaction is limited to whatever is necessary to achieve certain goals, whether the goal be the completion of work assignment or the playing of a basketball game. Even within the informal economic system there are parallel racial structures. Private, informal behavior of a primary group nature is subject to virtually complete segregation. In short, despite their common status as subordinate groups within the prison, a sharp cleavage remains between black and white prisoners.

There are, however, links across the racial line. These links are created by the mutuality of interests of different groups with respect to what might be considered focal concerns of prisoners—drugs, sex, keeping the peace, and meeting the public. The circumstances of confinement compel a substantial degree of biracial interaction to meet these needs. Such cooperation remains tenuous, however, dependent as it is upon the compatibility of black and white interests. Underlying the cooperation are strong sentiments of suspicion and hostility that continually threaten the existing relationships. It is the recognition of the ease with which racial violence may erupt, coupled with a belief that such violence will only benefit the custodians, that provides the foundation for cooperative efforts between the white ''mafia'' and the black ''revolutionaries'' to keep the peace.

Predicated as it is upon the ever present threat of racial violence, the informal means of conflict resolution developed by these two groups suggests the nature of race relations among the prisoners at ECI. Of central importance to the structure of race relations is the close proximity between a numerically superior but non-solidary white group and a small but solidary black minority. There is little sense of solidarity between two groups, but neither has the power to dominate the other. Mutual avoidance is the prevailing pattern of interaction, but complete polarization is prevented by instrumental ties at various points. The cornerstone of the structure is the continual accomodation of conflict by the leaders of both groups. Thus, while there are bonds of functional interdependence between black and white inmates, in the final analysis race relations among the prisoners at ECI is a balance of power.

9 Conclusion

From September 1970 to September 1971 the structure of race relations at ECI constituted a system in a precarious state of equilibrium. This system was not integrated by value consensus but by the more tenuous bonds of coercion, complementary interests, and interdependence in pursuit of these interests.[1] The coercive power of the dominant group, the custodians, had been weakened by both the policies of humanitarian reform and a series of court decisions. The custodial hierarchy was anomic, and the custodians in rebellion against the prison administration. The reform policies had also undermined the solidarity of the white inmates. Among them was a small group of highly respected and feared leaders drawn from the ranks of organized crime. The primary interests of these leaders lay in completing their sentences as quickly and comfortably as possible with a minimum of trouble and disruption. Order and stability between the custodians and white prisoners was maintained by the coincidence of interests between the custodians and these white leaders. In return for their mediation of crisis situations, the white leaders were granted privileges and immunity from punishment by the staff.

Contrary to its effect upon the custodians and the white inmates, the policy of humanitarian reform facilitated an increase in black solidarity. It permitted the black prisoners the freedom of interaction necessary to articulate the ideology of black nationalism with their status as prisoners. This process occurred in and through an Afro-American Society to which the vast majority of black prisoners belonged. The solidarity of this group presented a serious challenge to the authority of the custodians and served to protect its members from arbitrary and capricious actions by the staff. However, overt conflict of a violent nature was minimized by the circumspection of the black leaders. The primary interests of the black "revolutionaries" who founded the organization were to politicize and educate the membership to prepare them to assume a role in the black movement after their release. Not only would confrontations with the prison staff jeopardize this goal, but such tactics had little chance of achieving meaningful change within the prison. Thus, these leaders were careful to distinguish between "legitimate" and "illegitimate" grievances against the staff and to mobilize the organization only in support of those grievances determined to be "legitimate" by an investigation.

This coincidence of interests in peaceful coexistence shared by the

197

white "mafia" and the black "revolutionaries" and backed by the numerical superiority of the white prisoners as opposed to the solidarity of the black prisoners constituted the cornerstone of race relations among the inmates. Between black and white prisoners there was little sense of a cross-racial solidarity. Most day to day activities were characterized by a clear pattern of mutual avoidance and segregation, although biracial interaction occurred in focal activities such as drugs, sex, and meeting the public. The key to harmonious relations, however, was the arrangement by which the white and black leaders intervened to prevent individual encounters from developing into group violence.

Beginning in September 1971, the stability of this structure was threatened by a combination of exogenous and endogenous forces. By way of conclusion, I will analyze how the structure of race relations was upset and the actions by which stability was restored. In the analysis I will draw upon many of the conditions discussed in previous chapters. Finally, I will present what I consider to be some major implications of the present research for further research concerned with race relations in correctional institutions.

The Aftermath of Attica

Late in the evening of November 18, 1971, eleven prisoners were transferred from ECI to various federal and state prisons across the country. Without prior notice, they were taken from their cells, stripped to their underwear, handcuffed and shackled, placed in state police cars, and driven immediately to their destinations. Five of those transferred were black; six were white. The blacks transferred included the President and Vice President of the Afro-American Society, the Executive Advisor to the President, and one of the directors of the organization. The whites transferred were an assortment of types having only one characteristic in common—they were all regarded as troublemakers by the prison administration. Only two, however, could be regarded as leaders. These two previously had been transferred to a nearby state following a disturbance at ECI in January,[2] only to be returned after a disturbance at the institution to which they had been transferred. From the time of their return until the time of their transfer, they had been confined in segregation.

At a news conference one week after the transfers, the Governor of the state explained that the action had been taken to avert a planned insurrection. As outlined by the Governor, prison officials had learned from diverse sources that the Afro-American Society was planning to present a list of "impossible" and "unreasonable" demands to the prison authorities. When the demands were not met, they planned to take hostages and to negotiate the demands under the threat of physical harm or death to the hostages. At the same time, certain white prisoners planned to use the disorder to make an escape. Whether or not the plans to riot and the plans to escape were the product of biracial coordination was never made clear, but the implication was that they were.

Subsequent to their transfer, the transferees filed a civil action suit against the state in the United States District Court. In its decision, delivered some fourteen months after the transfers, the court ordered the return of the transferees to ECI. This decision was founded largely on the opinion that the way the transfers had been effected violated the prisoners' rights to due process and equal protection. The decision of the court, however, did not affirm that the administrative decision to transfer the prisoners was arbitrary and capricious, because in the court's opinion prison officials did believe that a conspiracy existed. And, while noting that the decision to transfer was not rooted in reliable evidence, the opinion held that it was not the province of the court to make a finding concerning the actual presence or absence of a conspiracy to riot.

This incident, involving as it did administrative action in the face of an alleged biracial conspiracy to riot and escape, provides a concise illustration of the dynamics of race relations in the prison. Drawing upon my presence and observations in the prison at the time, subsequent interviews with key informants, and testimony given in the civil action suit, I will attempt in this chapter to reconstruct the events leading to the transfer, and to present an interpretation of the incident. I will attempt to show that a combination of internal changes at ECI and external forces in the form of disturbances at other prisons shattered the structure of race relations described in the preceding chapters, and that the transfer was an adjustive reaction by which the prison administration sought to restore the former equilibrium. However, a note of caution must be introduced. An incident of this nature involves a tangle of vested interests that color perception, recall, and testimony. These facts render a definitive analysis of this event extremely difficult. Bearing this caution in mind, then, the following reconstruction and interpretation can be regarded as no more than plausible.

The Blacks

The killing of George Jackson at San Quentin in August 1971 was widely interpreted by black prisoners as the assassination of a revolutionary hero by white racists. One month later, the bloodletting at Attica lent further credence to the beliefs of many young blacks, and black prisoners in particular, that white authorities harbor designs of genocide. At ECI, the impact of these external events was exacerbated by changes that had

Table 9-1
Chronology of Events at ECI, August-November, 1971

August 3	Election of new leadership in Afro-American Society.
August 3-31	Disintegration of Afro-American Society.
September 1	Beginning of attempts by new black leaders to protect their position and regain solidarity by aggression against the staff.
September 8	Biracial disturbance in print shop; formation of a new Inmate Council.
September 8-30	"Mafia" attempt to draw closer to black leaders and at same time to convince administration to return two white "wise guys" "to take care of the race problem."
October 5	Discovery of a homemade bomb in cell of black inmate.
October 13	Retirement of several senior officers.
October 28	Discovery of sawed bars in North State Wing.
October 30	Blacks force guard captain to discard two disciplinary reports.
October 31	Work stoppage by officers' union.
November 1	Meeting at which black and white leaders turn against each other.
November 5	Deputy and Assistant Wardens inform Director of Corrections of plans to riot and escape.
November 8	Black leaders present racial grievances to Warden.
November 15	Warden first informed of planned riot.
November 18	Transfer of 11 prisoners to other institutions.

occurred within the Afro-American Society. In June 1971, the founder and then President of the Afro-American Society was released from prison and succeeded in office by the Vice-President. Both of these prisoners were "revolutionaries," but whereas the founder had been a highly respected prisoner with a large measure of charisma, his successor was not.

The new President was a Muslim from outside the state and had little if any relationship to the network of partnership alliances that cemented black solidarity. During his brief tenure, the dissensus between "revolutionaries" and "half-steppers" over such issues as drug use and homosexuality became open and intense. At a special election early in August, the new President and other "revolutionaries" were voted out of office and replaced by "half-steppers," the new President being a well-known pimp and drug dealer previously excluded from membership. For the next month, the "revolutionaries" remained as marginal members of the organization with little influence over its members.

As was noted in Chapter 5, the new President presented the membership with a new definition of the situation. By defining prison as an exceptional situation, by dissociating prison behavior from "street" behavior, and by defining a "revolutionary" as one who could be counted upon in a crisis, the new President legitimized drug use, homosexuality, and immersion in the underlife of the institution. As a result of these new definitions, drug use appeared to increase dramatically and the organization quickly began to show signs of disintegration as the educational and political programs established by the "revolutionaries" were neglected and ceased to function.

The killing of George Jackson and the events at Attica, however, presented the new leaders with a crisis of legitimacy. After the killing of Jackson, the remaining "revolutionaries" seized the occasion to point out in private conversations with other members the widening gap between the members' professed identities as black "revolutionaries" and their actual prison behavior. The "revolutionaries" argued for a change of leadership and a redirection of the organization to its original purposes. At a meeting on September 1, 1971 the President attempted to meet this crisis:

Now is there anybody here that wants to quit? [No answer.] I been hearing about brothers runnin' around in corners grumblin' 'bout the organization, sayin' I ain't runnin' it right. Anybody got anythin' to say 'bout that? [No response.] There anybody here thinks he can do a better job than me? [Silence.] Okay, then, everythin's cool. I don't wanna hear no more of this talk. I know things been fallin' apart in here and I mean to tighten 'em up startin' right now.

The fact that conflict with an out-group may serve to increase in-group solidarity and result in a centralization of group leadership has been recognized by theorists as diverse as Spencer, Simmel, and Weber.[3] It was precisely this tactic that the leaders of the Afro-American Society adopted in an effort to protect their position and regain group solidarity. The distinction between "legitimate" and "illegitimate" grievances was abandoned as the new leaders adopted a more aggressive posture with respect to the custodians. This new posture became clear just one week after the above statements. According to informants, rumors spread that a newly arrived and unknown white inmate had been placed in segregation and beaten severely by two officers. Several white leaders approached the blacks to arrange a meeting with the Warden, and the suggestion was made that the meeting be backed by a show of force. Rather than conduct their own investigation to determine the legitimacy of the grievance before consenting to a confrontation, as had been the practice in the past, the new black leaders consented to the demonstration.

At workcall on September 8, approximately 100 prisoners, with blacks and whites in almost equal numbers, barricaded themselves in the print shop and demanded a meeting with the Warden. While the prisoners continued to occupy the shop, the Warden met with five white and five black representatives. He promised to conduct his own personal investigation of the incident and to suspend any correctional officers suspected of brutality. He maintained, however, that the prisoner in question had not been beaten. To prove his point, he took one black and one white representative to the isolation cell where the prisoner substantiated the Warden's contentions. When the representatives returned to the shop with this information, the demonstration ended quietly.

Evidence of the increasing aggressiveness of the black prisoners in September and October is found in the disciplinary reports for those months. In September the number of reported infractions involving blacks (16) was double the number reported in July (7); the number reported in October (23) was triple the number reported in July. Three incidents, however, were of particular significance during this period. During the first week of October, a homemade bomb was discovered during the search of a black inmate's cell. Apparently, the organization took no action in support of this individual perhaps because he had been suspended from the organization for a similar offense several months previously. Nonetheless, coming in the wake of Attica the discovery of this bomb started rumors among the staff of a planned uprising by the blacks. As the Warden later recalled in court, the news of the discovery "went around the prison like wildfire, and there were a lot of rumors, tensions, that we were going to be blown up, you know, the revolution is coming."

Then, on October 30, an incident occurred that brought nearly the entire membership of the Afro-American Society into a direct confrontation with the staff. The President of the organization and another leader were observed assaulting a third black prisoner in the yard. On being approached by two officers, they ran but were discovered later in the chapel. The captain informed them that they were being reported for assault and ordered them to return to their cells. They refused and he reported them for disobeying an order. Still, they refused to return to their cells voluntarily. The captain might have used force to place them in their cells, but the wing was filled with inmates returning from an afternoon movie. He decided to leave them out of their cells for dinner and to lock them in after the early evening count. After the evening meal, however, the captain received a call from the wing. The black inmates refused to enter their cells for the count. Entering the wing, the captain was confronted by 30 to 35 black prisoners and backed into a corner. They demanded that the disciplinary reports be discarded and that both leaders be allowed out of their cells. Cornered, and with only a skeleton crew on duty, he assented to these demands.

The third incident occurred in the week following October 30. In a private meeting with the Warden, the leaders of the Afro-American Society presented him with a list of grievances entitled "Grievances Requiring Administrative Redress." The grievances included eleven items: (1) assignment of black inmates to better jobs, (2) black representation on the Classification and Disciplinary Boards, (3) the elevation of a black correctional officer to the rank of lieutenant, (4) support by the Warden for the legislative bill sponsored by the Afro-American Society to create three high-ranking positions for blacks in the Department of Corrections, (5) incorporation of a soul food and pork-free diet in the prison menu, (6) suspension of guards who are "exposed as overt or subtle racists," (7) extension of the same respect and courtesy to black visitors as is shown to white visitors, (8) encouragement of the prison staff to cooperate with the Afro-American Society's programs, (9) collective investigation by the administration and black representatives of "crisis problems" involving black inmates, (10) the hiring of a part-time black physician, and (11) extension of unrestricted telephone access to one Director of the Afro-American Society to allow him to conduct organizational business with the community.

After listening to these grievances, the Warden promised to consider them and to pursue an investigation of some of the specific complaints upon which they were based. A meeting to discuss the grievances further was set for the next week, but never occurred because other events intervened. As will be made clear below, the presentation of these grievances occurred in a tension-ridden atmosphere. Despite this fact and his promises to investigate the grievances, however, the Warden failed to communicate the substance of the meeting to either his superior or his subordinates. It was not until November 25, after the transfers had been made, that this meeting and the substance of the demands were made known to others by the Warden. On that date, he made the following public statement:

At no time did I feel this was an ultimatum or a face down situation. I don't think they meant it that way either. I think they wanted me to hear them out.

In sum, internal leadership changes within the Afro-American Society combined with the impact of the killing of George Jackson and the Attica massacre impelled the black prisoners to adopt a more aggressive posture toward the white staff. At first this aggression took the form of biracial cooperation in action on grievances in which black prisoners had no immediate interest; this was followed by increasing confrontations with the staff over disciplinary procedures; and finally the black leaders presented the Warden with a list of specifically racial grievances to which they demanded administrative redress. Along with this increased aggression on the part of the blacks came changes in the tactics of white leaders, and it is to these changes that I turn now.

The Cons

As noted in the previous chapter, the interests of the white "mafia" and the black "revolutionaries" had been comparable: both groups sought to avoid open conflict either among themselves or with the staff, and they had developed a relatively successful means of resolving incipient conflicts. With the ascent of the "half-steppers" to leadership in the Afro-American Society and their need to protect their leadership position within the organization by aggressive action against the staff, however, the interests of the white and black leadership became increasingly incompatible, and eventually the means of conflict resolution was dissolved. This did not happen, however, until after the "mafia" had made several attempts to maintain the status quo.

Between September and November, the "mafia" attempted in various ways to counter the threat posed to their position and interests by black aggression. As early as September, black informants I was interviewing were remarking that their relationship with the "mafia" was undergoing changes. Where previously their contact had been limited largely to resolving conflicts, in September the "mafia" began to draw closer to the blacks. They began to supply the leaders of the Afro-American Society with such amenities as steak sandwiches and pizza from outside the prison, favors that they alone were able to secure through the guards. On several occasions, they or their close associates provided blacks with free marijuana and heroin. On yet another occasion, the "mafia" offered to provide the funds for a popular black prisoner to retain a private counsel to represent him in appealing his conviction. While such overtures of friendship were not comprehensible to the blacks at the time, in retrospect they appear to have been attempts by the "mafia" to gain some influence over the black leadership and thereby neutralize the threat they posed.

Simultaneous with these overtures, the "mafia" were apparently seeking to use their influence with the staff for the same end. In separate interviews during October the Warden, a senior captain, and the President of the officers' union told me they each had been approached by the "mafia" with a request concerning two "wise guys" in segregation. These were two of the four inmates who had been transferred from ECI in January and subsequently returned. The request that each of the above received was to return these two individuals to the prison population "so we can take care of the race problem." Evidently, the "mafia" believed that the return of these two would provide them with the physical power necessary to control the blacks by coercion. Their request was not granted, however.

Still a third tactic apparently employed by the "mafia" to restrain the blacks was the establishment of a formal Inmate Advisory Council to the Warden. The formation of this council occurred quite unexpectedly during the previously mentioned biracial disturbance of September 8 to protest the alleged mistreatment of a white inmate. During the meeting with the Warden one white representative, a "wise guy," used this confrontation to propose the formation of an elected council with equal representation of black and white prisoners. Faced with 100 prisoners barricaded in the print shop and ready to riot, the Warden reluctantly agreed to this proposal and directed the representatives to form a steering committee and develop a statement of purpose and a proposal for an election.

This steering committee was established in the week following the confrontation. It was chaired by the Secretary of the Afro-American Society and a ranking member of the white "wise guys." The other members were five black leaders appointed by the Afro-American Society and five whites, "wise guys" who were self-selected and not previously involved with the inmate organization. In subsequent meetings with the staff, the committee announced the purposes of the council to be the peaceful resolution of grievances with the staff. No election of a permanent council was ever held, however. Rather, in the next two months the steering committee began to function as a council. To articulate grievances they formed several subcommittees, each of which was to investigate a different aspect of the prison's operation and prepare a report on grievances requiring redress. The various reports were to be assembled as a document and presented to the Warden for negotiation.

The formation of the new council represented a change in the relative prominence of white inmate leaders, specifically the displacement of the white "politicians." Prior to the formation of this council, the Warden had viewed the "politicians" and black leaders as an informal council, and as previously noted the "politicians" had had the support of the "mafia" to prevent encroachments upon their position by the "wise guys." Now, in September, the "politicians" were replaced as informal advisors to the Warden by a self-appointed group of "wise guys," and while opposed to the new council, the "politicians" withdrew from their position without any apparent conflict. It is unlikely that this change could have occurred without the intercession of the "mafia" in support of the new council. Did the "mafia" initiate this coup? This question cannot be answered, but probably they did not. A more plausible explanation would seem to be that the "wise guys" saw in the confrontation of September 8 a chance to usurp the position of the "politicians" thereby increasing their own influence and privileges within the institution. Faced with a *fait accompli,* the "mafia" may then have supported the new council in the belief that the physical power represented by the "wise guys" on the council would be a more effective resource than the verbal abilities of the "politicians" in restraining the aggressive activities of the blacks. Some limited evidence for this interpretation may be found in the fact that within a month after the formation of the council the black representatives were expressing frustration at the unwillingness of the white representatives to make any decision or take any action without first consulting the "mafia."

The increase in black aggression against the staff in September and October, then, appears to have precipitated several changes in both the structure and tactics of the white prisoner leadership, changes undertaken in an effort to preserve the stability of the structure of race relations. None of these changes, however, proved to be effective. The prison administration refused to return the two powerful white leaders to the population, and the incident of October 30, when the black prisoners refused to enter their cells, demonstrated the inability of either closer ties by the "mafia" or the new council to restrain black aggression. When the guard captain entered the wing on October 30, he found the black and white co-chairmen of the council attempting to persuade the black prisoners to enter their cells and to allow the council to negotiate with the custodians concerning the disciplinary action to be taken against the President of the Afro-American Society and the other black inmate. Rather than heed these requests, as we have seen, the black prisoners cornered the captain and forced him to agree that no action would be taken against these two black leaders. It thus became apparent to both the custodians and the white prisoner leaders that the council was an ineffective instrument to contain racial conflict.

As perhaps the white leaders feared, the actions of the blacks on October 30 precipitated a sharp reaction from the custodians. On Sunday, October 31, the officers refused to report for work. While the inmates remained locked in their cells, the guards gathered on the grounds outside the walls and demanded a meeting with the Warden. When the Warden arrived, the officers presented him with a list of demands. These included the following: (1) that 25 to 30 new officers be hired, (2) that a committee of officers be appointed to draft a set of custodial rules and regulations, and (3) that prisoners remain locked in their cells until the demands were met and order was restored. Except for the hiring of new officers, a matter over which he had no control, the Warden agreed to the demands and to meet with representatives of the Officers' Union on the next day to discuss the problems further.

On Monday, with the prisoners still in their cells, the Warden held several meetings: with his superiors, with the superior officers, and with representatives of the union. Late in the day, a meeting was scheduled with the superior officers, union representatives, and inmate leaders to air grievances and to inform the prisoners of the agreements with the union. Having been locked in their cells for nearly 48 hours, the inmate representatives entered the meeting in an angry mood.[a] Initially, their anger was directed at the union representatives, but as the Warden steered the discussion to the causes of the strike, the anger of the whites was deflected onto

---

[a] I was not at this meeting, as the Warden believed that my presence might prove disruptive. However, I was in adjoining room working on inmate records and able to overhear a good portion of the discussion, and later to reconstruct the discussion through interviews with the Warden and two prisoners.

the blacks. One white, the Co-chairman of the Inmate Council, accused the President of the Afro-American Society (who was not present) of not being a "man" because he had not taken the consequences of his action and thus had brought "heat" on everybody because of a personal "beef."

The blacks, who had been quiet to this point in the meeting, responded to these accusations with what was apparently the real reason for their refusal to enter their cells on October 30. A long-standing grievance of the blacks, as we noted in Chapter 6, was the relative immunity from punishment of certain white leaders. They had never before voiced their anger at this subtle form of discrimination. To do so would violate the norms proscribing "ratting" and those enjoining inmates to "do your own time" and "mind your own business." In their eyes, however, the accusations against the President of their organization absolved them from adherence to the code in this situation. Without naming specific individuals, they recounted an incident that had occurred two weeks earlier. According to them, two superior officers had turned their backs while several white leaders assaulted an inmate who had been a police informer in the case against one of them. The incident of October 30, they argued, was similar. Thus, either the white leaders should be punished or the black leaders not punished.

As a result of the meeting, the Warden was confronted with another serious problem that could further endanger the stability of the institution. To take action on the accusations of the blacks would place him in conflict with the correctional officers and white inmate leaders and would probably upset the arrangements by which the officers and the "mafia" averted crisis situations. Moreover, the flagrant violation of prison etiquette by the black leaders effectively ended cooperative relations between black and white prisoner leaders. From the time of this meeting until the transfers of November 18, the Inmate Council did not meet, and after being released from their cells, black and white leaders avoided each other completely. Thus, by November 1, the informal means of conflict resolution that had maintained racial harmony for the preceding eighteen months was shattered. It was in the midst of this tension that the black leaders prepared their list of grievances and presented them to the Warden. These grievances, particularly the items concerning the suspension of guards found to be "subtle racists" and the collective investigation with black representation of "crisis problems" involving black prisoners, were outgrowths of the conflict over the incident of October 30 and were symbolic of the racial polarization that had developed over the preceding months.

The Custodians

The mood of the custodians in the fall of 1971 can best be described as panic stricken. For several years the officers had been living in the belief that they no longer retained effective control over the institution. Now the uprising at Attica and the mounting aggressiveness of the black prisoners within their own institution placed them in fear for their lives. Just before the incident of October 30, two incidents compounded their fear. First, as a result of a new pension plan, all officers over 55 years of age and with 20 or more years of service had to be retired immediately. This action resulted in the loss of eight officers, four of them being senior captains and lieutenants, and in their replacement by young and relatively inexperienced men. Personnel turnover thus further weakened the capacities of the custodians to confront the crisis. Second, on October 28, a guard discovered that the bars on a window in North State wing had been sawed. This discovery sparked a rumor that many of the long-time inmates housed in that wing, most of whom are white, had been planning a mass escape on that evening. Coming two days after this discovery, the incident of October 30, where a guard captain was forced to accede to the demands of the black prisoners, created among the officers a dire fear for their own personal security as well as the security of the institution. The President of the officers' union described the mood of the custodians at the time:

You know how a forest fire will burn down into the roots of trees and spread underground? That's the way it was. It was gettin' outta hand. Even inmates who are quiet and don't give you any trouble were acting cocky and not following orders. The personnel were vulnerable. The structure of the institution was vulnerable. Somethin' hadda be done.

As we have seen, in an effort to do something about the situation, the union President organized a work stoppage to demand more officers and more stringent custodial regulations and forced inmates to remain locked in their cells for several days. However, the ensuing meeting with the Warden and inmate leaders resulted in an impasse, the officers being accused by black inmates of ignoring existing regulations in the cases of select white inmates. Following this meeting of November 1, the initiative passed out of the hands of the inmates, the officers, and the Warden and into the hands of the Director of Corrections.

It will be recalled from Chapter 3 that the Warden was isolated and his power to a large extent neutralized by the informal relationships existing between the Director of Corrections and the Assistant and Deputy Warden. By this time, some eighteen months after his appointment, the Warden was in fact completely removed from the channels of communication between his superiors and subordinates. By November 5, these channels were flooded with information about a planned disturbance. On that date the Deputy and Assistant Wardens first communicated to the Director of Corrections that two reliable informants had advised them that a disturbance was being planned. Over the next week, additional information was gathered and these three individuals met several times to evaluate the data. As constructed from these data, the plot involved the presentation of "impossible" and "unreasonable" demands by the Afro-American Society, an uprising when the demands were rejected, and an escape by a large group of white inmates. The later court testimony of these officials indicated that beyond this broad outline the investigation produced several versions of the plot differing in such details as the number of conspirators involved, the identity of several of them, whether or not hostages were to be taken, and when the disruption was to occur. Moreover, there apparently was no information concerning the substance of the demands to be made. Despite these ambiguities, the Director of Corrections testified that he made no attempt to learn the identity of the informants, the manner in which they had proved themselves to be reliable, or their means of access to the information. Nor did he consult with the Warden. Rather, the reality of a conspiracy was accepted, a list of probable conspirators was developed, and plans were laid for their transfer to other institutions.

By law, only the Warden has the authority to approve transfers from ECI. The Warden, however, was not informed of the alleged plot until November 15, ten days after the information was communicated to the Director of Corrections. Both in private conversations with me and in his later court testimony he indicated that he had serious doubts about the information and desired to conduct a more detailed investigation before taking any action. In meetings on November 15 and 16, however, he found it impossible to argue with his superiors, who were convinced of the reality of a conspiracy. As he later stated to me: "We were caught up in our own momentum. We had to do something." He thus acceded to the proposals for a transfer.

It is likely that the Warden did not argue strongly against the conspiracy theory. As evidence of this, there is his own testimony that during this time it never occurred to him that the impossible demands that were to touch off the disturbance may have been the very grievances already submitted to him. His meeting with the Afro-American leaders concerning their grievances did not become known to his superiors until after the transfers. Nor, apparently, did it occur to him that the rumor of an escape by the whites may have been related to the bar cutting of October 28. Subsequent investigation, however, revealed no evidence of other demands or any other reliable evidence of a planned escape. Moreover, like the Director of Corrections, the Warden apparently made no effort to learn the identity of the informants. At a court hearing nearly a year after the transfers, he admitted that he still did not know who the informants had been.

In fact, the Warden had much to gain by the transfers and much to lose by opposing them. The transfers offered a solution to many of the problems he was facing. First, they afforded a means of stemming the tide of black aggression that had been sweeping the institution since September. Second, they provided him with a means to avoid a confrontation with several senior officers and white inmate leaders over the issue of "subtle racism" in disciplinary measures. Third, in all likelihood the transfers would pacify the outraged officers demanding more stringent custodial regulations. On the one hand, the transfers afforded the Warden an opportunity to defuse an extremely tense situation. On the other hand, to oppose the transfers would in all probability have aggravated these tensions. The officers, if they learned of a suspected conspiracy and the failure to affect a transfer, would stage another strike to bring the matter to public attention. The inmates might also be incited to a disturbance. To oppose the transfers would place the responsibility for any future disturbances, be they spontaneous or the result of a conspiracy, on the shoulders of the Warden.

Thus, on November 17, the corrections officials outlined their information to the Governor and received his permission for the transfers. Arrangements were completed and the transfers made the following night.

Conclusion

Whether in fact there was a biracial conspiracy to riot and escape is a moot question. Granting this, however, the allegation of a biracial conspiracy does not appear plausible in light of the events at ECI in September and October 1971; nor is it plausible in light of the structure of race relations at the institution during the year prior to these events. Moreover, in the court hearings following the transfer, the prison authorities were unable to produce any tangible evidence of either a riot or a planned escape. The only tangible evidence of a conspiracy offered by the prison authorities was a display of contraband uncovered in a search of the prison after the transfers. Some of the more suggestive items included in this display were the following: a homemade bomb and diagrams for firearms found in the cell of a black inmate; a long rope found in the cell of a white inmate and a grappling hook found in the kitchen where he worked; a 12-volt battery and butane gas found in the cell of a black inmate; an assortment of knives and other weapons. Investigation of this display by the counsel for the transferees showed that the bomb was the one found one month prior to the transfers and that the diagrams for firearms had in fact been uncovered several months previously; that the rope in the display was not the one found in the prisoner's cell, the one found by the officer who searched the cell being a short jump rope given to the prisoner by the recreation officer; that the battery and gas had been authorized by the Deputy Warden himself and were used for a stereo reverberator and a cigarette lighter respectively; and that the assortment of weapons had in fact been found in various shakedowns of the prison over several months. In the opinion of the court, "the display offer(ed) precious little support to defendants. . . . there was, in general, nothing taken which would not have turned up in any search at any time."

The data presented above suggest a more plausible interpretation than a biracial conspiracy. A combination of events—the murder of George Jackson, Attica and leadership changes in the Afro-American Society —combined to precipitate a period of expressive protest on the part of the black inmates. By expressive protest I mean basically what Coser has termed "non-realistic conflict": conflicts which "are not occasioned by the rival ends of the antagonists, but by the need for tension release of at least one of them."[4] The events at San Quentin and Attica confirmed the beliefs of black prisoners that the white custodians harbored designs of genocide, and at the same time they threw into bold relief the contradiction between the "ideal selves" of the black prisoners and their actual prison behavior. This latter consequence was used by a few committed "revolutionaries" in an attempt to regain their positions of leadership. The ensuing black aggression against the white staff, then, initially served several ends: to vent frustrations, to affirm identity claims, and to protect the leadership positions of the "half-steppers." Within a short span of time, however, the protest took on an instrumental character, becoming oriented to the promotion of specific interests. Presumably, as aggressive action proved to be effective in numerous incidents such as that on October 30 the expectations of black prisoners with respect to achieving particular interests by force were raised, leading to an increased use of coercive resources.[5] The culmination of the transition from expressive to instrumental protest was reached in the submission to the Warden of eleven specific grievances requiring redress.

The expressive protest activity of the black prisoners quite obviously posed a threat to the interest of the white "mafia" in peaceful coexistence both with the staff and with the blacks. As we have seen, increasing aggressive activity by the blacks was accompanied by structural and tactical changes in the white leadership. These changes appear to have been attempts to contain black aggression by influence on the one hand and coercion on the other. Neither tactic succeeded presumably because the interests of the blacks, at first expressive and later instrumental, increasingly diverged from those of the whites. In the end, several of the grievances submitted to the Warden by the blacks were in direct opposition to those of those of the white leaders, arising from a long felt but unarticulated perception of racial discrimination by means of selective enforcement of rules by the custodians. Thus, the pursuit of particularistic instrumental interests by the blacks destroyed the preceding year's most effective means of resolving racial conflicts among inmates.

In his analysis of strikes and mutinies, Lammers notes that it is common for individuals at different levels of the hierarchy toward which the protest is directed to define the protest differently.[6] Specifically, he notes that commanding officers tend to share the views of the mutineers, to see protests as strikes to secure certain interests, while higher authorities incline to view all such protests as directed at the seizure of power and the implementation of radical changes. Such a process seems to have occurred at ECI. As we have seen, the Warden, when presented with the grievances of the black prisoners, did not consider them an ultimatum but rather as grievances to be negotiated. His failure to relay this information to his superior, however, paved the way for the Director of Corrections to define the apparently instrumental protest as a conspiracy to riot. Thus, rumors concerning demands to be made by black prisoners apparently emerged from the grievances presented to the Warden and were combined with other unrelated incidents such as the discovery of a bomb and of sawed window bars. The result was to cause the Director of Corrections to define the protest activity as a biracial conspiracy to riot and escape. While not in agreement with this definition of the situation, the Warden was not able to alter it due to his isolation in the chain of command, the demands of the custodians and the actual protests of the blacks. The Warden thus acquiesced to the transfer decision.

In sum, the precarious balance of power among the hacks, the blacks and the cons that constituted race relations at ECI in 1970-1971 was upset by a combination of external and internal events that provoked a marked increase in aggressive activity by the black prisoners. This aggression triggered counter-measures by both the white inmate leaders and the white staff to contain the threat. These measures proved ineffective, with the result that rumors of a biracial conspiracy to riot and escape were accepted uncritically by the authorities and five black leaders along with six miscellaneous white inmates were transferred to prisons across the country. In this manner the stability of the institution was restored, at least temporarily.

Some Implications For Further Research

The purpose of this research has been to explore. By probing deeply into the life within one prison, it has sought to describe and to analyze the structure of race relations as it existed in that prison at one point in time. At ECI during the period of study, the structure of race relations may be best represented as a system grounded in a delicate balance of power among the custodians, the black inmates, and the white inmates. As in the free community, this structure was the result of a complex interaction among a number of conditions on personal, social, and cultural levels. Among the more important of these conditions were the following: (1) humanitarian reforms of the prison social structure; (2) a policy of managed racial integration by the prison administration; (3) racial prejudice and black revolutionary ideology imported into the prison; (4) the size and relative solidarity of the groups in contact; and (5) interests shared by segments of the black and white inmate populations as a result of common deprivations.

No claim is made here that ECI is a typical or representative institution. Nonetheless, the data on race relations at ECI provide a basis for hypotheses to guide future comparative research. Hypotheses could be adduced concerning the operation of each of the above variables. In the following section, however, I shall concern myself with only one: the formal structure of correctional institutions. The formal structure of ECI was one of the major conditions impinging upon race relations and is thus of some theoretical importance in the explanation and understanding of race relations in prisons. Further, it is of considerable practical importance since, unlike many other factors, it is susceptible to directed change. Taking ECI as an example of a reform institution whose formal structure is a derivative of the dual goals of custody and rehabilitation, the question becomes what might be the nature of race relations in correctional institutions with differing organizational structures? Two ideal types present themselves as opposed possibilities. One is the purely custodial institution; the second is the purely treatment institution.

Race Relations in the Custodial Prison

The Custodial Prison. Nearly thirty years ago, Robin Williams noted that there exist three strategies to reduce intergroup conflict: (1) reduce the hostility underlying the conflict; (2) displace hostility onto substitute targets; and (3) repress the conflict by coercion.[7] The custodial prison attempts to implement the third possibility.

The custodial prison is rooted in a conception that convicted felons are inherently evil and dangerous.[8] The prison exists for two purposes: (1) to exact retribution, and (2) to protect society. These goals are most visibly symbolized in the physical structure of the institution. While there is considerable diversity in specific architectural details, custodial prisons in general resemble medieval fortresses. They are surrounded by high walls, on top of which are placed gun towers and powerful searchlights and beyond which are a secondary line of defense in the form of chain-link and barbed-wire fences. There is usually only one way in and out of the institution, and this is controlled by a series of electronically operated steel bar doors, as are all internal passage ways. Inmates are housed in small cells with barred doors operated by the custodial staff.

The formal organization is the prototype of Gouldner's "punishment-centered bureaucracy'' in that it is based upon the imposition of rules and upon obedience for its own sake.[9] Policies and rules designed to exact retribution and protect society are formulated by a centralized power and implemented through a bureaucratic chain of command whose primary function is to enforce the rules. Typically, these rules extend to the most minute details of inmate life. Compliance with rules is expected and not rewarded. Deviations are viewed as willful, malicious insubordination and punished swiftly and severely. The behavior of the custodians is likewise governed by detailed regulations enjoining them to remain distant, impersonal, authoritarian, and unchallengeable in their relations with prisoners. These latter rules exist to define the role relationship between custodians and prisoners so as to induce in the prisoners an awe and acceptance of the dominance of custodial power and thus to minimize the need to resort to actual physical coercion to secure compliance.

Upon entering the institution, prisoners are subjected to a ritualized series of debasements including a shaving of the head, the dispossession of all personal effects, and the assignment of a uniform and a number, which thereafter is the symbol of their identity in reference to the formal structure. Contact of inmates with the external world is sharply curtailed: visits are severely restricted and closely monitored; mail is closely censored; and access to the mass media is prohibited. In the extreme situation, such as the early Pennsylvania System, the isolation of the inmate was extended even to other inmates by means of continual solitary confinement. More commonly, however, prisoners perform exhausting physical labor during the day under the watchful eyes of the custodians who are responsible not only for the performance of the work but also perhaps for the enforcement of a ''silent system'' wherein prisoners are not permitted to communicate with each other. Movement from the cells to work and to eat are by means of regimented mass formations, and working and eating are followed by confinement to the cell.

Race Relations. Given conditions such as those described, the nature of race relations would be greatly affected by two variables: (1) the equality of repression, and (2) the proportion of the prisoner population which is black. At one extreme, where repression is egalitarian and there is a small proportion of black inmates, the social significance of racial differences may be minimized relative to distinctions between staff and inmates, and race relations may in effect be eliminated. In response to the severe deprivations and control to which prisoners are subject, there may emerge an encompassing inmate culture emphasizing solidary opposition to the staff and loyalty to other inmates. Given the existence of such a subculture, the detachment from external reference groups fostered by the formal organization may facilitate the internalization of standards by prisoners, which may in effect neutralize pre-existing attitudes of racial prejudice. Inmates of the other race may come to be seen as exceptions, as different from those of their race on the outside, and evaluated in terms of standards specific to the prison situation. Further, the dual conditions of a high degree of regimentation and extreme material deprivation may at once prevent extensive primary grouping, thereby impeding structural differentiation along racial lines, and force prisoners into functionally interdependent relations irrespective of race. To the extent that prejudice is so neutralized and cross-racial convict solidarity is developed, protracted opposition to the staff may minimize the significance of race along the vertical dimension as the custodians come to define themselves as a ruling class in opposition to a unified class of subordinates.

In fact, however, such an outcome appears unlikely. Under conditions in the custodial prison, the initiative lies more with the custodians than with the inmates. It is the custodians who regulate access to rewards, administer punishments, and thus determine the presence or absence of egalitarian repression. Egalitarian repression is then highly problematic. As at ECI, the guards in most prisons are overwhelmingly white, and we may assume that they carry with them into the prison the same racial prejudices as do the officers at ECI. Thus, the surveillance and controls to which black prisoners are subject may exceed those to which white prisoners are subject. Moreover, assuming that the mechanisms of control in the custodial prison are more effective in repressing confrontation tactics than are the controls at ECI, there may be considerable racial discrimination in the imposition of punishments. Discrimination may also exist in the area of rewards. As Sykes has shown [10] and I have noted on several occasions, even in the most custodial of prisons coercive powers fail to secure compliance to routine directives. What emerges in prisons are tacit alliances between staff and inmates in which officers may overlook violations of rules and actually provide inmates with illicit comforts and valuable information in return for their cooperation. As we have seen at ECI, black inmates did not have equal access to such rewards, and there is no reason to assume equal access in a highly custodial institution with a low proportion of black prisoners. Finally, a highly coercive prison is likely to increase solidarity among white prisoners and thus to neutralize the power advantage of a numerically smaller but more solidary black population. Given a high degree of repressive control by the custodians, black prisoners may in fact become scapegoats for aggression by white inmates. In an effort to buttress their position, the custodians may channel onto black prisoners aggressions of the white inmates that are instigated by the frustrations of prison life. For example, white prisoners may be permitted to aggrandize themselves at the expense of black prisoners, while similar responses by black prisoners may be severely punished. In brief, in a highly custodial prison where blacks are a distinct minority in the prison population, shared prejudices and tacit alliances between the custodians and white inmates are likely to establish and maintain a structure of race relations in which black inmates are a distinctly subordinate class and a target for displaced aggression by white prisoners. While in all likelihood there would be a high incidence of racial conflict among inmates under such conditions, overt conflict between staff and inmates would be minimized as white hostility is displaced onto black prisoners; and the repressive power of the custodians would inhibit hostile actions from the small proportion of blacks.

In custodial prisons where blacks constitute a large proportion of the prisoner population, particularly in prisons where they are a majority, somewhat different outcomes than those hypothesized above might be expected. As the proportion of black inmates increases, the isolation from the outside imposed by the prison and the regimentation imposed by the staff are likely to prove ineffective in preventing the identification of black prisoners with the black revolutionary movement. New arrivals into the prison may serve as links to the external world; besides, a large number of black prisoners would undoubtedly develop a network of communication among themselves even under the most adverse circumstances. Moreover, the combination of extreme repression and high isolation from the outside world may well encourage the circulation of rumors exaggerating the possibility of a black revolution and/or the degree of outside support that may be forthcoming in the event of a rebellion within the prison. Thus, a combination of large numbers, a high degree of solidarity resulting from an identification with a revolutionary movement, and rumors may increase among black prisoners expectations of success in overt conflict with the custodians. Under conditions of inegalitarian repression, black aggression is likely to be directed at white prisoners as well. But in a situation of egalitarian repression, a condition which may well be directly related to the proportion of black prisoners in the population, white prisoners may be politicized and included in the movement against the custodians. In any event, because the conditions of the custodial prison preclude inmate organization for the negotiation of grievances, the movement against the custodians is likely to involve violence to some degree.

Thus, despite the high degree of coercive power embedded in the custodial prison, a large proportion of black prisoners seems likely to result in protracted and occasionally violent racial conflict. Moreover, any concessions by the custodians may further increase expectations of success and, while temporarily alleviating the conflict, only lead to further confrontations in the future. The effort to maintain control in the purely custodial prison with a large black population may thus lead the institution into a spiral of increasingly repressive measures such as the "maxi-maxi-security" prisons proposed in New York as the result of Attica.

Race Relations in the Therapeutic Community

From the perspective of race relations, the custodial prison may be viewed as an attempt to reduce racial conflict by repression. In contrast, the therapeutic community may be seen as an attempt to reduce racial conflict by reducing prejudice and hostility. There is abundant evidence to show that prejudice and hostility can be reduced by bringing members of antagonistic groups into contact under certain conditions. For example, after systematically generating conflict and hostility between groups of adolescent boys, Sherif was able to induce intergroup cooperation by introducing "superordinate" goals that were compelling to members of both groups but beyond the capacity of one group alone to attain.[11] Similarly, research in natural settings indicates that racial prejudice may be reduced even among highly prejudiced people as a result of contacts between status equals that occur in non-threatening social settings in which significant others are perceived as approving the contact and when the contact is of sufficient duration and intimacy to challenge existing stereotypes.[12] The therapeutic community is a setting within which all of these conditions may be realized.

The Therapeutic Community. Therapeutic communities are predicated upon the postulate that the most effective therapy for the offender is one in which the institutional setting is an experiment in social living, so that by learning to adjust to life within the institution, the offender at the same time learns the necessary values, attitudes, and skills to lead a law-abiding life in free society. Within a therapeutic community, all aspects of the institution are coordinated to the single goal of rehabilitation.[13]

Like prisons, therapeutic communities differ greatly in physical arrangements. Some are small units within larger custodial structures. Others are small, single units, often former residences. However, the full implementation of the concept, of which there are a few examples, involves the establishment of an actual community composed of perhaps 200 residents and a sizeable complement of staff. In keeping with the concept of community, the physical arrangement de-emphasizes custody. There are no walls or bars, although a fence may surround the facility at a considerable distance from its center. The community center is likely to be modeled after a town square—with adimistrative offices, a school, a vocational training facility, a chapel, a recreation building, and perhaps quarters for visitors. Arranged around the square in a manner to simulate neighborhoods are the cottages for residents. Each cottage is likely to house some 15 to 20 residents in private rooms and to contain a kitchen and dining area.

In comparison to prisons, therapeutic communities are non-bureaucratic. There is a minimum of clearly defined rules, and decision-making is decentralized to facilitate the goal of individualized treatment.

The staff are either trained professionals or lay personnel who receive extensive and continuous training in treatment skills, and both groups are expected to be guided by standards of professional expertise in the performance of their functions. Open communication among staff members is encouraged at frequent staff meetings whose aims are to arrive at consensual decisions on therapeutic and administrative matters and to scrutinize role relationships among the staff and between staff and clients. In their relations with clients, the staff is expected to minimize status distinctions, to encourage open and spontaneous communication, and to develop close, personal relations in an effort to gain client cooperation and identification with the staff and the goals of the institution. Through their relations with clients, staff gather material on behavior and attitudes that is discussed at staff meetings and provides the data upon which decisions regarding therapy are made. Misconduct by clients is interpreted as symptomatic of an underlying problem, and any punishment is consistent with therapeutic recommendations. Punishment is thus minimized and highly individualized.

The client is expected to develop a life as similar as possible to life in the free community through involvement in the work, educational, religious, and recreational programs provided. Consistent with this orientation to life after release, clients are encouraged to maintain contact with the external world through the mass media and through extensive visits and mail from family and friends. At the same time, clients are encouraged to develop close peer group relations. At the heart of the program is the residential unit, which is also the primary treatment unit. Relations within residential units are expected to resemble family relations. Group therapy sessions are conducted within the residential unit, perhaps on a daily basis. Further, each cottage is largely a self-governing unit, and administrative and maintenance problems are resolved by means of group decisions.

Race Relations. Within the therapeutic community, racial conflict and prejudice may be reduced as a by-product of the rehabilitative process. A policy of managed integration in which black and white clients are assigned to residential units in numbers equal to their proportion of the total population would maximize opportunities for intimate equal status contact, presumably of sufficient duration to challenge stereotypes. The problems involved in the governance and maintenance of the residential units would introduce superordinate goals into the relationship. Frequent interracial group therapy sessions may be used to promote interracial understanding through examination of the bases of racial antagonisms and by making clear common values, beliefs, and interests. Other aspects of the institutional program may also be used to the same end. For example, competitive sports between residential units may strengthen allegiances to cottage members regardless of race. And the educational program may include material and group discussions on the problems of race relations in this country, the contributions of black Americans, and the history of Africa. In short, given the rather pleasant, non-oppressive amd non-threatening environment embodied in the concept of a therapeutic community, a policy of managed integration may succeed in the establishment of what I have referred to previously as interracial cohesion, i.e., primary groups in which race ceases to function as a barrier to spontaneous interaction.

Interracial cohesion does not, however, appear to be the inevitable result of interracial contact within a therapeutic community. Other factors associated with the structure of such institutions have the potential for exacerbating racial prejudice and conflict. Despite the attempt of the staff to minimize status distinctions between themselves and the clients, it is unlikely that they will be perceived as status equals by clients. A large portion of the interracial contact within the institution will be contact between individuals of unequal status. In the case of black staff and white clients, this may not prove to be a problem as available evidence indicates that prejudice among whites is reduced by contact with blacks of higher status as well as with blacks of equal status.[14] Data from a recent study, however, suggest that even within equal status contact situations, blacks frequently perceive whites as paternalistic, and when this occurs the contacts may not decrease prejudice.[15] On the basis of this finding, it would seem possible that attempts by white staff members to establish close relationships with black clients may only result in a definition of the white staff as paternalistic and increase prejudice among black clients.

Another factor with the potential to inadvertently increase racial antagonism is the leadership structure of the institution. The non-bureaucratic nature of the therapeutic community of necessity increases its reliance on personalized, perhaps charismatic leadership, both among the staff and the clients. Personnel turnover at both levels, then, is likely to prove a critical problem for the institution. As leaders leave, one possible result is a disintegration of established group relationships and a concomitant increase in conflict among individuals. Given the salience of race as a symbol of group identity, any institutional crisis of this sort may eventually result in realignment of the institution's personnel, both staff and clients, into mutually antagonistic racial groups.

Yet another problem derives from the ideology of the institution as reflected in its openness to the outside and the freedom granted to clients. A quite probable result is a request from the black clients to form a black cultural association. One would think that such a request could not be denied without running counter to the ideology of the therapeutic community and also precipitating racial conflict. But although such an association may prove to be a valuable resource in the rehabilitation of black inmates, it may also counter efforts to encourage equal status contact. The activities of a black cultural association may easily become so engrossing for black clients as to confine interracial contacts to the residential units, perhaps even encouraging patterns of racial avoidance within them. Further, as has happened on many college campuses, the formation of a black cultural association may be followed by requests or demands for racially segregated residential units. To deny such a request would inevitably increase black hostility toward the institution and its staff and thus frustrate the strategy of gaining client cooperation and identification with the goals of the institution; to grant it, however, may well negate opportunities for equal status contact among the clients and in fact increase racial hostilities as a result of competition between residential units.

Thus, the character of race relations within therapeutic communities is a clouded question. On the one hand, many features of life within such a setting are conducive to the development of interracial cohesion and a concomitant reduction in prejudice. On the other hand, other features have equal potential to intensify racial conflict and hostility. In the final amalysis, it may be that to the extent they succeed in replicating life within free communities, therapeutic communities also replicate the patterns of race relations found in those communities—that institutional race relations are nothing more or less than particular manifestations of race relations in the surrounding society.

Concluding Remarks

Because an increasingly larger proportion of those confined in our correctional institutions are black, research into the conditions affecting race relations in these institutions is essential. The above remarks were intended as tentative hypotheses for such research. In no way were they intended to be guidelines for practical decision-making. However, administrative decisions cannot always wait for an adequate basis in research, and this fact requires a few remarks concerning the problem of race relations as it relates to correctional policies.

Both custodial and reform prisons such as ECI seem destined to intensify racial hostilities and to be rocked by periodic outbursts of racial violence. Attempts to repress such conflict and violence could eventually transform prisons into institutions bearing a strong resemblance to the Nazi concentration camps. The other alternative is to attempt to fully institutionalize the goal of rehabilitation in the form of therapeutic communities. Such institutions, as has been pointed out, are not entirely free from conditions that may inflame racial antagonisms, but it would seem that many of these conditions, such as separatist demands, are a concomitant of the size of the institution. Small therapeutic centers, containing fifteen to twenty clients, may thus prove to be both an effective means of rehabilitating offenders and reducing racial conflict and hostility.

The transition from prisons to therapeutic communities, even given community acceptance, is likely to prove precarious, however. By definition, therapeutic communities lack strong external controls and are highly dependent upon a skilled staff able to gain the trust and cooperation of clients. To transfer inmates directly from a prison to therapeutic communities is to run a high risk that aggression built up as a result of incarceration will be vented in the absence of coercive controls. To transfer correctional staff members from prison to therapeutic communities without an extensive period of retraining may well produce acute role conflict. In short, efforts to move directly from prisons to therapeutic communities run a high risk of precipitating a period of collective disturbances sufficient to alienate the outside community. A more gradual strategy is likely to prove more successful. Initially, several small therapeutic communities, staffed by professionals and drawing their clients from new commitments by the courts, could be established. Concurrently, as fewer offenders are sent to the prison, correctional staff members released from duties in the prison might be trained at the existing treatment centers and then used in new centers. In this way, the population in prisons would be decreased over several years, staff members retrained, and the number of small therapeutic communities increased.

EPILOGUE, 1988

Race Relations in the Prison: Fifteen Years of Research

Looking back nearly 15 years since its first publication, I am proud of the contribution *Hacks, Blacks and Cons* has made to our knowledge of prison life and of the place it has come to occupy in a tradition of research spanning half a century. The book, along with several others published about the same time, focussed on facets of the prison which had been neglected. In doing so, these works revised then dominant conceptions of the prison as a total institution and opened new areas of inquiry. In this epilogue, I assess how the observations I made in Rhode Island in the early 1970s have stood the test of this subsequent research.

The Hacks

Writing in 1975, David Fogel observed that while "academicians for the last generation have been fascinated with the discovery of inmate types, cultures and, more recently, inmate political groups...precious little is known about the guard..." (p. 70). Despite having been a correctional officer, I was conditioned to overlook those whom Gordon Hawkins (1976:105) rightly characterizes as "the key figure(s) in the penal equation." The depth of this blindness is seen in the early proposals for study wherein I conceptualized the custodians, not as people, but as features of the environment to which the prisoners have to adapt!

That I corrected my original conceptions had less to do with my prior experience or with my sensitivities as an observer than it did to the obvious troubles in the ranks at the time. The adoption of rehabilitation as a major goal of prisons with the expectation that guards would be active agents in that process, the softening of the custodial regimen, the recognition that prisoners retained constitutionally guaranteed rights that the federal courts must protect, along with the centralization and bureaucratization of corrections reduced the status of the officers, made their role more ambiguous and uncertain, their person less safe and thereby created an alienated, anomic and angry custodial force which refused to be ignored.

Virtually the same process of deterioration which I witnessed in Rhode Island was observed at about the same time by James Jacobs (1977) at Stateville in Illinois. Lucien Lombardo (1981:140) described the typical officer at New York's Auburn prison in the mid-1970s as a "classic example of the alienated worker," and, in a survey of officers in a mid-western state, Poole and Regoli (1981) found their respondents scored high on scales measuring all five senses of alienation: powerlessness, meaninglessness, normlessness, isolation and self-estrangement.

It is scarcely surprising then that Cheek and Miller (1983) report that rates of stress-related illnesses such as hypertension, ulcers and heart disease were higher among a sample of New Jersey correctional officers than those found for a national sample of police officers. And the major cause of job-related stress, they found, is not the danger posed by inmates but the "double bind" created by the lack of clear guidelines for job performance, the lack of communication with management, inoperable rules developed by persons far removed from the work setting, and the lack of recognition given to the fact that officers are also managers (Cheek and Miller, 1983; Whitehead and Lindquist, 1986).

Experienced officers in many states are now able to decrease their felt stress by taking advantage of recently negotiated contracts which contain provisions requiring that posts be assigned to the most senior officer bidding for it (Wynne, 1978:169-176). Increasingly, the most experienced officers retreat from responsibility by bidding into posts such as the wall towers or perimeter security, assignments formerly considered undesirable but which have the advantage of minimizing contact with inmates. This leaves the most sensitive positions to younger officers. Lacking the "personalized authority" (Lombardo, 1981:74-77) by which experienced officers are able to manage prisoners, many of these younger officers seek only to minimize their troubles by courting acceptance with the inmates while others, probably the majority, become repressive, operating strictly by the book (Jacobs and Retsky, 1975:22-24; Poole and Regoli, 1980a). The first tactic further contributes to the deterioration of relationships within the custodial hierarchy by fostering mistrust; the second creates a more volatile situation by escalating possibly minor incidents into major confrontations. Together they contribute to the exceptionally high annual turnover among correctional officers, which in some institutions averages nearly 40 percent per year (Corrections Compendium 1983), further undermining the stability and security of the institution.

Under the pressure of affirmative action and in the belief that minority officers would help ease racial tensions in the prison, administrators began active programs to recruit black and Hispanic officers in the early seventies. Far from easing racial tension, however, the infusion of minorities appears to have introduced it into the custodial force. Skin color and language are not the only ways in which minority officers differ from their co-workers; they are also younger, better educated and more likely to have grown up in large metropolitan areas. Moreover, the recency of their hiring, apart from any racial discrimination, places them disproportionately in the lower ranks, thus increasing the social distance between the line officers and their superiors.

Superior officers regard minorities with mistrust and suspicion. In their eyes, affirmative action has lowered recruitment standards, minorities are uncommitted to the job, identify with inmates rather than their fellow officers and are responsible for much of the increase in contraband and violence. To this line officers add charges of reverse discrimination (Fox, 1982:72-73; Jacobs, 1977:185-86; Owen, 1985), and minorities, for their part, believe themselves to be discriminated against. Over half of the non-white officers interviewed by Jacobs and Grear (1977), for example, complained that race was a problem on the job. Believing that their union does not fairly represent them, minority officers in New York formed the Minority Correctional Officer Association to combat discrimination both within the Department of Correctional Services and the union itself (Zimmer and Jacobs, 1981:535).

Despite, or perhaps because of the perceptions of superior officers, researchers have found few significant racial differences in attitudes and beliefs among officers (Jacobs and Kraft, 1978; Crouch and Alpert, 1982) except perhaps that black officers, while less punitive toward inmates, nonetheless prefer to maintain greater social distance from them (Toch and Klofas, 1982; Whitehead et. al., 1987; Jurik, 1985b). Why officers should be so similar in their attitudes despite the differences in their backgrounds is an open question. It may be that the constraints of the role are so great that all officers develop a similar "working personality." It seems more likely, however, that during the six to nine months probationary period in most prisons there is a highly selective process which screens out recruits whose attitudes and behavior are at variance from those of the top echelon (Jacobs and Grear, 1977; Jurik and Winn, 1987).

Yet another force causing trouble in the ranks in recent years has been the introduction of female officers into custodial positions in male prisons. The 1972 amendment to the Civil Rights Act of 1964 contained a provision extending the obligation of non-discrimination to public sector employers including criminal justice agencies. Whether this should or should not apply to employment of women in contact positions in male prisons has been the subject of considerable litigation. As yet, there are no clear guidelines for a legally acceptable balance among women's right to equal employment opportunities, inmates' rights to privacy and the state's interest in secure prisons (Zimmer, 1986:4-8). In the meantime, women are being hired to work in male prisons and assigned to contact positions within those facilities.

In the most complete study of sexual integration of the custodial ranks, Zimmer (1986) reports that male officers in New York and Rhode Island are unanimously and intensely opposed to the presence of female officers in male prisons. Women, they argue, can neither compel the routine obedience of prisoners nor be counted upon in emergencies requiring the use of physical force, and, as they are at risk of sexual victimization, they must be protected. In sum, in the eyes of the male officers, the presence of women impairs security, places additional burdens on male officers and increases the danger that all face. Moreover, male officers do not see assignment of females to non-contact positions as a solution. In their minds, these choice positions belong to those with seniority. The anger of the male guards is directed not only at their female co-workers but extends to the "radical" bureaucrats and liberal judges who have mandated the changes and to the weak administrators who have acquiesced to them.

Every female officer interviewed by Zimmer reported at least one incident of sexual harassment on the job. These incidents involved mainly fellow officers rather than inmates and ranged from statements about the type of woman who would want such a job to rumors of sexual intimacies with inmates or poor performance evaluations after refusing the sexual advances of superior officers. Perceiving neither administrative nor union support, many women resign their position. Those who remain cope with the harassment on an individual basis as best they can. While satisfied with their jobs, they become significantly alienated from their co-workers (Jurik, 1985a).

As yet, there is no hard evidence concerning the impact of female officers on institutional security and there are as many reasons for believing that they may enhance security as there are reasons for believing they impair it. Male prisoners may, by the presence of women, be motivated toward more socially acceptable behavior and, perceiving fewer psychic gains, they may be less inclined to engage in cofrontation tactics. By displaying greater understanding and being more hesitant to rely on force, female officers may in fact prevent violence. In the end, however, the impact on security, if any, may have less to do with women's dispositions and capacities than to the reactions of male officers to their presence. Continued harassment of women and discrimination against both women and minorities may factionalize custodial forces to the point where communication, coordination and teamwork are impossible.

Thus, the picture presented of an alienated, anomic and angry custodial force appears to have been accurate and not merely a local phenomenon due to idiosyncratic factors unique to Rhode Island. Nationwide sociopolitical forces (some specific to corrections and others made more sensitive by the nature of prisons) have transformed the world of the guard. And, in reaction, guards have "hit the bricks."

At the time of my research in Rhode Island, the officers withdrew from the state employees' union and established their own. There followed a turbulent period of several years during which the new union organized a number of job actions. By the mid-1970s, correctional officers in nearly half the states had unionized and, in virtually every case, had staged job actions. In Ohio, for example, there was at least one job action per year in the years 1971-1975 (Wynne, 1978:202). In April 1979 nearly all of New York State's seven thousand officers walked off the job and remained on strike for seventeen days requiring the call up of over 12,000 National Guardsmen (Zimmer and Jacobs, 1981). In 1981, Michigan guards locked up prisoners against orders, triggering a riot that resulted in 160 injuries (Hart, 1981).

These actions, of course, involve bread and butter issues of salaries, benefits and pensions. More deeply, however, they concern the guards' frustration and anger at the humanitarian reform of the prison and the judicial constraints on custodial power. Among their demands are stricter rules and harsher punishments for inmates, increases in staff-inmate ratios, and the elimination of many reforms. Many of these demands are beyond the power of administrators to grant, and the job actions often seem less directed at the administration than at the public, to draw its attention to the situation and thereby to place pressure on the legislature and the courts.

Unions have been successful in gaining many of their objectives. Pay and benefits have improved substantially and the guards now have a voice in the formation of policy independent of their position in the organization, a voice which has been influential in increasing the resources allocated for custodial operations and the imposition of stricter rules for inmate behavior (Wynne, 1978b). Ultimately, however, it is possible that the unions will further fragment and frustrate their members. In both New York and Rhode Island, for example, union interest in protecting the seniority provisions for job assignments forced them to support senior female officers seeking posts in male prisons, an action which, as we have seen, caused intense resentment among male officers (Zimmer, 1986:65-72). In both California and New York, unions engaged in partially successful litigation to block affirmative action promotion programs, an action which led to the formation in both states of separate organizations for minority officers (Irwin, 1980:22; Zimmer and Jacobs, 1981:535). And, finally, the expectations of the rank and file, arising out of intense anger, may be unrealistically high. Many of the issues which most concern line officers (such as court imposed restrictions) are not susceptible to change through collective bargaining, and those which are, usually result in compromises which may alienate members from leaders. The 1979 strike in New York, for example, was partly a rebellion by the rank-and-file against union leadership for not bargaining firmly enough with the state (Zimmer and Jacobs, 1981).

Blacks and Cons

In his now classic study of the prison, *The Society of Captives* (1958), Gresham Sykes delineated the major "pains of imprisonment" and the way in which inmates collectively adapt to those deprivations. Although recognizing that the "inmate population is shot through with a variety of ethnic and social clevages..." (Sykes, 1958:81) and that the focal concerns of prisoners may vary with their backgrounds, Sykes emphasized what he perceived as the "hard core concensus" among those confined. With few exceptions (e.g. Irwin, 1970) this perspective dominated sociological research on the prison during the 1960s and early 1970s, and race relations in the prison was ignored. I tried to make clear in this book that the pre-prison experiences of blacks and whites cause them to experience and adapt to prison differently. For black prisoners, discrimination is their most salient concern. In clinical interviews with 471 inmates, Johnson (1976) found that blacks were strikingly different from both Hispanic and white prisoners in their concern with being victims of inequity and abuse and in tending to express fear of being unable to control their anger and resentment at this perceived victimization. Similarly, Toch (1977:97-104) found that, of eight environmental concerns of prisoners, the most important to blacks was freedom. Inmates expressing a high degree of concern for freedom are those who see themselves as placed in childlike roles, deprived of due respect, continually harassed in both serious and petty ways, angry at their lack of autonomy and raging at their inability or fear of expressing resentment.

The pain of incarceration for whites does not seem to be related to any single focal concern. Like blacks, a good number of whites see themselves as victims of unjust treatment, and, like Hispanics, they show great concern for their separation from significant others. Many more whites, however, suffer a serious loss of self-esteem as a result of incarceration. They are more likely than minority prisoners to develop a view of their lives as devoid of value and of themselves as despicable and inadequate. And finally, white inmates express more concern for their personal safety and are more likely to express fear that they will be unable to bear the stresses of confinement (Johnson, 1976:68-79; Toch, 1977:127).

It appears that life in the black central city ghetto is functional for survival in the walled ghetto of the prison. The ghetto inhabitants' sense of themselves as victims, reinforced daily by the facts of their existence and given expression in both "soul" and radical political ideology, provides a rationale by which criminals may shift responsibility for their acts from themselves to the system. It is scarcely surprising then that survey research finds that black inmates are more politically radical and prisonized than are white inmates (Alpert, 1979; Fox, 1982; Goodstein and MacKenzie, 1984).

Moreover, these attitudes among black inmates seem to result from the experience of blacks in the wider society whereas among whites they derive from experience with the criminal justice system: blacks enter prison radical and prisonized; whites become so in prison (Alpert, 1979; Goodstein, 1984).

The adaptiveness of the black ghetto subculture to the prison is also evident in the social organization of prisoners. The concern for safety in the ghetto, along with the instability of the family, gives rise to a strong peer group orientation which is a source of special relations of mutual aid and affection frequently given the status of kinship as in "going for cousins" (Anderson, 1978:21). Black prisoners in Rhode Island in the early 1970s were made cohesive through a network of personalized relations among "partners." Such relationships have been described as the building blocks of black street gangs (Keiser, 1969:13-18) and the larger prisons today are dominated by racial and ethnic gangs. Jacobs (1977:ch. 6) has documented how four gangs (three black, one Hispanic) developed in Stateville following a crackdown on gang activity in Chicago. In his view, the intrusion of the gangs has changed the very principles by which inmates "do time" — from "doing your own time" to "doing gang time." Gangs have closed down individual entrepreneurs and monopolized the *sub rosa* economy, thereby transforming the nature of the inmate social system. In California, conflict between two Chicano gangs over control of the drug trade became so intense that officials there segregated the gangs into different institutions (Irwin, 1980:189-191; Moore, 1978:114-116). Most recently, racial and ethnic gangs have emerged in Texas prisons following the implementation of the judicial decree in *Ruiz v. Estelle* which, among other things, banned the system of inmate building tenders and turnkeys by which control had been maintained (Marquart and Crouch, 1985).

Whatever cohesion and solidarity there may have been among white prisoners in the past was presumably a product of their common deprivation in prison. In lessening this deprivation, reforms of the prison eroded the basis of white convict solidarity so that the white prisoner population was no longer an organized collectivity but a congeries of small cliques with diverse orientations. Similar observations to those I made in Rhode Island have since been made in both juvenile and adult facilities in all regions of the country (see, for example, Bartollas et al., 1976; Davidson, 1974; Dishotsky and Pfefferbaum, 1979, 1981; Feld, 1977; Jacobs, 1977). Toch (1977:177-205) describes the retreat of many white prisoners into subsettings within the larger prison in which they can relax with a small number sharing similar interests and orientation. Irwin (1980:147), observing the same phenomenon in California, compares it to the tactics of slum residents who, out of fear and mistrust, restrict the range of their interaction to their household and close friends.

In only a few institutions, most notably in California, have white inmates formed gangs. These have been explicitly and primarily a response to the perceived threat posed by black and Hispanic gangs and have been modeled along the lines of the Ku Klux Klan or the American Nazi Party. Generally, however, these groups are small, although they may make up for lack of numbers with their high internal cohesion and virulent racism (e.g. Dishotsky and Pfefferbaum, 1979; 1981). Their presence suggests at least the possibility that convict solidarity, rooted in opposition to staff, could be replaced with a similarly defensive solidarity rooted in racial and ethnic antagonism.

If, as I have argued, the culture of the inner city ghetto is functional for survival in the prison, then one would expect that black inmates would show fewer symptoms of psychological distress than would whites. There now exists a fair amount of research on the mental health of prisoners. With one exception (Goodstein and MacKenzie, 1984), research supports this hypothesis. Jones (1976:70-71, 80-83) reports that among the inmates at the Tennessee State Penitentiary a much lower percentage of blacks than whites reported symptoms of distress and that while one-third of the whites have considered suicide, only three percent of the blacks have. These results are consistent with others conducted in a medium custody federal institution (Fagan and Lira, 1978) and at the Utah State Prison (Oldroyd and Howell, 1977) and with Johnson's (1976:41-55) study of self-injury which found blacks to be grossly underrepresented among those who had experienced psychological crises and breakdowns in a New York prison. In a recent study of 9,103 inmates released from the New York prison system between July 30, 1982 and September 1, 1983, Toch, Adams and Greene (1987) found that black releasees were less likely than others to have received mental health services during their confinement but that those who did were disproportionately diagnosed as paranoid schizophrenic or anti-social; whites were primarily diagnosed as having affective or anxiety disorders. Differences in diagnosis partly explained the higher level of disciplinary infractions reported for blacks. Thus, it seems that culture not only influences adaptations to confinement; it also shapes the forms of psychopathology which develop there.

Intergroup Relations

Staff-Inmate

In maintaining security and order in the prison the guard has recourse to a formal system of rewards and punishments. Because this formal system frequently is inadequate, guards as often, if not more often, rely on an informal system involving friendship, allowing their authority to be corrupted in return for compliance, and violence. Race influences the operation of both these systems in very complex ways. In Rhode Island, as documented in Chapter 5, an anomic custodial force was threatened by the radicalism and solidarity of the black inmates and kept them under closer surveillance, but at the same time were made cautious by their fears of aggressive confrontations. Black inmates were thus reported for infractions more than were whites, but officers were careful to distinguish between major and minor offenses in the cases of blacks, and the Disciplinary Board imposed less severe penalties. The official statistics on reports and penalties are misleading as to the actual level of infractions, however, because a small white inmate elite were virtually immune from punishment.

To my knowledge, no single piece of research in the intervening years has dealt with the full complexity of staff-inmate race relations to the degree it was treated in this study, nor does it all conclude that race is a major factor in staff-inmate relations. Most research, however, is consistent with the processes I described.

Jacobs (1977:161-162) found a pattern of group confrontation at Stateville similar to what I found in Rhode Island at about the same time. At Stateville, gangs forced officers to back down from writing reports and were able to negotiate with superior officers over the appearance of their members at disciplinary boards. Conversely, in Texas prior to 1981, the recruitment of inmates to run the living areas reinforced a "white con power structure" (Marquart and Crouch, 1985:566-67) and the frequent use of "tune-ups," and "ass-whippings" was disproportionately directed against black inmates (Marquart, 1986). With the abolition of the building tender system, the "white con power structure" has been destroyed and officers appear to have lost control to black and Hispanic gangs (Marquart and Crouch, 1985).

Even in the absence of confrontation, the racial biases of the predominantly white custodians are apt to lead them to see black inmates as more aggressive. Held, Levine and Swartz (1979), for instance, found no differences between black and white inmates in their ratings of their own aggressiveness but found that the officers rated the blacks as more aggressive and the black inmates received more disciplinary reports than the whites. However, the racial differences in reports were for infractions in which the guards had the most discretion (e.g. disobeying an order, verbal aggression); there were no differences in more objective offenses such as attempted escape, assault and theft.

The most complete studies of the intersection of race and discipline are those conducted by Poole and Regoli (1980b) and by Flanagan (1982, 1983). Using data collected from questionnaires completed by 198 inmates of a southern prison and compiled from institutional records, Poole and Regoli found that while blacks did not report more infractions in the preceding month, they received more reports. Because they are more likely to be reported, they accumulate a more serious prior record which, in turn, affects response to the instant offense. In fact, prior record and rule-breaking interact with race in influencing the response. For whites, only the seriousness of the current offense directly affects the disciplinary response; for blacks, both the seriousness of the current offense and prior record affect the response with the effect of the latter being considerably more powerful. Poole and Regoli conclude that

Prior record, itself shown to be partly a product of discriminatory response, influenced subsequent sanctioning decisions, thus amplifying the racial bias.... and (served) to confirm stereotypic expectations that blacks are dangerous and threatening... and to justify differential response in succeeding disciplinary actions (1980b:944-45).

Flanagan's research was conducted on a weighted sample of 758 inmates released from fourteen facilities in a northeastern state during 1973-76. Unlike other researchers, he examined the annual infraction rate over the inmate's entire sentence. He found race was significantly related to the rate of infractions but only among older inmates who had no history of drug use and were convicted of offenses other than homicide (Flanagan, 1983). However, he did not find race to be related to the severity of sanctions imposed though sanction severity was influenced by prior record, age of the inmate and type of facility (Flanagan, 1982).

The differences in the findings reported by Poole and Regoli, on the one hand, and those of Flanagan, on the other, may be due to methodological differences or perhaps differences in the organization of black prisoners. Flanagan did not test for an interaction between race and prior record which Poole and Regoli found crucial in interpreting differences in sanction severity. This may account for Flanagan's negative finding. However, it could also be that the black inmates in the northeast are more politicized and solidary than those in the south. Younger black inmates may be able to intimidate officers whose biases are then only displayed against older blacks, and the disciplinary board may moderate sanctions against blacks in an attempt to avoid racial disturbances much as I found happening in Rhode Island. In either event, the conclusion that racial tension and hostility pervade staff-inmate relations remains; in the one case it is expressed in discrimination by staff and in the other by intimidation of staff by prisoners.

Inmate to Inmate

Every observer of race relations in the prison has noted the extent to which they are characterized by segregation and avoidance despite administrative attempts at integration (e.g. Jacobs, 1977; Feld, 1977). The extent of racial and ethnic closure was roughly measured by John Slosar (1978) in a study of two federal youth centers. When asked to choose two friends with whom they would like to take a trip to town, white inmates selected other white inmates four to ten times more often than would be expected by chance and blacks selected other blacks twenty to thirty-five times more often than dictated by chance (Slosar, 1978:88).

This prevailing pattern of segregation and avoidance is underlaid by tension and conflict. The level of violence in the contemporary prison is exceedingly high. Using anonymous prisoner reports, Fuller and his colleagues (1977) estimated that 77 of every 100 prisoners in North Carolina are assaulted each year. Nationwide, the homicide rate in prisons stands at nearly three times higher than in the surrounding society (Lester, 1987). Much of this violence is interracial. Of the incidents documented by Fuller et al. (1977), forty percent crossed racial lines; of these, eighty-two percent involved a black aggressor and a white victim.

In some institutions blacks seem to dominate whites totally. For example, in a juvenile institution with equal numbers of black and white residents, Bartollas et al. (1976:53-81) found that a boy's status was determined by, and inversely proportional to, the level of exploitation to which he permitted himself to be subjected. The researchers described the "exploitation matrix" as follows:

At the top is normally a black leader called a "heavy." He is followed closely by three or four black lieutenants. The third group, a mixture of eight to sixteen black and white youths, do the bidding of those at the top. This group is divided into a top half of mostly blacks, known as "alright guys," with the bottom half composed mostly of whites, designated as "chumps." One or two white scapegoats become the sexual victims of the first three groups (Bartollas et al., 1976:72).

This degree of dominance seems unusual by comparison to other studies (e.g. Bartollas and Sieverdes, 1981; Feld, 1977) and may have been related to a rather active cooperation of the staff in maintaining black hegemony (Bartollas et al., 1976:106-125). The sexual domination of whites by blacks which I found in Rhode Island, however, is by now a matter of general agreement. A number of studies report that roughly two-thirds of all sexual assaults involve black aggressors and white victims (Jones, 1976; Lockwood, 1980; Scacco, 1975). I, and most other researchers, have interpreted this victimization as expressive of racial antagonism. Lockwood (1980:106-107), however, in what is the most detailed study of the problem, says that neither aggressors nor victims emphasized racial antagonism and argues that the root cause is the threat that incarceration poses to the sexual identity of young males. Sexual assault is a response to the problem by those who have been socialized in a subculture of violence. True as this may be, racism still must be seen as an important element. Those socialized into the subculture of violence are disproportionately minorities. How else can one explain Lockwood's observations that "most informants reported young slender white men were the highest object of desire" and that the "white target brings the highest status to the aggressor" (Lockwood, 1980:32)?

Despite the attention it has received, sexual aggression is only one aspect of the conflict and violence in the prison. There has always existed an illegal economy through which inmates have sought to meet their needs for desirable food, good coffee, and cigarettes, not to mention alcohol and drugs. As a result of the reforms of the past twenty years, the affluence of the surrounding society has spilled over the walls and created a more visible and pronounced stratification within. In many institutions, prisoners who can afford them are permitted luxuries such as televisions, stereos, musical instruments, virtually unlimited supplies of books and food, and even street clothing. And, as a result of more liberal policies and the power and connections of gangs, drugs, alcohol and cash have become more readily available. All of this has stimulated increased economic competition and conflict. Individual "merchants," largely white, have been driven out of business by "racketeers" backed by large gangs, mainly black and Hispanic. These gangs now struggle with each other over sources of supply and control of markets while small cliques differentiated by race, prey upon one another in an attempt to raise their standard of living (Irwin, 1980:206-212; Kalinich, 1980).

Unlike sexual aggression, the violence surrounding economic conflict tends to be instrumental and leaders attempt to control and moderate it. As I noted, an agreement to regulate and manage conflict was arrived at between a white "Mafia" clique and black leaders in Rhode Island. Jacobs (1977:155-56) has described how gang leaders at Stateville reached an accommodation by pledging to abide by a set of "international rules." Similarly, violence between a black and a Chicano gang in Jackson, Michigan was avoided by an agreement over relative market shares in the drug trade (Kalinich, 1980:44). Due to the mistrust which surrounds such arrangements, however, they tend to be tenuous and are heavily dependent upon the personal relations between the leaders who enter into them and their ability to control the behavior of their followers. The release or transfer of a leader, challenges to his position, or independent actions by small cliques can destroy the precarious equilibrium and plunge the prison into violence.

For a brief period of time in the early 1970s, it appeared that prisoners might bridge racial and ethnic clevages. Black, white and Hispanic inmates, politicized by the civil rights and antiwar movements, came to see racism as a facet of the prison administration's efforts to divide and conquer them. A series of unity strikes at San Quentin, followed by a number of other dramatic prison related events across the country, focussed attention on the prison and drew groups as diverse as the American Friends Service Committee and the Black Panthers into coalitions with prisoner organizations. In many institutions, these prisoner organizations were recognized and empowered by reform-minded administrators and reform was pursued through litigation and negotiation.

It was the threat posed by this movement which pushed the guards to unionize and to counter prisoner demonstrations and strikes with their own job actions. As fear of "crime in the streets" rose, the public lost sympathy with the concerns of prisoners and the officers were able to force a return to a stricter custodial regimen. Inmate leaders were segregated or transferred, followers were harassed and, ultimately, political organizations, in the most generic sense of the term, were banned (Berkman, 1979; Irwin, 1980).

Irwin (1980) argues that the prisoners' movement, though indirectly causing an increase in violence against staff, afforded the only possibility to develop a new and peaceful order in the prison. In repressing the movement, "administrators stopped the development of alternative group structures that could have prevented the rise of hoodlum gangs involved in rackets, formed on racial lines, and engaged in extreme forms of prisoner-to-prisoner violence" (Irwin, 1980:151).

The New Mexico riot of 1980 lends considerable support to Irwin's argument. Unlike the Attica riot in 1971 in which a high degree of inmate organization was evident, the riot in New Mexico was notable for its fragmentation, lack of leadership and extreme brutality. The major factors predisposing the inmates to riot were the abolition of a large number of programs administered by prisoners and which involved the majority of the population in meaningful activity, the failure to implement court-ordered reforms, and the imposition after 1975 of a more custodial regime (Colvin, 1982; Useem, 1985). In the course of the riot, former leaders, who had been active in litigation and the administration of programs, were unsuccessful in a bid to take control and negotiate with the administrators. In addition, the entire black population retreated from participation, organizing to protect themselves from other inmates, and 33 prisoners, most of them "snitches" recruited by the guards, were brutally murdered. Comparing New Mexico to Attica, a long-term observer of prisons was led to comment *"anarchy within the walls replaced unity; atavism replaced ideology; prisoners destroyed their own"* (Dinitz, 1981:9; emphasis in original).

Conclusion

Racial tension and hostility is endemic to America. It is unrealistic to expect to cure in the prison what is one of society's most serious and persistent problems. Nonetheless, it is clear that racial conflict is heightened by the conditions in the contemporary prison. The construction of smaller facilities near metropolitan areas, the continued active recruitment of minority staff, the development and implementation of better classification procedures, the implementation of effective grievance systems and the institution of parole guidelines would all serve to moderate racial tensions. Here, however, I will focus on other organizational changes more directly related to the roles of officers and prisoners: the professionalization of the officers' role and the inclusion of both officers and inmates in decision making. In making these suggestions, I am under no illusion concerning the level of support they now have among administrators. Nonetheless, I am convinced that lawful, stable and safe prisons can only be achieved through such collaborative efforts.

Despite the reactionary posture of officers' unions and in contradiction to popular stereotypes, prison guards are not loutish brutes. Most believe in the rehabilitative potential of prisoners and are favorable to the provision of treatment services (Jacobs, 1981; Shamir and Droz, 1981; Teske and Williamson, 1979). Moreover, they maintain less social distance between themselves and inmates and display more sympathetic understanding of inmate problems than is commonly supposed. Lombardo (1981:59-73), for instance, reports that virtually all those in his sample of officers at Auburn helped inmates with institutional problems and that a majority at times became directly involved with the personal problems of prisoners even to the point of taking the initiative in finding out if an inmate has a problem.

Formal recognition of the officers' role in the provision of human services might be one step toward reducing trouble in the ranks. The primary focus of such a role would not be intervention to change post-prison behavior (though this may be an indirect result), but to assist prisoners in coping with the day-to-day stresses of confinement through the provision of both advice and assistance in solving institutional and personal problems, referral to appropriate treatment services when necessary, finding comfortable niches within the prison environment for those under stress, and so on (Johnson, 1981; Johnson and Price, 1981; Lombardo, 1985). Most officers perform such functions informally but hide it from both peers and superiors whom they perceive as opposed to it (Kaufman, 1981; Klofas and Toch, 1982). Formal incorporation of these duties into the officers' role would allow for training, permit the establishment of networks between officers and other workers who provide more specialized services and elevate the status of the officer. An experimental program in

Maryland along these lines, in which line officers were given appropriate training and assigned casework management responsibilities for 7-10 inmates along with their custodial duties, has met with considerable success (Ward and Vandergoot, 1981).

Such duties, unlike the vague prescriptions of rehabilitation, may actually enhance the officers' custodial function. Most officers, especially experienced officers, rely less on legal authority or coercion in managing inmates than they do on what Lombardo (1981:74-77) terms "personalized authority" and Hepburn (1985) characterizes as "expert power." By displaying sympathetic understanding and the ability to help solve problems while maintaining a professional detachment, officers can extend the bases of their power.

Such a role redefinition, however, cannot be imposed from above nor is it likely to arise spontaneously from the ranks. It can only develop within the context of organizational changes which address the sources of threat felt by the officers. With considerable justification, officers feel jeopardized by reforms and judicial constraints which they perceive as reducing their abilities to control prisoners in an increasingly hostile environment. And they feel powerless to influence policy or management operational decisions (Fox, 1982). A more participatory style of management which includes them is required to reduce this sense of threat. At the highest level this might take the form of a union-management council to address policy issues. At lower levels a number of task forces might be established to investigate operational problems and make recommendations for their solution. To ensure the proper training, officers might be granted sabbaticals to study management, organizational problem-solving, and dispute resolution, side benefits of which would include gaining their participation and at least a temporary reduction in their level of stress. Moreover, involving female and minority officers as equals with white male officers and administrators in the solution of common problems would be more likely to reduce tensions between them than would programs explicitly established for this purpose (see, for example, the references in Chapter 9, footnote 12) and may help to establish a racially and sexually integrated staff to serve as a model of effective cooperation.

The successful inclusion of officers within the decision-making process and the resultant decrease in the sense of powerlessness and threat may then permit meaningful sharing of power with inmates. Again, in suggestng this, I am under no illusion about the success of attempts at inmate self-government in the past nor with the current level of opposition to such programs among both officers and administrators. Yet it seems that the failure of such experiments in the past has been almost a self-fulfilling prophecy. Initiated haphazardly under pressure from prisoners or by a lone administrator with a vision, with little or no thought given to the impact on the officers, these fragile arrangements have been doomed to failure from the moment of their inception. Even programs now branded as failures, however, seem to have had some beneficial effects. A study at Walla Walla, for example, found that participants in the inmate self-government system established in the early 1970s showed significant increases in self-esteem, self-confidence, tolerance of others and acceptance of law and order (Regan and Hobson, 1978). In a juvenile institution, Feld (1977:186, 204-205) found collaborative decision making concerning the establishment of rules and the imposition of sanctions defused racial violence. Moreover, there is perhaps no other way to counter the dominance of gangs and oulaw cliques than by the development of prisoner leaders who are able to articulate inmate interests, negotiate them through legitimate channels and secure meaningful changes.

The construction of smaller and more autonomous institutions and the prior development of collaborative decision making with officers should make the empowerment of prisoners less threatening. Experimentation with different kinds and degrees of prisoner participation to determine what is feasible could then be conducted. Even then, of course, there is no guarantee that such changes will actually reduce violence and rapacity. Our only other choice is to continue our attempts at repressing violence—attempts which have met with no more success than have experiments with self-government. And if we attempt to maintain order in prisons through a reign of terror, we will, in the long run, all suffer the consequences.

References

Alpert, G. (1979) "Patterns of Change in Prisonization: A Longitudinal Analysis." *Criminal Justice and Behavior* 6:159-74.

Anderson, E. (1978) *A Place in the Corner.* Chicago: University of Chicago Press.

Bartollas, G., S.J. Miller and S. Dinitz (1976) *Juvenile Victimization: The Institutional Paradox.* New York: Halsted Press.

Bartollas, C. and C.M. Sieverdes (1981) "The Victimized White in a Juvenile Correctional System." *Crime and Delinquency.* 27:534-43.

Berkman, R. (1979) *Opening the Gates: The Rise of the Prisoners' Movement.* Lexington, MA: Lexington Books.

Cheek, F. and M.S. Miller (1983) "Experience of Stress for Correctional Officers: A Double Bind Theory of Correctional Stress." *Journal of Criminal Justice* 11:105-120.

Colvin, M. (1982) "The 1980 New Mexico Prison Riot." *Social Problems* 29:449-63.

Corrections Compendium (1983) *National Survey of Correctional Staff Turnover.* Lincoln, NE: Contact.

Crouch, B. and G. Alpert (1982) "Sex and Occupational Socialization Among Prison Guards: A Longitudinal Study." *Criminal Justice and Behavior* 9: 959-76.

Davidson, T.R. (1974, reissued 1983) *Chicano Prisoners: The Key to San Quentin.* Prospect Heights, IL: Waveland Press, Inc.

Dinitz, S. (1981) "Are Safe and Humane Prisons Possible?" *Australian and New Zealand Journal of Criminology* 14:3-19.

Dishotsky, N.I. and A. Pfefferbaum (1979) "Intolerance and Extremism in a Correctional Institution: A Perceived Ethnic Relations Approach." *American Journal of Psychiatry* 138:1438-43.

———— (1981) "Racial Intolerance in a Correctional Institution: An Ecological View." *American Journal of Psychiatry* 138:1057-62.

Fagan, T.J. and F.T. Lira (1978) "Profile of Mood States: Racial Differences in a Delinquent Population." *Psychological Reports* 43:348-50.

Feld, B.C. (1977) *Neutralizing Inmate Violence.* Cambridge, MA: Ballinger Books.

Flanagan, T.J. (1982) "Discretion in the Prison Justice System: A Study of Sentencing in Institutional Disciplinary Proceedings." *Journal of Research in Crime and Delinquency* 19:216-37.

———— (1983) "Correlates of Misconduct Among State Prisoners." *Criminology* 21:29-40.

Fogel, D. (1975) "*... We are the Living Proof...*": The Justice Model for Corrections. Cincinnati: Anderson Publishing Co.

Fox, J.G. (1982) *Organizational and Racial Conflict in Maximum Security Prisons.* Lexington, MA: Lexington Books.

Fuller, D., T. Orsagh and D. Raber (1977) "Violence and Victimization within the North Carolina Prison System." Paper presented at the meeting of the Academy of Criminal Justice Sciences.

239

240

Goodstein, L. and D.L. MacKenzie (1984) "Racial Differences in the Adjustment Patterns of Inmates—Prisonization, Conflict, Stress and Control." In D. Georges-Abeyie (ed.), *The Criminal Justice System and Blacks,* 271-306. New York: Clark Boardman Co.

Hart, W. (1981) "In Michigan, Officers Rebel Then Inmates Riot." *Corrections Magazine* 7(4):52-56.

Hawkins, G. (1976) *The Prison: Policy and Practice.* Chicago: University of Chicago Press.

Held, B.S., D. Levine and V.D. Swartz (1979) "Interpersonal Aspects of Dangerousness." *Criminal Justice and Behavior* 6:49-58.

Hepburn, J. (1985) "The Exercise of Power in Coercive Organizations: A Study of Prison Guards." *Criminology* 23:145-64.

Irwin, J. (1970) *The Felon.* Englewood Cliffs, NJ: Prentice-Hall.

_____ (1980) *Prisons in Turmoil.* Boston: Little Brown.

Jacobs, J.B. (1977) *Stateville: The Penitentiary in Mass Society.* Chicago: University of Chicago Press.

_____ (1981) "What Prison Guards Think: A Profile of the Illinois Force." In R.R. Ross (ed.), *Prison Guard/Correctional Officer,* 41-53. Toronto: Butterworth and Co.

_____ (1983) *New Perspectives on Prisons and Imprisonment.* Ithaca: Cornell University Press.

Jacobs, J.B. and L.J. Kraft (1978) "Integrating the Keepers: A Comparison of Black and White Prison Guards in Illinois." *Social Problems* 25:304-318.

Jacobs, J.B. and H.G. Retsky (1975) "Prison Guard." *Urban Life* 4:5-29.

Johnson, R. (1976) *Culture and Crisis in Confinement.* Lexington, MA: Lexington Books.

_____ (1981) "Informal Helping Networks in Prison: The Shape of Grass-Roots Correctional Intervention." In R.R. Ross (ed.), *Prison Guard/Correctional Officer,* 105-25. Toronto: Butterworth and Co.

Johnson, R. and S. Price (1981) "The Complete Correctional Officer: Human Services and the Human Environment of the Prison." *Criminal Justice and Behavior* 8:343-73.

Jones, D.A. (1976) *The Health Risks of Imprisonment.* Lexington, MA: Lexington Books.

Jurik, N.C. (1985a) "An Officer and a Lady: Organizational Barriers to Women Working as Correctional Officers in Men's Prisons." *Social Problems* 32:375-85.

_____ (1985b) "Individual and Organizational Determinants of Correctional Officer Attitudes Toward Inmates." *Criminology* 23:523-39.

Jurik, N.C. and R. Winn (1987) "Describing Correctional Security Drop-outs and Rejects." *Criminal Justice and Behavior* 14:5-25.

Kalinich, D.B. (1980, reissued 1986) *Power, Stability and Contraband: The Inmate Economy.* Prospect Heights, IL: Waveland Press, Inc.

Kauffman, K. (1981) "Prison Officers' Attitudes and Perceptions of Attitudes: A Case of Pluralistic Ignorance." *Journal of Research in Crime and Delinquency* 18:272-94.

Keiser, R.L. (1969) *The Vice Lords: Warriors of the Streets.* New York: Holt, Rinehart and Winston.

Klofas, J. and H. Toch (1982) "The Guard Subculture Myth." *Journal of Research in Crime and Delinquency* 19:238-54.

Lester, D. (1987) "Suicide and Homicide in USA Prisons." *Psychological Reports* 61:126.

Lockwood, D. (1980) *Prison Sexual Violence.* New York: Elsevier.

Lombardo, L.X. (1981) *Guards Imprisoned: Correctional Officers at Work.* New York: Elsevier.

_____ (1985) "Mental Health Work in Prisons: Inmate Adjustment and Indigenous Correctional Personnel." *Criminal Justice and Behavior* 12:17-28.

Marquart, J.W. (1986) "Prison Guards and the Use of Physical Coercion as a Mechanism of Social Control." *Criminology* 24:347-66.

Marquart, J.W. and B.M. Crouch (1985) "Judicial Reform and Prisoner Control: The Impact of *Ruiz v. Estelle* on a Texas Penitentiary." *Law and Society Review* 19:557-86.

Moore, J.W. (1978) *Homeboys: Gangs, Drugs and Prison in the Barrios of Los Angeles.* Philadelphia: Temple University Press.

Oldroyd, R.J. and R.J. Howell (1977) "Personality, Intellectual and Behavioral Differences between Black, Chicano and White Prison Inmates in the Utah State Prison." *Psychological Reports* 41:187-91.

Owen, B.A. (1985) "Race and Gender Relations Among Prison Workers." *Crime and Delinquency* 31:147-59.

Poole, E.D. and R.M. Regoli (1980a) "Role Stress, Custody Orientation and Disciplinary Actions: A Study of Prison Guards." *Criminology* 18:215-26.

_____ (1980b) "Race, Institutional Rule Breaking and Disciplinary Response: A Study of Disciplinary Decision-Making in Prison." *Law and Society Review* 14:931-46.

_____ (1981) "Alienation in Prison: An Examination of the Work Relations of Prison Guards." *Criminology* 19:251-70.

Regens, J.L. and W.G. Hobson (1978) "Inmate Self-Government and Attitude Change: An Assessment of Participation Effects." *Evaluation Quarterly* 2: 455-79.

Scacco, A. (1975) *Rape in Prison.* Springfield, IL: Charles C. Thomas.

Slosar, J.A., Jr., (1978) *Prisonization, Friendship and Leadership.* Lexington, MA: Lexington Books.

Shamir, B. and A. Drosz (1981) "Some Correlates of Prison Guards' Beliefs." *Criminal Justice and Behavior* 8:233-49.

Sykes, G.M. (1958) *The Society of Captives: A Study of A Maximum Security Prison.* Princeton, NJ: Princeton University Press.

Teske, R.H. and H.E. Williamson (1979) "Correctional Officers' Attitudes Toward Selected Treatment Programs." *Criminal Justice and Behavior* 6:59-66.

Toch, H. (1977) *Living in Prison: The Ecology of Survival.* New York: Free Press.

Toch, H., K. Adams and R. Greene (1978) "Ethnicity, Disruptiveness and Emotional Disorder Among Inmates." *Criminal Justice and Behavior* 14:93-109.

Toch, H. and J. Klofas (1982) "Alienation and Desire for Job Enrichment Among Correctional Officers." *Federal Probation* 46:35-44.

Useem, B. (1985) "Disorganization and the New Mexico Prison Riot." *American Sociological Review* 5:677-88.

Ward, R.J. and D. Vandergoot (1981) "Correctional Officers with Case Loads." In R.R. Ross (ed.), *Prison Guard/Correctional Officer,* 127-33. Toronto: Butterworth and Co.

Whitehead, J.T. and C.A. Lindquist (1986) "Correctional Officer Job Burnout: A Path Model." *Journal of Research in Crime and Delinquency* 23:23-42.

Whitehead, J.T., C.A. Lindquist and J. Klofas (1987) "Correctional Officer Professional Orientation: A Replication of the Klofas-Toch Measure." *Criminal Justice and Behavior* 14:468-86.

Wynne, J.M., Jr. (1978) *Prison Employee Unionism: The Impact on Correctional Administration and Programs.* Washington: U.S. Government Printing Office.

Zimmer, L. (1986) *Women Guarding Men.* Chicago: University of Chicago Press.

Zimmer, L. and J.B. Jacobs (1981) "Challenging the Taylor Law: Prison Guards on Strike." *Industrial and Labor Relations Review* 34:531-44.

Notes

Notes to Chapter 1
Introduction

1. Michael T. Kaufman, "Troubles Persist in Prison at Auburn" *The New York Times,* May 17, 1971, p. 37.

2. "Wainwright Says Black Prison Majority Feared," *Sentinel Star* (Orlando). May 28, 1973, p. 2.

3. Ibid.

4. James Bacchus, "Sumter Tense—'Riots Could Happen Again'," *Sentinel Star* (Orlando), May 28, 1973, p.2.

5. The source of this estimate is The President's Commission on Law Enforcement and the Administration of Justice, *The Challenge of Crime in a Free Society* (New York, Avon Books, 1968), p. 386.

6. Donald Clemmer, *The Prison Community* (2d ed.; New York: Holt, Rinehart and Winston, 1958).

7. These labels were taken from Hugh Cline, "The Determinants of Normative Patterns in Correctional Institutions," *Scandanavian Studies in Criminology,* Vol. 2, ed. Niles Christie (Oslo: Oslo University Press, 1968), pp. 173-84.

8. Gresham M. Sykes, *The Society of Captives: A Study of a Maximum Security Prison* (Princeton, N.J.: Princeton University Press, 1958), ch. 9; Gresham M. Sykes and Sheldon M. Messinger, "The Inmate Social System," *Theoretical Studies in Social Organization of the Prison* (Pamphlet #15; New York: Social Science Research Council, 1960), pp. 13-19.

9. Lloyd McCorkle and Richard Korn, "Resocialization Within the Walls," *The Annals of the American Academy of Political and Social Science* 293 (May 1954), 88.

10. Sykes and Messinger, pp. 6-9.

11. Sykes, ch. 4; Sykes and Messinger, pp. 8-10.

12. Stanton Wheeler, "Socialization in Correctional Communities," *American Sociological Review* 26 (October 1961), 697-712; Peter G. Garabedian, "Social Roles and Processes of Socialization in the Prison Community," *Social Problems* 11 (Fall 1963), 139-52; Charles R. Tittle and Drollene P. Tittle, "Social Organization of Prisoners: An Empirical Test," *Social Forces* 43 (December 1964), 216-221; Charles R. Tittle, "Inmate Organization: Sex Differentiation and the Influence of Criminal Subcultures," *American Sociological Review* 34 (August 1969), 492-505.

13. Erving Goffman, *Asylums: Essays on the Social Situation of Men-*

tal Patients and Other Inmates (Garden City: Doubleday Anchor Books, 1961), pp. 14-48.

14. Clemmer, p. 119.

15. Wheeler, Table 4, p. 703.

16. Daniel Glaser, *The Effectiveness of a Prison and Parole System* (abridged ed.; Indianapolis: Bobbs-Merrill, 1969), pp. 64-65.

17. Tittle, p. 498.

18. The concept of latent culture was developed by Becker and Geer building on Gouldner's conceptualization of latent social roles. See Howard S. Becker and Blanche Geer, "Latent Culture: A Note on the Theory of Latent Social Roles," *Administrative Science Quarterly* 5 (September 1960), 304-313. Also see Alvin W. Gouldner, "Cosmopolitans and Locals: Toward an Analysis of Latent Social Roles—I," *Administrative Science Quarterly* 2 (September 1959), 281-306.

19. John Irwin and Donald R. Cressey, "Theives, Convicts and the Inmate Culture," *Social Problems* 10 (Fall 1962), 142-55.

20. Ibid., p. 152.

21. John Irwin, *The Felon* (Englewood Cliffs, N.J.: Prentice-Hall, 1970), p. 66.

22. David A. Ward and Gene G. Kassebaum, *Women's Prison: Sex and Social Structure* (Chicago: Aldine, 1965), ch. 3.

23. Rose Giallombardo, *Society of Women: A Study of a Women's Prison* (New York: John Wiley and Sons, 1966), chs. 8-9.

24. Bernard Berk, "Organizational Goals and Inmate Organization," *American Journal of Sociology* 71 (March 1966), 522-34.

25. Ibid., Table 3, p. 529.

26. David Street, Robert Vinter, and Charles Perrow, *Organization For Treatment: A Comparative Study of Institutions for Juveniles* (New York: The Free Press, 1966), p. 236.

27. Ibid., pp. 199-200.

28. Ibid., pp. 229.

29. Thomas P. Wilson, "Patterns of Management and Adaptations to Organizational Roles: A Study of Prison Inmates," *American Journal of Sociology* 74 (September 1968), 146-57.

30. Charles R. Tittle, *Society of Subordinates: Inmate Organization in a Narcotics Hospital* (Bloomington: Indiana University Press, 1972).

31. Ibid., p. 66, p. 73.

32. Ibid., p. 79.

33. Ibid., pp. 89-94.

34. Ibid., pp. 98-101.

35. See, for example, Pierre L. van den Berghe, *Race and Racism: A Comparative Perspective* (New York: John Wiley and Sons, 1967), ch. 5; and *South Africa: A Study in Conflict* (Middletown, Conn.: Wesleyan University Press, 1965).

36. Julian Pitt-Rivers, "Race, Color, and Class in Central America and the Andes," *Daedalus* 92 (No. 2), 253-75. Reprinted in Norman R. Yetman and C. Hoy Steele (eds.), *Majority and Minority: The Dynamics of Racial and Ethnic Relations* (Boston: Allyn and Bacon, 1971), pp. 91-102.

37. John Biesanz and Luke M. Smith, "Race Relations in Panama and the Canal Zone," *American Journal of Sociology* 57 (July 1951), 7-14.

38. Herbert Blumer, "Reflections on Theory of Race Relations," *Race Relations in World Perspective,* ed. Andrew Lind (Honolulu: University of Hawaii Press, 1955), p. 5.

39. Clemmer, p. 319.

40. Muzafer Sherif, "Superordinate Goals in the Reduction of Intergroup Conflict," *American Journal of Sociology* 57 (January 1958), 349-56; Seymour Feshbach and Robert Singer, "The Effects of Personal and Shared Threats Upon Social Prejudice," *Journal of Abnormal and Social Psychology* 54 (May 1957), 411-16.

41. For example, see David G. Mandelbaum, *Soldier Groups and Negro Soliders* (Berkeley: University of California Press, 1952). pp. 117-27.

42. For a discussion of the difference between humanitarianism and treatment see Don C. Gibbons, *Changing the Lawbreaker: The Treatment of Delinquents and Criminals* (Englewood Cliffs, N.J.: Prentice-Hall, 1965), pp. 129-35.

43. Irwin has made a similar observation with repect to convict organization in California prisons. Irwin, pp. 64-66.

44. These decisions are too numerous to cite here. An excellent review of this litigation can be found in South Carolina Department of Corrections, *The Emerging Rights of the Confined* (Columbia: The Correctional Development Foundation, 1972), ch. 3.

45. Ibid., p. 62 citing *Sostre v. McGinnis,* 442 F. 2d 178, 202 n, 48 (2d Cir., 1971).

46. DeBro has presented a case study of how the opposition of prison administrators to the recognition of the Black Muslims stimulated racial conflict throughout an entire prison system. Julius DeBro, "The Black Revolution in Prison: A Case Study of Separatism," (paper presented at the annual meeting of the American Sociological Association, New York, August 1973).

47. Tad Szulc, "George Jackson Radicalizes the Brothers in Soledad and San Quentin," *The New York Times Magazine,* August 1, 1971, p. 16.

48. This section follows closely an outline for methodological accounts of fieldwork suggested by John Lofland in *Analyzing Social Settings: A Guide to Qualitative Observation and Analysis* (Belmont, Cal.: Wadsworth, 1971), pp. 131-32.

49. Morris and Charlotte Schwartz, "Problems in Participant Observation," *American Journal of Sociology* 60 (January 1955), 343-54.

50. Schatzman and Strauss analogize mapping operations to the use of tracers, chemical elements injected into the body, in physiological research. Leonard Schatzman and Anselm Strauss, *Field Research: Strategies for a Natural Sociology* (Englewood Cliffs, N.J.: Prentice-Hall, 1973) p. 83. In this section I draw heavily upon their framework in an effort to systematize the observational process I followed. As is perhaps the case in most methodological accounts, however, the actual process was not nearly as systematic as the *ex post facto* explication of it might make it appear.

51. Schatzman and Strauss, p. 52.

52. Ibid., pp. 71-72.

53. Lofland, pp. 119-21.

54. Ibid., p. 122; Schatzman and Strauss, pp. 100-101, 104-105.

55. For a definition and discussion of social types, see Samuel Strong, "Social Types in a Minority Community," *American Journal of Sociology* 48 (March 1943), 563-73.

56. For a fuller discussion of working hypotheses in fieldwork, see Blanche Geer, "First Days in the Field: A Chronicle of Research in Progress," *Sociologists at Work,* ed. Phillip E. Hammond (New York: Basic Books, 1964), ch. 11.

Notes to Chapter 2
The Prison

1. This and the following paragraph are based upon Cressey's excellent analysis of custodial and treatment prisons as ideal types. See Donald R. Cressey, "Prison Organizations," *Handbook of Organizations,* ed. James G. March (Chicago: Rand McNally, 1965), pp. 1037-53.

2. Don C. Gibbons has presented an incisive discussion of the distinction between humanitarianism and treatment. See Don C. Gibbons, *Changing the Lawbreaker: The Treatment of Delinquents and Criminals* (Englewood Cliffs, N.J.: Prentice-Hall, 1965), pp. 129-35.

3. Ibid., This tendency has long been noted and of concern to researchers investigating prison social organization. McCorkle and Korn, for instance, argued that the defense of humanitarian reforms as rehabilitative might precipitate a return to highly repressive structures if recidivism rates

are not lowered as a result of the changes. Lloyd McCorkle and Richard Korn, "Resocialization Within the Walls," *Annals of the American Acadamy of Political and Social Science* 293 (May 1954), 94-5.

4. Robbery, combining as it does the elements of personal violence and property loss, has been termed the "bellwether offense in the crime index." Moreover, it is becoming an increasingly black offense. In 1960, 55.5 percent of all persons arrested for robbery were black. By 1969 this had increased to 69.1 percent. See John E. Conklin, *Robbery and the Criminal Justice System* (Philadelphia: J.B. Lippincott, 1972), pp. 3-4, 32.

5. The data in this study are not adequate to test for racial discrimination in sentencing. The issue is an extremely complicated one, involving not only sociological variables such as the race of the offender and the race of the victim, but also legal variables such as the number of bills of indictment in connection with the act. One extensive investigation of sentencing in Philadelphia found that controlling for such legal variables was sufficient to account for racial disparities in sentencing. See Edward Green, "Inter- and Intra-Racial Crime Relative to Sentencing," *Journal of Criminal Law, Criminology, and Police Science* 55 (September 1964), 348-58. At ECI there was no uniform racial difference in sentences for similar crimes. For example, the mean sentence of whites convicted of Robbery was 12.5 years; for blacks it was 8.3 years. On the other hand, blacks convicted of Violation of Narcotics Laws received a mean sentence of 6.6 years; whites had a mean sentence of 2.8 years.

6. This assertion is based on the results of considerable research in small groups. For an excellent summary see Edwin J. Thomas and Clinton F. Fink "Effect of Group Size," *Small Groups: Studies in Social Interaction,* ed. A. Paul Hare, Edgar F. Borgatta, and Robert F. Bales (New York: Alfred A. Knopf, 1965), pp. 525-36.

Notes to Chapter 3
The Hacks

1. Gresham M. Sykes, *The Society of Captives: A Study of a Maximum Security Prison* (Princeton, N.J.: Princeton University Press, 1958), ch. 3. Sykes argues that physical coercion is an ineffective means of securing compliance on a routine basis, that punishment is an ineffective measure when men are living close to allowable limits of physical punishment, and that the rewards are administered in such a manner as to be defined as punishment. The result is that guards must often sacrifice a degree of their authority in their efforts to secure compliance.

2. Emile Durkheim, *The Division of Labor in Society,* trans. George Simpson (New York: The Free Press, 1964), Book 3, ch. 1; *Suicide,* trans.

John A. Spaulding and George Simpson (New York: The Free Press, 1951), Book 2, ch. 5.

3. Robert K. Merton, *Social Theory and Social Structure,* (2d rev. ed.; New York: The Free Press, 1957), pp. 132-39.

4. A second prominent use of the concept is to refer to a psychological state of isolation. See Robert M. MacIver, *The Ramparts We Guard* (New York: Macmillan, 1950), pp. 84-85; David Reisman, Reuel Denney, and Nathan Glazer, *The Lonely Crowd* (New Haven: Yale University Press, 1950), pp. 287 ff; Leo Srole, "Social Integration and Certain Corollaries; An Exploratory Study," *American Sociological Review* 21 (December 1956), 709-16.

5. Alvin W. Gouldner, *Patterns of Industrial Bureaucracy* (New York: The Free Press, 1954), chs. 4-5.

6. For a detailed analysis of the ways in which pressure groups may influence correctional administrators see Lloyd E. Ohlin, "Conflicting Interests in Correctional Objectives," *Theoretical Studies in Social Organization of the Prison* (New York: Social Science Research Council, pamphlet #15, 1960), pp. 111-129.

7. Role conflict here is used to refer to two or more inconcistent but equally legitimate sets of behavioral expectations associated with a single position. The problem of role conflict of correctional officers has been the subject of some study. See Oscar Grusky, "Role Conflict in Organization: A Study of Prison Camp Officials," *Administrative Science Quarterly* 3 (March 1959), 452-72: Donald R. Cressey, "Contradictory Directives in Complex Organizations: The Case of the Prison," *Administrative Science Quarterly* 4 (June 1959), 1-19; Lloyd E. Ohlin, "The Reduction of Role Conflict in Institutional Staff," *Children* 5 (March-April 1958), 65-69.

8. Merton, p. 134.

9. Ibid., pp. 141-57.

10. Sykes, pp. 52-53; Also, Sykes, "The Corruption of Authority and Rehabilitation, *Social Forces* 34 (March 1956), 257-62.

11. Merton, p. 156.

Notes to Chapter 4
The Cons

1. Samuel A. Strong, "Social Types in a Minority Group," *American Journal of Sociology* 48 (March 1943), 563-73.

2. Ibid., p. 565.

3. Orrin, E. Klapp, "Social Types: Process and Structure," *American Sociological Review* 23 (December 1958), 674-78.

4. Ibid., p. 674.

5. Gresham M. Sykes, *The Society of Captives: A Study of a Maximum Security Prison* (Princeton, N.J.: Princeton University Press, 1958), chs. 4-5.

6. Rose Giallombardo, *Society of Women: A Study of a Women's Prison* (New York: John Wiley and Sons, 1966), ch. 8.

7. Klapp, p. 677.

8. Sykes, ch. 4.

9. Richard M. McCleery, *Policy Change in Prison Management* (East Lansing, Mich.: Governmental Research Bureau, Michigan State University, 1957), pp. 31-32. McCleery analyzes how a liberal revolution in the administration of Oahu prison undermined the position of the "old cons" resulting in a period of inmate violence led by "young toughs."

10. John Irwin, *The Felon* (Englewood Cliffs, N.J.: Prentice Hall, 1970), pp. 26-29.

11. Thomas Matthiesen, *The Defences of the Weak* (London: Tavistock Publications, 1965), p. 12, 23.

12. Goffman has conceptualized behavior of this sort as role distance. Erving Goffman, *Encounters* (New York: Bobbs-Merrill, 1961), ch. 2.

13. For a fuller discussion of this aspect of prison homosexuality, see John H. Gagnon and William Simon, "The Social Meaning of Prison Homosexuality," *Federal Probation* 32 (March 1968), 23-29. It is also discussed by Sykes. See Sykes, pp. 71-72.

14. Most studies of prisons identify an active, aggressive role variously labeled a "wolf" or a "jocker." For example, Sykes, pp. 95-99. A comparable role at ECI was the "ripper." "Rippers," however, are black and thus not treated here. There were no labels applied to white inmates playing an active role, perhaps because, as we shall see, the primary aggressors are seldom white.

15. Coser notes that renegades and heretics may serve to strengthen a solidary group, but disrupt one which is non-cohesive. Lewis Coser, *The Functions of Social Conflict* (New York: The Free Press, 1956), pp. 69-71.

16. Rose Giallombardo has used this concept to describe the type of solidarity found among a population of female offenders. See her *Society of Women,* pp. 15-16, 106. While she ascribes this to the previous sex role socialization of women, it may well be a form of inmate solidarity that emerges under conditions of lessened deprivation and oppression rather than a particularly feminine adaptation.

Notes to Chapter 5
The Blacks

1. E. U. Essien-Udom, *Black Nationalism: A Search for an Identity in America* (Chicago: University of Chicago Press, 1962), pp. 6-7.

2. E. Franklin Frazier, *The Negro in the United States* (rev. ed.; New York: Macmillan, 1957), pp. 680-81.

3. Nathan Glazer and Daniel P. Moynihan, *Beyond the Melting Pot* (Cambridge, Mass.: M.I.T. Press, 1963), p. 53.

4. L. Singer, "Ethnogenesis and Negro Americans Today," *Social Research* 29 (Winter 1962), 419-32.

5. Ulf Hannerz, *Soulside: Inquiries into Ghetto Culture and Community* (New York: Columbia University Press, 1969), ch. 9.

6. Robert Blauner, *Racial Oppression in America* (New York: Harper and Row, 1972), ch. 4.

7. Hannerz, p. 144.

8. Charles Keil, *Urban Blues* (Chicago: University of Chicago Press, 1966), p. 152.

9. Thomas Kochman, "Rapping in the Ghetto," *Soul,* ed. Lee Rainwater (Chicago: Aldine, 1970), p. 52.

10. Ibid., pp. 56-64.

11. Hannerz, p. 146.

12. Ibid.

13. Ibid.

14. See, for example, Elliot Liebow, *Tally's Corner: A Study of Negro Streetcorner Men* (Boston: Little, Brown, 1967), pp. 64-71. Liebow suggests that the "present-time" orientation of blacks, and other lower class groups, is not an infantile unconcern with the future as has been suggested by some writers. Quite to the contrary, he argues, the absence of a "deferred gratification pattern" results from a realistic appraisal of the future as being filled with trouble, failure, and despair.

15. John Horton, "Time and Cool People," *Soul,* pp. 43-45.

16. Hannerz, pp. 145-46.

17. Hortense Powdermaker, *After Freedom* (New York: Viking Press, 1939), pp. 259-60. Brotz has observed that the "no black culture" argument assumes that an ethnic group must possess a homeland, a distinctive language and a religion to possess a distinct culture. Howard Brotz, *The Black Jews of Harlem* (New York: The Free Press, 1964), pp. 129-30. Given the above considerations on "rapping," the South and the "old time religion" one could argue quite reasonably that blacks possess a distinctive ethnic culture even given these restrictive assumptions.

18. I have adopted these titles from illustrations used by Hannerz, p. 149.

19. Both Keil and Hannerz have commented upon the ideological aspects of soul music. Keil, pp. 164-66; Hannerz, p. 150.

20. William J. Wilson, "Revolutionary Nationalism 'versus' Cultural Nationalism: Dimensions of the Black Power Movement," *Sociological Focus* 3 (Spring 1970), 43-51.

21. Cited by Robert G. Weisbord, *Ebony Kinship: Africa, Africans, and the Afro-American* (Westport, Conn.: Greenwood Press, 1973), p. 184.

22. For example, a survey by the Opinion Research Corporation revealed that 86 percent of the blacks in their sample believed that black children should be taught subjects in school that add to feelings of racial pride, and a study by Campbell and Schuman found that 42 percent of the blacks surveyed believed that black school children should study an African language. Opinion Research Corporation, *White and Negro Attitudes Toward Race Related Issues and Activities* (Princeton, N. J.: Opinion Research Corp., 1968); Angus Campbell and Howard Schuman, "Racial Attitudes in Fifteen American Cities," *National Advisory Commission on Civil Disorders, Supplemental Studies* (Washington: Government Printing Office, 1968), p. 6.

23. Weisbord, p. 187.

24. Ibid., p. 145.

25. Alex Poinsett, "Inawapasa Watu Weusi Kusema Kiswahili," *Ebony*, (December 1968) p. 163, cited by Weisbord, p. 191.

26. William H. Grier and Price M. Cobbs, *Black Rage* (New York: Bantam Books, 1969), pp. 36-37.

27. Lee Lockwood, *Conversation with Eldridge Cleaver–Algiers* (New York: Delta Books, 1970), p. 113.

28. Julius Lester, *Revolutionary Notes* (New York: Richard W. Baron, 1969), pp. 190-91.

29. S. E. Anderson, "Revolutionary Black Nationalism and the Pan-African Idea," *The Black 70's,* ed. Floyd B. Barbour (Boston: Porter Sargent, 1970), pp. 99-126.

30. Ibid., p. 112.

31. Ibid., p. 114.

32. Ibid., p. 116.

33. Ibid., p. 115.

34. Ibid., p. 114.

35. Hannerz inclines toward this view but Blauner tends to see the "soul" movement as the first step in a culture building process. Hannerz,

pp. 195-200; Robert Blauner, "Black Culture: Lower Class Result or Ethnic Creation," *Soul,* pp. 152-66.

36. George Jackson, *Soledad Brother: The Prison Letters of George Jackson* (New York: Bantam Books, 1970), p. 87.

37. Ibid., p. 21.

38. Regardless of ideological conflict, the existence of such mechanisms would appear to be necessary for the stability of a group such as the Afro-American Society, in which there are close ties and a high degree of personal involvement. See Lewis Coser, *The Functions of Social Conflict* (New York: The Free Press, 1956), pp. 61-64.

39. In Theodore Newcomb's terms, the "toms" function as a negative reference group for "half-steppers," as opposed to the positive reference group represented by the "revolutionaries." Unwilling or unable to attain the ideal standards of the "revolutionaries," "half-steppers" validate their identity claims more by reference to what they are not than by reference to what they should be. This process also occurs in their relation with the white staff. See Theodore M. Newcomb, *Social Psychology* (New York: Dryden Press, 1950), p. 227. From another perspective, Coser comments upon the functionality of a small group of renegades for the preservation of group solidarity (Coser, p. 71).

Notes to Chapter 6
Hacks, Blacks and Cons: Discipline

1. Sykes has made similar observations with respect to the structure of rewards at the New Jersey State Prison. Gresham M. Sykes: *The Society of Captives: A Study of a Maximum Security Prison* (Princeton, N.J.: Princeton University Press, 1958), pp. 51-52.

2. For example, see Robin M. Williams, Jr., *Strangers Next Door: Ethnic Relations in American Communities* (Englewood Cliffs, N.J.: Prentice-Hall, 1964), pp. 50-53, 97-108, 144-61.

3. Herbert Blumer, "Race Prejudice as a Sense of Group Position," *Pacific Sociological Review* 1 (Spring 1958), 1-7.

4. Ibid., p. 4.

5. Ibid., p. 5.

6. Ibid., p. 6-7. There is a considerable body of research attesting to the importance of definitions of the situation in shaping attitudes and behavior. One of the earliest and most interesting is Dietrich C. Reitzes, "The Role of Organizational Structures: Union versus Neighborhood in a Tension Situation," *Journal of Social Issues* 9, No. 1 (1953), 37-44. A recent study suggests that the relation between personal attitudes and

perceptions of the position of reference groups in the shaping of behavior is interactive in nature. See Alan C. Acock and Melvin L. DeFleur, ''A Configurational Approach to Contingent Consistency in the Attitude-Behavior Relationship,'' *American Sociological Review* 37 (December 1972), 714-26.

7. Alvin W. Gouldner, *Wildcat Strike: A Study in Worker-Management Relations* (New York: Harper Torchbooks, 1954), p. 165.

8. David Mechanic, ''Sources of Power of Lower Level Participants in Complex Organizations,'' *Administrative Science Quarterly* 7 (December 1962), 352-57.

9. Sykes, pp. 53-58.

10. Ibid. Also see R. A. Cloward, ''Social Control in the Prison,'' *Theoretical Studies in Social Organization of the Prison* (New York: Social Science Research Council, pamphlet #15, 1960), pp. 20-48.

11. While the concept of identity is fraught with definitional ambiguities, it is virtually an axion of symbolic interactionism that one's identity is developed and sustained through interactive processes. For a provocative attempt to draw together symbolic interaction and exchange theory by postulating the validation of identity as one of the major rewards that actors seek in their interaction with others, see George J. McCall and J. L. Simmons, *Identities and Interactions: An Examination of Human Associations in Everyday Life* (New York: The Free Press, 1966), especially pp. 72-81.

12. A somewhat similar pattern of activating alliances has been noted in a study of a black fighting gang. See R. Lincoln Keiser, *The Vice Lords: Warriors of the Streets* (New York: Holt, Rinehart and Winston, 1969), ch. 3. Also the concept of ''ordered segmentation'' developed by Suttles is quite similar to the pattern observed here. Gerald D. Suttles, *The Social Order of the Slum: Ethnicity and Territory in the Inner City* (Chicago: University of Chicago Press, 1968), pp. 10-37.

13. For an explication of the concept of relative deprivation in terms of reference group theory emphasizing the importance of the socially structured visibility of the reference group, see Robert K. Merton, *Social Theory and Social Structure* (2d rev. ed.; New York: The Free Press, 1957), especially pp. 227-36 and 336-40.

Notes to Chapter 7
Blacks and Cons: Routine Activities

1. Studies in natural settings include the following: John Biesanz and Luke M. Smith, ''Race Relations in Panama and the Canal Zone,''

American Journal of Sociology 57 (July 1951), 7-14; Lewis M. Killian, "The Adjustment of Southern White Migrants to Northern Urban Norms," *Social Forces* 33 (October 1953), 66-69; Melvin L. Kohn and Robin M. Williams, Jr., "Situational Patterning in Intergroup Relations," *American Sociological Review* 21 (April 1956), 164-74; Bernard Kutner et al., "Verbal Attitudes and Overt Behavior Involving Racial Prejudice," *Journal of Abnormal and Social Psychology* 47 (October 1952), 649-52; R.T. LaPiere, "Attitudes versus Action," *Social Forces* 13 (December 1934), 230-37; Joseph D. Lohman and Dietrich C. Reitzes, "Deliberately Organized Groups and Racial Behavior," *American Sociological Review* 19 (June 1954), 342-44. Studies in more experimental settings include the following: Alan C. Acock and Melvin L. DeFleur, " A Configurational Approach to Contingent Consistency in the Attitude-Behavior Relationship," *American Sociological Review* 37 (December 1972), 714-26; Melvin L. DeFleur, and Frank R. Westie, "Verbal Attitudes and Overt Acts," *American Sociological Review* 23 (December 1958), 667-73; Lawrence S. Linn, "Verbal Attitudes and Overt Behavior: A Study of Racial Discrimination," *Social Forces* 43 (March 1956), 353-64; Lyle G. Warner and Melvin L. DeFleur, "Attitude as an Interactional Concept: Social Constraint and Social Distance as Intervening Variables Between Attitudes and Action," *American Sociological Review* 34 (April 1969), 153-69.

2. Kohn and Williams, pp. 164-174.

3. Charles C. Moskos, Jr., "Racial Integration in the Armed Forces," *American Journal of Sociology* 72 (September 1966), 132-48.

4. Harvey Molotch, "Racial Integration in a Transition Neighborhood," *American Sociological Review* 34 (December 1969), 878-93. While the definition of these types is the same as those presented by Molotch, I have changed the term of one concept. What Molotch referred to as "transracial solidarity" I have termed "interracial cohesion." This change was made to be consistent with the previous distinction I made between solidarity and cohesion, i.e., between bonds of loyalty among a class of individuals and sentiments of liking within primary groups.

5. In Sykes' study 31.5 percent of the prisoners were unemployed for various reasons. G.M. Sykes, *The Society of Captives: A Study of a Maximum Security Prison* (Princeton: Princeton University Press, 1958), pp. 26-7. In contrast, only 9.7 percent of the 186 sentenced men in maximum security at ECI were unemployed. Nine of these were in segregation, eight were in the hospital, and one was considered too old to work.

6. Suttles has made the point that much interracial avoidance behavior is not the result of racial prejudice *per se*. Rather, it is often the result of what he has termed "ordered segmentation." That is, residents of slum areas are sensitive to cues from others that bespeak dependability and

trustworthiness and seek to surround themselves with people who possess characteristics that signify such traits to them. Race is only one such characteristic and may at times be less important than others. Gerald D. Suttles, *The Social Order of the Slum: Ethnicity and Territory in the Inner City* (Chicago: University of Chicago Press, 1968). Much the same process likely operates in the prison as a response to the physical and psychic dangers present. That is, much of the racial segregation is due less to patterns of exclusion than to patterns of inclusion.

7. In view of Sherif's experiments, the fears of the administration concerning competition between all-black and all-white teams would seem to be justified. However, these same experiments cast doubt upon the Warden's hopes that biracial cooperation on intramural athletic teams will reduce racial conflict and promote understanding. In Sherif's experiments, the superordinate goals that resulted in a reduction of conflict were "urgent," "compelling," and "appealing." As will be made clear in the following pages, the goal of winning intramural contests at ECI are not invested with such importance by the participants. See Muzafer Sherif et al., *Intergroup Conflict and Cooperation: The Robbers' Cave Experiment* (Norman: University of Oklahoma Book Exchange, 1961).

8. "Cadillac" was president of the Afro-American Society at the time. The way his entry into the game precipitated a change in group support of the teams and in the play of "Tickie" is quite similar to Whyte's observations on how a streetcorner gang maintained its leadership structure by harassing lower status members who challenged the leader in bowling. See William F. Whyte, *Street Corner Society* (enlarged ed.; Chicago: University of Chicago Press, 1955), p. 24. While I never observed other blacks competing with "Cadillac" being harassed, in any competition he had the support of the black spectators and usually emerged the winner.

9. As originally formulated by Park and in its later usage by Stonequist, the concept of marginal man referred to individuals who were caught between memberships in two societies with entirely different cultural traditions. See Robert E. Park, "Human Migration and the Marginal Man," *American Journal of Sociology* 33 (July 1928), 881-93; and Everett V. Stonequist, *The Marginal Man* (New York: Charles Scribner's Sons, 1937). Here I am using the concept on a level of social organization below that of total societies. As used here, the concept refers to individuals who because of racial barriers and conflicting reference groups are unable to attain full and legitimate membership in either racial group.

10. A brilliant analysis of this form of exchange in pre-literate societies is Marcel Mauss, *The Gift,* trans. Ian Cunnison (New York: W.W. Norton, 1967).

11. Several recent investigations of ghetto areas have commented upon

the presence and central importance of similar patterns of behavior for lower class black males. See Elliot Liebow, *Tally's Corner: A Study of Negro Streetcorner Men* (Boston: Little, Brown, 1967), chs. 4-5; Ulf Hannerz, *Soulside: Inquiries into Ghetto Culture and Community* (New York: Columbia University Press, 1969), ch. 5.

Notes to Chapter 8
Blacks and Cons: Focal Concerns

1. Muzafer Sherif, "Superordinate Goals in the Reduction of Intergroup Conflict," *American Journal of Sociology,* 63 (January, 1958), 349-50.

2. Exchange refers to a relation in "which one person or group acts for the express purpose of receiving a reward" from another. Cooperation is "joint or collaborative behavior toward some goal in which there is a common interest." Robert A. Nisbet, *The Social Bond: An Introduction to the Study of Society* (New York: Alfred A. Knopf, 1970), pp. 63, 66.

3. David A. Ward and Gene G. Kassebaus, *Women's Prison: Sex and Social Structure* (Chicago: Aldine, 1965); Rose Giallombardo, *Society of Women: A Study of a Women's Prison* (New York: John Wiley and Sons, 1966); Esther Heffernan, *Making It in Prison: The Square, the Cool, and the Life* (New York: John Wiley and Sons, 1972), ch. 5.

4. Donald Clemmer, *The Prison Community* (2d. ed.; New York: Holt, Rinehart and Winston, 1958), ch. 10; Gresham M. Sykes, *The Society of Captives: A Study of a Maximum Security Prison* (Princeton N.J.: Princeton University Press, 1958), pp. 95-99; Arthur V. Huffman, "Sex Deviation in a Prison Community," *Journal of Social Therapy* 6 (Third Quarter, 1960), 170-81; John H. Gagnon and William Simon, "The Social Meaning of Prison Homosexuality," *Federal Probation,* 32 (March 1968), 23-29.

5. See Chapter 4 for a discussion of the meaning of these terms, and for a discussion of homosexual marriages among white inmates.

6. Several studies in institutions for females have noted that racial differences appear to function as a substituted for sex differences in homosexual marriages and that two disproportionate number of such unions involve black and white partners. See Giallombardo, p. 3 and diagrams on pp. 177, 183.

7. John Dollard, *Caste and Class in a Southern Town* (3d ed.; Garden City N.Y.: Doubleday Anchor Books, 1957), chs. 7, 14, 17; Gordon W. Allport, *The Nature of Prejudice* (Garden City N.Y.: Doubleday Anchor Books, 1958), ch. 23; Calvin C. Hernton, *Sex and Racism in America* (New

York: Grove Press, 1965); William H. Grier and Price M. Cobbs, *Black Rage* (New York: Bantam Books, 1968), chs. 3-5.

8. Dollard, chs. 7, 14, 17; Grier and Cobbs, chs. 3-5; Hernton, ch. 3.

9. J.W. Johnson, *Along This Way* (New York: Viking Press, 1933), p. 170 quoted by Dollard, p. 135. For an indication of the impact of black-white sexual confict on the psychological development of one black militant leader, and the significance he attributes to the role of white sexual dominance as a factor in racial conflict, see Eldridge Cleaver, *Soul on Ice* (New York: Dell, 1968). See especially the essays entitled "The Allegory of the Black Eunuchs" and "The Primeval Mitosis," wherein he analyzes the structure of American race relations from a perspective that blends Marxism with Freudianism.

10. A study of sexual assaults in the Philadelphia prison system revealed that in 56 percent of the incidents the aggressor was black and the victim was white. None of the incidents involved white aggressors and black victims. In 29 percent of the incidents, both the aggressor and the victim were black and in 15 percent both were white. See Alan J. Davis, "Sexual Assaults in the Philadelphia Prison System and Sheriff's Vans," *Trans-Action* 6 (December 1968), p. 15. In general, these findings conform to the estimates of my informants at ECI. The lower frequency of interracial assaults involving black aggressors and the higher frequency of intraracial assaults involving blacks may be the result of several factors. First, in the Philadelphia system 80 percent of the population were black. There were thus proportionately fewer potential white victims. Moreover, the larger the black population, the more likely it will become polarized into conflicting factions, for example between what I have termed "revolutionaries" and "half-steppers," thus making sexual assaults among blacks more likely. Second, the time of the studies may be important. The ideology of brotherhood did not become a strong force at ECI until 1967. The study in Philadelphia was from June 1966 to July 1968. It is possible then that the brotherhood ideology, a major factor preventing intraracial sexual assaults among blacks, was not fully institutionalized at that time. In any event, the findings of this study confirm my main contention that the majority of sexual assaults involve black aggressors and white victims.

11. Leonard Berkowitz, *Aggression: A Social Psychological Analysis* (New York: McGraw-Hill, 1962), ch. 2.

12. In this regard, see the essays by Cleaver and the analysis by Grier and Cobbs, ch. 4

13. Berkowitz, ch. 4.

14. Ibid., ch. 5

15. Seating arrangements are indicative of both leadership and the quality of interraction. Based upon the findings of Sommer that leaders

prefer end positions around rectangular tables and that competing individuals most frequently place themselves diagonally opposite each other, the black representatives at this meeting would appear to be leaders of an aliented faction. See Robert Sommer, "Leadership and Group Geography," *Sociometry* 24 (March 1961), 99-110; "Further Studies of Small Group Ecology," *Sociometry* 28 (December 1965); 337-48.

Notes to Chapter 9
Conclusion

1. Despite the common equation of value consensus with the concept of social system, the two are logically gratuitous. The assumption that value consensus is a prerequisite to the existence of a social system is found largely in the work of Parsons and is correlative with his postulate of dynamic equilibrium as a property of social systems. Critiques of this position maintain that a system model may be retained without either of these restrictive assumptions. For examples of such critiques, see Pierre van den Berghe, "Dialectic and Functionalism: Toward a Theoretical Synthesis,"*American Sociological Review,* 28 (October, 1963), 695-705; R. A. Schermerhorn, *Comparative Ethnic Relations: A Framework for Theory and Research,* (New York: Random House, 1970), especially Chapter 1.

2. This incident was a threatened disturbance at a banquet sponsored by the "Jay Cees." It was discussed previously in Chapter 4.

3. See, for example, Lewis Coser, *The Functions of Social Conflict,* (New York: The Free Press, 1956), pp. 87-93.

4. Coser, p. 49.

5. Drawing upon findings in experimental psychology, Blalock has hypothesized that the mobilization of resources in pursuit of a goal is a multiplicative function of the strength of the goal and the expectation of success in attaining it. Hubert M. Blalock, Jr., *Toward a Theory of Minority Group Relations,* (New York: John Wiley and Sons, 1967), pp. 126-31. On this basis, we would expect black aggression to increase in direct relation to the degree to which the officers were intimidated and had acceded to the pressure.

6. Cornelius J. Lammers, "Strikes and Mutinies: A Comparative Study of Organizational Conflicts Between Rulers and Ruled," *Administrative Science Quarterly 14* (December 1969), p. 562.

7. Robin M. Williams, Jr., *The Reduction of Intergroup Tensions: A Survey of Research on Problems of Ethnic, Racial, and Religious Group Relations* (New York: Social Science Research Council, Bulletin #57, 1947), pp. 61-62.

8. The following description draws heavily upon that presented by Donald R. Cressey, "Prison Organizations," *Handbook of Organizations,* ed. James G. March (Chicago: Rand McNally, 1965), pp. 1037-53.

9. Alvin W. Gouldner, *Patterns of Industrial Bureaucracy* (New York: The Free Press, 1954), pp. 24, 207-28.

10. Gresham M. Sykes, *The Society of Captives: A Study of a Maximum Security Prison* (Princeton, N.J.: Princeton University Press, 1958), ch. 3.

11. Muzafer Sherif et al., *Intergroup Conflict and Cooperation: The Robbers Cave Experiment* (Norman, Okla.: Oklahoma University Book Exchange, 1961), pp. 151-91.

12. The following list is only a sample of the more important research bearing upon this hypothesis. Morton Deutsch and Mary E. Collins, *Interracial Housing: A Psychological Evaluation of a Social Experiment* (Minneapolis: University of Minnesota Press, 1951); Daniel M. Wilner, Rosabelle P. Walkley, and Stuart W. Cook, *Human Relations in Interracial Housing* (Minneapolis: University of Minnesota Press, 1955); Robin M. Williams, Jr., *Strangers Next Door: Ethnic Relations in American Communities* (Englewood Cliffs, N.J.: Prentice-Hall, 1964), ch. 7; Barbara K. MacKenzie, "The Importance of Contact in Determining Attitudes Towards Negroes," *Journal of Abnormal and Social Psychology* 43 (October 1948), 417-41; John Harding and Russel Hogrefe, "Attitudes of White Department Store Employees Toward Negro Co-Workers," *Journal of Social Issues* 8, No. 1 (1952), 18-28; Ernest Works, "The Prejudice-Interaction Hypothesis From the Point of View of the Negro Minority Group," *American Journal of Sociology,* 67 (July 1961), 47-52; Barry S. Brown and George W. Albee, "The Effect of Integrated Hospital Experiences on Racial Attitudes—a Discordant Note," *Social Problems* 13 (Spring 1966), 324-33; Bernard Meer and Edward Freeman,"The Impact of Negro Neighbors on White Home Owners," *Social Forces* 45 (May 1966), 11-19; W. Scott Ford, "Interracial Public Housing in a Border City: Another Look at the Contact Hypothesis," *American Journal of Sociology* 78 (May 1973), 1426-47.

13. The following description draws upon those provided by Cressey, pp. 1037-53 and Don C. Gibbons, *Changing the Lawbreaker* (Englewood Cliffs, N.J.: Prentice-Hall, 1965), pp. 157-74. Also see Maxwell Jones, *The Therapeutic Community* (New York: Basic Books, 1953) and *Beyond the Therapeutic Community* (New Haven: Yale University Press, 1968).

14. Jeanne B. Watson, "Some Social and Psychological Situations Related to Change in Attitude," *Human Relations* 3 (January 1950), 15-56.

15. Ford, p. 1441.

Bibliography

Books

Adams, R. N., and J. J. Preiss, (eds.). *Human Organization Research*. Homewood, Ill.: The Dorsey Press, 1960.

Allport, Gordon W. *The Nature of Prejudice*. Garden City, N. Y.: Doubleday Anchor Books, 1958.

Berkowitz, Leonard. *Aggression: A Social Psychological Analysis*. New York: McGraw-Hill, 1962.

Blalock, Hubert M., Jr. *Social Statistics*. New York: McGraw-Hill, 1960.

————. *Toward a Theory of Minority Group Relations*. New York: John Wiley and Sons, 1967.

Blau, Peter M. *Exchange and Power in Social Life*. New York: John Wiley and Sons, 1964.

Blauner, Robert. *Racial Oppression in America*. New York: Harper and Row, 1972.

Blumer, Herbert. *Symbolic Interactionism: Perspective and Method*. Englewood Cliffs, N.J.: Prentice-Hall, 1969.

Brotz, Howard. *The Black Jews of Harlem*. New York: The Free Press, 1964.

Bruyn, Severyn T. *The Human Perspective in Sociology: The Methodology of Participant Observation*. Englewood Cliffs, N.J.: Prentice-Hall, 1966.

Cleaver, Eldridge. *Soul On Ice*. New York: Dell, 1968.

Clemmer, Donald. *The Prison Community*. 2d. ed. New York: Holt, Rinehart and Winston, 1958.

Conklin, John E. *Robbery and the Criminal Justice System*. Philadelphia: J. B. Lippincott, 1972.

Coser, Lewis. *The Functions of Social Conflict*. New York: The Free Press, 1956.

Cressey, Donald R. (ed.). *The Prison: Studies in Institutional Organization and Change*. New York: Holt, Rinehart and Winston, 1961.

Deutsch, Morton, and Mary E. Collins. *Interracial Housing: A Psychological Evaluation of a Social Experiment*. Minneapolis: University of Minnesota Press, 1951.

Dollard, John. *Caste and Class in a Southern Town*. 3d ed. Garden City, N. Y.: Doubleday Anchor Books, 1957.

Durkheim, Emile. *Suicide*. Translated by John A. Spaulding and George Simpson. New York: The Free Press, 1951.

————. *The Division of Labor in Society*. Translated by George Simpson. New York: The Free Press, 1964.

Essien-Udom, E. U. *Black Nationalism: A Search for an Identity in America*. Chicago: University of Chicago Press, 1962.

Etzioni, Amitai. *A Comparative Analysis of Complex Organizations*. New York: The Free Press, 1961.

Filstead, William J. (ed.). *Qualitative Methodology: Firsthand Involvement With the Social World*. Chicago: Markham, 1970.

Frazier, E. Franklin. *The Negro in the United States*. Rev. ed. New York: Macmillan, 1957.

Giallombardo, Rose. *Society of Women: A Study of a Women's Prison*. New York: John Wiley and Sons, 1966.

Gibbons, Don C. *Changing the Lawbreaker: The Treatment of Delinquents and Criminals*. Englewood Cliffs, N. J.: Prentice-Hall, 1965.

Glaser, Barney G. and Anselm Strauss. *The Discovery of Grounded Theory: Strategies for Qualitative Research*. Chicago: Aldine, 1967.

Glaser, Daniel. *The Effectiveness of a Prison and Parole System*. Abridged ed. Indianapolis: Bobbs-Merrill, 1969.

Glazer, Nathan and Daniel P. Moynihan. *Beyond the Melting Pot*. Cambridge, Mass.: MIT Press, 1963.

Goffman, Erving. *Asylums: Essays on the Social Situation of Mental Patients and Other Inmates*. Garden City, N.Y.: Doubleday Anchor Books, 1961.

————. *Encounters*. New York: Bobbs-Merrill, 1961.

Gouldner, Alvin W. *Patterns of Industrial Bureaucracy*. New York: The Free Press, 1954.

————. *Wildcat Strike: A Study in Worker-Management Relations*. New York: Harper Torchbooks, 1954.

Grier, William H., and Price M. Cobbs. *Black Rage*. New York: Bantam Books, 1969.

Hannerz, Ulf. *Soulside: Inquiries into Ghetto Culture and Community*. New York: Columbia University Press, 1969.

Heffernan, Esther. *Making It in Prison: the Square, the Cool and the Life*. New York: John Wiley and Sons, 1972.

Hernton, Calvin C. *Sex and Racism in America*. New York: Grove Press, 1965.

Hesslink, George K. *Black Neighbors: Negroes in a Northern Rural Community*. New York: Bobbs-Merrill, 1968.

Irwin, John. *The Felon*. Englewood Cliffs, N. J.: Prentice-Hall, 1970.

Jackson, George. *Soledad Brother: The Prison Letters of George Jackson*. New York: Bantam Books, 1970.

Jones, Maxwell. *The Therapeutic Community*. New York: Basic Books, 1953.

_____. *Beyond the Therapeutic Community*. New Haven: Yale University Press, 1968.

Junker, Buford H. *Field Work: An Introduction to the Social Sciences*. Chicago: University of Chicago Press, 1960.

Keil, Charles. *Urban Blues*. Chicago: University of Chicago Press, 1966.

Keiser, R. Lincoln. *The Vice-Lords: Warriors of the Streets*. New York: Holt, Rinehart and Winston, 1969.

Lee, Frank F. *Negro and White in Connecticut Town*. New Haven: College and University Press, 1961.

Lester, Julius. *Revolutionary Notes*. New York: Richard W. Baron, 1969.

Liebow, Elliot. *Tally's Corner: A Study of Negro Streetcorner Men*. Boston: Little, Brown, 1967.

Lincoln, C. Eric. *The Black Muslims in America*. Boston: Beacon Press, 1961.

Lockwood, Lee. *Conversation with Eldridge Cleaver-Algiers*. New York: Delta Books, 1970.

Lofland, John. *Analyzing Social Settings: A Guide to Qualitative Observation and Analysis*. Belmont, Cal.: Wadsworth, 1971.

McCall, George J., and J. L. Simmons. *Identities and Interactions: An Examination of Human Associations in Everyday Life*. New York: The Free Press, 1966.

_____(eds.). *Issues in Participant Observation: A Text and Reader*. Reading, Mass.: Addison-Wesley, 1969.

McCleery, Richard M. *The Strange Journey*. Chapel Hill, N.C.: University of North Carolina Extension, 1953.

_____. *Policy Change in Prison Management*. East Lansing, Mich.: Governmental Research Bureau, Michigan State University, 1957.

MacIver, Robert M. *The Ramparts We Guard*. New York: Macmillan, 1950.

Mandelbaum, David G. *Soldier Groups and Negro Soldiers*. Berkeley: University of California Press, 1952.

Matthiesen, Thomas. *The Defences of the Weak*. London: Tavistock Publications, 1965.

Mauss, Marcel. *The Gift*. Translated by Ian Cunnison. New York: W. W. Norton, 1967.

Merton, Robert K. *Social Theory and Social Structure*. 2d rev. ed. New York: The Free Press, 1957.

Newcomb, Theodore. *Social Psychology*. New York: Dryden Press, 1950.

Nisbet, Robert A. *The Social Bond: An Introduction to the Study of Society*. New York: Alfred A. Knopf, 1970.

Opinion Research Corporation. *White and Negro Attitudes Toward Race Related Issues and Activities*. Princeton, N.J.: Opinion Research Corporation, 1968.

Powdermaker, Hortense. *After Freedom*. New York: Viking Press, 1939.

President's Commission on Law Enforcement and the Administration of Justice. *The Challenge of Crime in a Free Society*. New York: Avon Books, 1968.

Rainwater, Lee (ed.). *Soul*. Chicago: Aldine, 1970.

Reisman, David; Reuel Denney; and Nathan Glazer. *The Lonely Crowd*. New Haven: Yale University Press, 1950.

Schatzman, Leonard, and Anselm Strauss. *Field Research: Strategies for a Natural Sociology*. Englewood Cliffs, N. J.: Prentice-Hall, 1973.

Schermerhorn, Richard A. *Comparative Ethnic Relations: A Framework for Theory and Research*. New York: Random House, 1970.

Sherif, Muzafer. *In Common Predicament: Social Psychology of Intergroup Conflict and Cooperation*. Boston: Houghton Mifflin Co., 1966.

Sherif, Muzafer; O. J. Harvey; B. J. White; W. R. Hood; and Carolyn W. Sherif. *Intergroup Conflict and Cooperation: The Robbers' Cave Experiment*. Norman, Okla.: University of Oklahoma Book Exchange, 1961.

Sherif, Muzafer, and Carolyn W. Sherif. *Groups in Harmony and Tension: An Integration of Studies on Intergroup Relations*. New York: Harper Brothers, 1953.

Skolnick, Jerome. *The Politics of Protest*. New York: Ballantine Books, 1969.

South Carolina Department of Corrections. *The Emerging Rights of the Confined*. Columbia, S. C.: The Correctional Development Foundation, 1972.

Spindler, George D. (ed.). *Being an Anthropologist: Fieldwork in Eleven Cultures*. Prospect Hts, IL: Waveland Press, Inc., 1970 (reissued 1986).

Stonequist, Everett V. *The Marginal Man*. New York: Charles Scribner's Sons, 1937.

Street, David; Robert Vinter; and Charles Perrow. *Organization For Treatment: A Comparative Study of Institutions for Juveniles*. New York: The Free Press, 1966.

Suttles, Gerald D. *The Social Order of the Slum: Ethnicity and Territory in the Inner City*. Chicago: University of Chicago Press, 1968.

Sykes, Gresham M. *The Society of Captives: A Study of a Maximum Security Prison*. Princeton, N. J.: Princeton University Press, 1958.

Theoretical Studies in Social Organization of the Prison. Pamphlet no. 15. New York: Social Science Research Council, 1960.

Tittle, Charles R. *Society of Subordinates: Inmate Organization in a Narcotics Hospital*. Bloomington: Indiana University Press, 1972.

van den Berghe, Pierre L. *South Africa: A Study in Conflict*. Middletown, Conn.: Wesleyan University Press, 1965.

_____. *Race and Racism: A Comparative Perspective*. New York: John Wiley and Sons, 1967.

_____(ed.). *Intergroup Relations: Sociological Perspectives*. New York: Basic Books, 1972.

Wagley, Charles, and Marvin Harris. *Minorities in the New World: Six Case Studies*. New York: Columbia University Press, 1964.

Ward, David A., and Gene G. Kassebaum. *Women's Prison: Sex and Social Structure*. Chicago: Aldine, 1965.

Webb, Eugene; Donald T. Campbell; Richard D. Schwartz; and Lee Sechrest. *Unobtrusive Measures: Nonreactive Research in the Social Sciences*. Chicago: Rand McNally, 1966.

Weisbord, Robert G. *Ebony Kinship: Africa, Africans, and the Afro-American*. Westport, Conn.: Greenwood Press, 1973.

Whyte, William F. *Street Corner Society*. Enlarged ed. Chicago: University of Chicago Press, 1955.

Williams, Robin M., Jr. *The Reduction of Intergroup Tensions: A Survey of Research on Problems of Ethnic, Racial, and Religious Group Relations*. New York: Social Science Research Council, Bulletin no. 57, 1947.

_____. *Strangers Next Door: Ethnic Relations in American Communities*. Englewood Cliffs, N. J.: Prentice-Hall, 1964.

Wilner, Daniel M.; Rosabelle P. Walkley; and Stuart W. Cook. *Human Relations in Interracial Housing*. Minneapolis: University of Minnesota Press, 1955.

Yinger, J. Milton. *Toward A Field Theory of Behavior*. New York: McGraw-Hill, 1965.

Articles

Acock, Alan C., and Melvin L. DeFleur. "A Configurational Approach to Contingent Consistency in the Attitude-Behavior Relationship." *American Sociological Review* 37 (December 1972), 714-26.

Anderson, S. E. "Revolutionary Black Nationalism and the Pan-African Idea." Pp. 99-126 in Floyd B. Barbour (ed.), *The Black 70's*. Boston: Porter Sargent, 1970.

Bacchus, James. "Sumter Tense—'Riots Could Happen Again'." *Sentinel Star* (Orlando), May 28, 1973.

Becker, Howard S. "Problems of Inference and Proof in Participant Observation." *American Sociological Review* 23 (October 1958), 652-60.

Becker, Howard S., and Blanche Geer. "Latent Culture: A Note on the Theory of Latent Social Roles." *Administrative Science Quarterly* 5 (September 1960), 304-13.

Berk, Bernard. "Organizational Goals and Inmate Organization." *American Journal of Sociology* 71 (March 1966), 522-34.

Bettleheim, Bruno. "Individual and Mass Behavior in Extreme Situations." *Journal of Abnormal and Social Psychology* 38 (October 1943), 417-52.

Bierstedt, Robert. "An Analysis of Social Power." *American Sociological Review* 15 (December 1950), 730-38.

Biesanz, John and Luke M. Smith. "Race Relations in Panama and the Canal Zone." *American Journal of Sociology* 57 (July 1951), 7-14.

Blumer, Herbert. "Reflections on Theory of Race Relations." Pp. 3-21 in Andrew Lind (ed.), *Race Relations in World Perspective*. Honolulu: University of Hawaii Press, 1955.

————. "Race Prejudice as a Sense of Group Position." *Pacific Sociological Review* 1 (Spring 1958), 1-7.

————. "Recent Research on Race Relations in the United States." *International Social Science Bulletin (UNESCO)* 10, No. 3 (1958), 403-47.

Bradbury, William C. "Evaluation of Research in Race Relations." *Inventory of Research in Racial and Cultural Relations* 5 (Winter-Spring 1953), 99-133.

Brown, Barry S., and George W. Albee. "The Effect of Integrated Hospital Experiences on Racial Attitudes—a Discordant Note." *Social Problems* 13 (Spring 1966), 324-33.

Campbell, Angus, and Howard Schuman. "Racial Attitudes in Fifteen American Cities." *National Advisory Commission on Civil Disorders, Supplemental Studies*. Washington: Government Printing Office, 1968.

Cline, Hugh. "The Determinants of Normative Patterns in Correctional Institutions." Pp. 173-84 in Nils Christie (ed.), *Scandanavian Studies in Criminology*, Vol. 2. Oslo: Oslo University Press, 1968.

Cressey, Donald R. "Contradictory Directives in Complex Organizations: The Case of the Prison." *Administrative Science Quarterly* 4 (June 1959), 1-19.

———. "Prison Organizations." Pp. 1037-53 in James G. March (ed.), *Handbook of Organizations*. Chicago: Rand McNally, 1965.

Davis, Alan J. "Sexual Assaults in the Philadelphia Prison System and Sheriff's Vans." *Trans-Action* 6 (December 1968), 8-16.

Dean, John P.; Robert L. Eichhorn; and Lois R. Dean. "Observation and Interviewing." Pp. 274-304 in John T. Doby (ed.), *An Introduction to Social Research*. New York: Appleton, Century, Crofts, 1967.

DeBro, Julius. "The Black Revolution in Prison: A Case Study of Separatism." Paper presented at the annual meeting of the American Sociological Association, New York, August, 1973.

DeFleur, Melvin L., and Frank R. Westie. "Verbal Attitudes and Overt Acts." *American Sociological Review* 23 (December 1958), 667-73.

Erikson, Erik. "The Concept of Identity in Race Relations." Pp. 227-53 in Talcott Parsons and Kenneth Clark (eds.), *The Negro American*. Boston: Beacon Press, 1966.

Feshbach, Seymour, and Robert Singer. "The Effects of Personal and Shared Threats Upon Social Prejudice." *Journal of Abnormal and Social Psychology* 54 (May 1957), 411-16.

Ford, Charles A. "Homosexual Practices of Institutionalized Females." *Journal of Abnormal and Social Psychology* 23 (January-March 1929), 492-544.

Ford, W. Scott. "Interracial Public Housing in a Border City: Another Look at the Contact Hypothesis." *American Journal of Sociology* 78 (May 1973), 1426-47.

Frazier, E. Franklin. "Sociological Theory and Race Relations." *American Sociological Review* 12 (June 1947), 265-71.

Gagnon, John H., and William Simon. "The Social Meaning of Prison Homosexuality." *Federal Probation* 32 (March 1968), 23-29.

Garabedian, Peter G. "Social Roles and Processes of Socialization in the Prison Community." *Social Problems* 11 (Fall 1963), 139-52.

Geer, Blanche. "First Days in the Field: A Chronicle of Research in Progress." Chapter 11 in Phillip E. Hammon (ed.), *Sociologists at Work*. New York: Basic Books, 1964.

Gibb, Cecil A. "The Sociometry of Leadership in Temporary Groups." Pp. 658-74 in A. Paul Hare, Edgar Borgatta, and Robert F. Bales (eds.),

268

Small Groups: Studies in Social Interaction. Rev. ed. New York: Alfred A. Knopf, 1965.

Gold, Raymond. "Roles in Sociological Field Observations." *Social Forces* 36 (March 1958), 217-23.

Gouldner, Alvin W. "Cosmopolitans and Locals: Toward an Analysis of Latent Social Roles—I." *Administrative Science Quarterly* 2 (September 1959), 281-306.

Green, Edward. "Inter- and Intra-Racial Crime Relative to Sentencing." *Journal of Criminal Law, Criminology, and Police Science* 55 (September 1964), 348-58.

Grusky, Oscar. "Role Conflict in Organization: A Study of Prison Camp Officials." *Administrative Science Quarterly* 3 (March 1959), 452-72.

————. "Organizational Goals and the Behavior of Informal Leaders." *American Journal of Sociology* 65 (July 1959), 59-67.

Harding, John, and Russell Hogrefe. "Attitudes of White Department Store Employees Toward Negro Co-Workers." *Journal of Social Issues* 8 No. 1 (1952), 18-28.

Huffman, Arthur V. "Sex Deviation in a Prison Community." *Journal of Social Therapy* 6 (Third Quarter, 1960), 170-81.

Hyman, Herbert. "Social Psychology and Race Relations." Pp. 3-48 in Irwin Katz and Patricia Gurin (eds.), *Race and the Social Sciences*. New York: Basic Books, 1969.

Irwin, John, and Donald R. Cressey. "Thieves, Convicts and the Inmate Culture." *Social Problems* 10 (Fall 1962), 142-55.

Kaufman, Michael T. "Troubles Persist in Prison at Auburn." *The New York Times*, May 17, 1971.

Killian, Lewis M. "The Adjustment of Southern White Workers to Northern Urban Norms." *Social Forces* 33 (October 1953), 66-69.

Klapp, Orrin E. "Social Types: Process and Structure." *American Sociological Review* 23 (December 1958), 674-78.

Kluckhohn, Florence. "The Participant Observer Technique in Small Communities." *American Journal of Sociology* 46 (November 1940), 331-43.

Kohn, Melvin L., and Robin M. Williams, Jr. "Situational Patterning in Intergroup Relations." *American Sociological Review* 21 (April 1956), 164-74.

Kutner, Bernard; Carol Wilkins; and Penny Yarrow. "Verbal Attitudes and Overt Behavior Involving Racial Prejudice." *Journal of Abnormal and Social Psychology* 47 (October 1952), 649-52.

Lammers, Cornelius J. "Strikes and Mutinies: A Comparative Study of

Organizational Conflicts Between Rulers and Ruled." *Administrative Science Quarterly* 14 (December 1969), 558-72.

LaPiere, R. T. "Attitudes versus Action." *Social Forces* 13 (December 1934), 230-37.

Linn, Lawrence S. "Verbal Attitudes and Overt Behavior: A Study of Racial Discrimination." *Social Forces* 43 (March 1965), 353-64.

Lohman, Joseph D., and Dietrich C. Reitzes. "Note on Race Relations in Mass Society." *American Journal of Sociology* 58 (November 1952), 240-46.

_____. "Deliberately Organized Groups and Racial Behavior." *American Sociological Review* 19 (June 1954), 342-44.

McCorkle, Lloyd, and Richard Korn. "Resocialization Within the Walls." *The Annals of the American Academy of Political and Social Science* 293 (May 1954), 88-98.

MacKenzie, Barbara. "The Importance of Contact in Determining Attitudes Towards Negroes." *Journal of Abnormal and Social Psychology* 43 (October 1948), 417-41.

Martinson, Robert. "Collective Behavior at Attica." *Federal Probation* 36 (March 1972), 3-7.

Mechanic, David. "Sources of Power of Lower Level Participants in Complex Organizations." *Administrative Science Quarterly* 7 (December 1962), 352-57.

Meer, Bernard, and Edward Freeman. "The Impact of Negro Neighbors on White Home Owners." *Social Forces* 45 (May 1966), 11-19.

Merton, Robert K. "Selected Problems of Fieldwork in a Planned Community." *American Sociological Review* 12 (June 1947), 304-12.

Minard, Ralph D. "Race Relations in the Pocahontas Coal Field." *Journal of Social Issues* 8 No. 1 (1952), 29-44.

Molotch, Harvey. "Racial Integration in a Transition Neighborhood." *American Sociological Review* 34 (December 1969), 878-93.

Moskos, Charles C., Jr. "Racial Integration in the Armed Forces." *American Journal of Sociology* 72 (September 1966), 132-48.

Ohlin, Lloyd E. "The Reduction of Role Conflict in Institutional Staff." *Children* 5 (March-April 1958), 65-69.

Otis, Margaret. "A Perversion Not Commonly Noted." *Journal of Abnormal Psychology* 8 (June-July 1913), 112-14.

Park, Robert E. "Human Migration and the Marginal Man." *American Journal of Sociology* 33 (July 1928), 881-93.

Pearlin, Leonard I. "Shifting Group Attachments and Attitudes Toward Negroes." *Social Forces* 33 (February 1954), 47-50.

Pitt-Rivers, Julian. "Race, Color and Class in Central America and the Andes." Pp. 91-102 in Norman R. Yetman and C. Hoy Steele (eds.), *Majority and Minority: The Dynamics of Racial and Ethnic Relations*. Boston: Allyn and Bacon, 1971.

Reitzes, Dietrich C. "The Role of Organizational Structures: Union versus Neighborhood in a Tense Situation." *Journal of Social Issues* 9, No. 1 (1953), 37-44.

––––––. "Institutional Structure and Race Relations." *Phylon* 20 (Spring 1959), 48-66.

Roebuck, Julian. "A Critique of 'Thieves, Convicts and the Inmate Culture'." *Social Problems* 11 (Fall 1963), 193-200.

Rose, Arnold M. "Intergroup Relations vs. Prejudice: Pertinent Theory for the Study of Social Change." *Social Problems* 4 (October 1956), 173-76.

Schrag, Clarence. "Leadership Among Prison Inmates." *American Sociological Review* 19 (February 1954), 37-42.

Schwartz, Morris and Charlotte Schwartz. "Problems in Participant Observation." *American Journal of Sociology* 60 (January 1955), 343-54.

Sherif, Muzafer. "Superordinate Goals in the Reduction of Intergroup Conflict." *American Journal of Sociology* 57 (January 1958), 349-56.

Singer, L. "Ethnogenesis and Negro Americans Today." *Social Research* 29 (Winter 1962), 419-32.

Sommer, Robert. "Leadership and Group Geography." *Sociometry* 24 (March 1961), 99-110.

––––––. "Further Studies of Small Group Ecology." *Sociometry* 28 (December 1965), 337-48.

Srole, Leo. "Social Integration and Certain Corallaries: An Exploratory Study." *American Sociological Review* 21 (December 1956), 709-16.

Strong, Samuel. "Social Types in a Minority Community." *American Journal of Sociology* 48 (March 1943), 563-73.

Sykes, Gresham M. "The Corruption of Authority and Rehabilitation." *Social Forces* 34 (March 1956), 257-62.

––––––. "Men, Merchants and Toughs: A Study of Reactions to Imprisonment." *Social Problems* 4 (October 1956), 130-38.

Szulc, Tad. "George Jackson Radicalizes the Brothers in Soledad and San Quentin." *The New York Times Magazine* (August 1, 1971) pp. 10-11, 16-23.

Thomas, Charles W., and Samuel C. Foster. "The Importation Model of Inmate Social Roles: An Empirical Test." *The Sociological Quarterly* 14 (Spring 1973), 226-34.

Thomas, Edwin J., and Clinton F. Fink. "Effect of Group Size." Pp.

525-36 in A. Paul Hare, Edgar F. Borgatta, and Robert F. Bales (eds.), *Small Groups: Studies in Social Interaction.* New York: Alfred A. Knopf, 1965.

Tittle, Charles R. "Inmate Organization: Sex Differentiation and the Influence of Criminal Subcultures." *American Sociological Review* 34 (August 1969), 492-505.

Tittle, Charles R., and P. Drollene. "Social Organization of Prisoners: An Empirical Test." *Social Forces* 43 (December 1964), 216-21.

Trice, H. M. "The 'Outsider's' Role in Field Study." *Sociology and Social Research* 41 (September 1955), 27-32.

van den Berghe, Pierre L. "Dialectic and Functionalism: Toward a Theoretical Synthesis." *American Sociological Review* 28 (October 1963), 695-705.

"Wainwright Says Black Prison Majority Feared." *Sentinel Star* (Orlando), May 28, 1973.

Warner, Lyle G., and Melvin L. DeFleur. "Attitude as an Interactional Concept: Social Constraint and Social Distance as Intervening Variables Between Attitudes and Actions." *American Sociological Review* 34 (April 1969), 153-69.

Watson, Jeanne B. "Some Social and Psychological Situations Related to Change in Attitude." *Human Relations* 3 (January 1950), 15-56.

Wellford, Charles E. "Factors Associated With Adoption of the Inmate Code." *Journal of Criminal Law, Criminology and Police Science* 58 (June 1967), 197-203.

Wheeler, Stanton. "Socialization in Correctional Communities." *American Sociological Review* 26 (October 1961), 697-712.

Williams, Robin M., Jr. "Racial and Cultural Relations." Pp. 423-64 in Joseph B. Gittler (ed.), *Review of Sociology: Analysis of a Decade.* New York: John Wiley and Sons, 1957.

Wilsnack, Richard W., and Lloyd E. Ohlin. "Preconditions for Major Prison Disturbances." (mimeographed paper, no date).

Wilson, Thomas P. "Patterns of Management and Adaptations to Organizational Roles: A Study of Prison Inmates." *American Journal of Sociology* 74 (September 1968), 146-57.

Wilson, William J. "Revolutionary Nationalism 'versus' Cultural Nationalism: Dimensions of the Black Power Movement." *Sociological Focus* 3 (Spring 1970), 43-51.

Works, Ernest. "The Prejudice-Interaction Hypothesis From the Point of View of the Negro Minority Group." *American Journal of Sociology* 67 (July 1961), 47-52.

272

Wulbert, Roland. "Inmate Pride in Total Institutions." *American Journal of Sociology* 71 (July 1965), 1-9.

Zald, Mayer. "The Correctional Institution for Juvenile Offenders: An Analysis of 'Organizational Character." *Social Problems* 8 (Summer 1960), 57-67.

———. "Power Balance and Staff Conflict in Correctional Institutions." *Administrative Science Quarterly* 6 (June 1962), 22-49.

Zelditch, Morris, Jr. "Some Methodological Problems of Field Studies." *American Journal of Sociology* 67 (March 1962), 566-76.

Zimbardo, Philip G. "A Pirandellian Prison." *New York Sunday Times Magazine* (April 8, 1973) pp. 38-60.

Index

Index

Accommodation, 45, 46, 80
"Administration men," 74-75, 85, 140-141
Administrative succession, 48-52
Africa, 95, 96, 104
Afro-American Society: and "brother," 99; conflict within, 100-101, 108-111; and conflict with staff, 40-42; formation of, 32-33; goals of, 33; leadership of, 100-101, 109-110; membership of, 91; programs of, 33, 99, 104, 108-109; re-establishment of, 44; segregation in, 163-165; and solidarity, 102, 107, 112; views of officers on, 127
Aggression, 112, 183-184, 206, 211, 216. *See also* Frustration-aggression
Ali, Muhammed, 108
Anderson, S.E., 97
Anomie: defined, 47; and goal conflict, 20, 52, 53; and humanitarian reform, 52-57; and prejudice, 126
Attica Correctional Institution: events at, 1, 21, 60, 127; impact upon ECI, 198-212
Attitudes, 6, 66, 147-148
Avoidance, 156-159 *passim,* 168
Axes of life, 63-64, 91

"Beacon, The": activities of, 33; formation of, 33; leaders of, 71-74; racial conflict in, 40; racial segregation of, 163
Berk, Bernard, 6
Bias, racial: and corruption of authority, 131; among custodians, 123-127; and discipline, 129-130, 136; and surveillance of blacks, 127-129
Biesanz, John, 8
Black Muslims, 10
Black nationalism: conflict with "soul," 97-98; cultural nationalism, 95-96; defined, 91; and race relations in prisons, 9; revolutionary nationalism, 96-97; and solidarity of black prisoners, 18-19, 101-103
Black rage, 182, 184
Blauner, Robert, 92
Blumer, Herbert, 8, 125
"Brothers": and conflict with staff, 132-135; and corruption of authority, 131; and mutual aid, 100; social type, 98-100
Bureaucracy, punishment-centered, 213-214
Bureaucratization, 48-49

Cell assignments, 153-156
Censoriousness, 72

Characteristics of prisoners, 33-38
Cleaver, Eldridge, 13, 96, 97, 101, 102, 104
Clemmer, Donald, 2, 9
Cliques: as form of prisoner organization, 4; and humanitarian reform, 5-7, 85-86; among white inmates, 67-84 *passim*
Cobbs, Price M., 96
Coercion: as form of custodial power, 47, 115-116; and humanitarian reform, 53-57; among prisoners, 69, 79-81, 183-186
Cohesion, 63, 67, 85, 107
Cohesion, interracial, 150, 178, 179-180, 219
Collective adaptations: and background characteristics, 38; of black prisoners, 98, 130; as result of deprivation, 2-7; of white prisoners, 63-64
Competition, 86, 153, 173, 192
Compliance, 115
Conflict: among administrators, 50-52; among black prisoners, 108-111, 200-201; ideological, 98, 101, 110, 113; non-realistic, 211; reduction of, 149, 213; staff-inmate, 42, 43, 68; among white prisoners, 75, 84, 86, 89
Conflict, interracial: instigation of, 188; in past, 39-42; among prisoners, 177, 182-186, 187-190, 194-195, 206-207; with staff, 133-135, 201-203
Conflict resolution, means of: dissolution of, 204, 206-207; among prisoners, 187-190; with staff, 190-192
Confrontation: effect on discipline, 135-137, 142, 144-145; tactic of black prisoners, 132-135
Conner, K. D., 1
Contact, interracial: equal status, 217-219; and focal concerns, 173; among officers, 124; opportunities for, 152, 154
Control by staff: immunity from, 138-139; 141-142, 144; and integration, 148-149, 154-156, 159, 170; neutralization of, 144
Cooperation, 17, 56-57, 131, 137-141
Cooperation, biracial: in conflict resolution, 187-192; in drugs, 176-178; in sports, 157-158; in homosexual behavior, 186; on public occasions, 193-195
Cooptation, 71
Correctional officers: anomie among, 52-57; class identification of, 124-125, 127; corruption of the authority of, 58-59, 61, 137-141; and disciplinary proce-

275

dures, 117; disposition of infractions by, 118- 119 ; as dominant group, 47, 125; intimidation of, 135-137, 145, 202; power of, 47, 54, 115, 133, 142; prejudice among, 123-127; reaction to Attica, 208; rebellion of, 59-61; role definition of, 47, 52, 53, 57; surveillance by, 127-130; union of, 60-61, work stoppages by, 59-60, 135, 206, 208

Corruption of authority: as adaptation by officers, 58-59; and discrimination, 142; and discipline, 141-143; inability of blacks to, 131-132; as tactic by white prisoners, 137-141

Coser, Lewis, 211

Court decisions, 43, 51, 54, 60, 199

Cressey, Donald R., 4

Cross pressures, 149, 154, 156, 170

Culture: black, 92; inmate, 2-9, 173; of poverty, 92, 94

Custodial orientation, 6, 9, 28, 30, 45

Custodians. *See* Correctional officers

Davis, Angela, 108

Deferred gratification, 93

Definitions of the situation: by black leaders, 110, 200-201; by correctional officers, 126; and homosexual behavior, 78, 185; and overt behavior, 48; race differences in, 124

Demands. *See* Grievances

Discipline: as aspect of staff-inmate relations, 115; and black resources, 116, 135-137; Board, 18, 55, 116-118, 137-142; discrimination in, 142-145; dispositions, 56, 116-123, 136-137; infractions, 117-123, 129-130, 136-141; prejudice and, 116, 129-130; procedures, 54, 116-117; reports, 55-56, 117, 136; and white resources, 116, 141-143

Discrimination, racial: black perceptions of, 116, 145; and conflict among prisoners, 193, 207; in the custodial prison, 215; and immunity of white elite, 142-143; officers' view of, 129

Disturbances: after Attica, 199-203; and discipline, 136-137; in past, 39-43; and prejudice, 126; and rebellion of officers, 59-60; threat of, 51, 67, 132-134

Dominance, sexual, 182

Dominant group, 47, 125

"Dope fiends," 81-83, 85, 89

Drugs: access to, 69, 140; "connecting," 82, 174-175; "dealing," 82, 175-176; demand for, 81; "fixing," 177-178; as genocide, 102-103; "getting beat," 82,

177; race relations in, 174-178; "scoring," 82, 176-178; "stashing," 82, 174-175

Durkheim, Emile, 47

Eastern Correctional Institution: formal organization, 26-28; goals and resources, 28-30; physical characteristics, 23-26; prisoner population, 33-38; reform of, 30-33

Escapes, 198-199, 208, 209

Ethnogenesis, 92

Exchange, 58, 166-167, 173

Exploitation, 69-70, 75, 164

"Fags": marriages of, 179-180; prostitution by, 180-181; as social type, 78-79

Focal concerns, 63-64, 112, 173

Formal organization: of Eastern Correctional Institution, 26-28; and race relations, 148-149, 170, 212-220

Frazier, E. Franklin, 91

Frustration-aggression, 184-186

Giallombardo, Rose, 5, 63

Glaser, Daniel, 4

Glazer, Nathan, 91

Goals, organizational, 28-30

Goal conflict, 47, 50-57, 61

"Good time," 115

Gouldner, Alvin, 48, 49, 126, 213

Grier, William H., 96

Grievances: black, 201-203, 207; inmate, 190

Guards. *See* Correctional officers

"Hacks." *See* Correctional officers

"Half-steppers": and conflict with staff, 201-204; as social type, 104-108

"Hanging out," 128, 167-168

Hannerz, Ulf, 92

Hibbler, Al, 92

"Hippies," 76-77

Homosexual behavior: as focal concern, 78-81; marriage, 78, 179-180; prostitution, 79, 180-181; race relations in, 179-187; rape, 182-186; seduction, 79, 186; as viewed by black prisoners, 103, 107; in women's prisons, 5, 179

Humanitarian reform: and anomie, 52-57; as compromise, 30-33; and convict solidarity, 6-7, 19, 85-88; defined, 9; and goal conflict, 14; and power of the custodians, 47, 126-127; and prejudice, 126; and race relations, 9-10, 19, 107; views of officers on, 54, 59

"Hustling," 93, 165-167

Identity: and aggression, 112, 182-186; black, 96, 102, 105; and conflict, 211; and confrontation, 132-134; convict, 3, 9, 102; and corruption of authority, 131-132; criminal, 186; pre-prison, 87-88

Ideology: of black nationalism, 95-97; and conflict, 101, 108-111; and confrontation, 132, 136; and solidarity, 98-101; "soul" as, 94-95

Indulgency pattern, 48

"Industrial time," 115

Inmate Advisory Council: formal, 204-205; informal, 51, 71

Inmate culture: code of solidarity, 3-5, 67, 85; and definition of homosexuality, 78, 185; focal concerns of, 3, 173; norms of, 3; and prejudice, 9, 214-215; socialization into, 3-7; subcultural orientations within, 4, 9; violation of by black prisoners, 207

Inmate social organization: of black prisoners, 98-112 passim; as collective adaptation, 3-7; deprivation model of, 3-5, 85; under differing conditions, 5-7; importation model of, 4-5, 85; among white prisoners, 64-88 passim; in women's prisons, 5

Innovation, 57

Integration, racial: in Army, 148; in cell assignments, 154-156; demographic, 150, 152-153, 155; and early black movement, 95; and limitations of space, 148, 159, 170; and policy of warden, 148-149, 156, 170; on public occasions, 193-195; in sports, 157; staff control, 148-149, 170; on work details, 151-153

Interaction, biracial: in cell blocks, 154-156; in conflict resolution, 187-192; defined, 150; in drug traffic, 174-178; in exchange relations, 166-167; in gym, 159-161; in homosexual behavior, 179-181; at movies, 161-163; opportunities for 152, 154, 157; in sports, 157-158; on work details, 152-153; in yard, 168

Interests: of black prisoners, 103-105, 193; complementary, 197; conflict of, 193, 207; of officers, 53, 60; of white prisoners, 65, 68, 81, 85, 193

Irwin, John, 4, 69

Jackson, George: cited, 10, 13, 103; killing of, 199, 201, 211; as role model, 101, 102, 104, 108

"Jay Cees": conflict within, 40; formation of, 32; goals of, 32; leadership of, 71-74; membership of, 32; programs, 33; segregation in, 163-165

"Jiving": 93

Karenga, Mulana Ron, 96

Kassebaum, Gene G., 5

Keil, Charles, 92

"Kids": 66, 80-81, 85, 140, 183

Klapp, Orrin E., 63

Kochman, Thomas, 93

Kohn, Melvin L., 148

Korn, Richard, 3

Lammers, Cornelius J., 211

Latent culture, 4

Leadership: of black prisoners, 134-135, 137, 211; changes in, 48-50, 110-111, 200-201; conflict among, 204-207; 211; of staff, 50-53, 61; of white prisoners, 67-74 passim

Lester, Julius, 97

McCleery, Richard M., 69

"Mafia": attempts to control black prisoners, 204-205; immunity from punishment, 138; as mediators, 70-71; 188-190; as social type, 67-68

Malcolm X, 101

Marginal Men, 163

Masculinity, affirmation of, 77, 184

Mechanic, David, 130

Merton, Robert K., 47, 53, 57, 59

Messinger, Sheldon M., 3

Molotch, Harvey, 150

Moskos, Charles C., Jr., 148

Moynihan, Daniel P., 91

Newton, Huey, 108

Normative orientations, 9, 76, 85

Norms, 3, 83-84, 148

Oppression, racial: and brotherhood, 99-100; and self-definition as political prisoners, 102-103; and "soul," 93-94; and sexual assault, 184-186

Organizational drift, 51

Organized crime, 65, 88

Oswald, Russell G., 1

"Others," 83

Pains of imprisonment, 3, 63, 88

Pan-African world, 97

Paradigmatic experience, 126

Parole, 115-116

"Partners," 100-101, 133-134, 136

Pennsylvania System, 214
Perrow, Charles, 6
Personnel turnover, 208, 219
Political prisoners, 10, 77, 102, 131
"Politicians": and conflict resolution, 190-192; displacement of, 205; immunity from punishment, 140-141; as social type, 71-74
Powdermaker, Hortense, 94
Power: of black prisoners, 130-135; of correctional officers, 47, 54, 115, 133, 142; and humanitarian reform, 126-127; and resources, 130-132; of white prisoners, 137-143
Prejudice: and behavior, 127; among black prisoners, 148; defined, 125; and discipline, 129-130; among officers, 116, 123-127; reduction of, 217; and surveillance, 127-129; among white prisoners, 147
Primary groups, 2-7 passim
Prison, custodial, 8-9, 213-214
Projection, 179, 181
Protest, 211
Punishment: basis of custodial power, 115-116; and confrontation, 136-137; immunity from, 137-141; race differences in, 120-121, 137, 142, 144-145
"Punks," 79-80, 180, 183-184

"Queens," 78

Race: and characteristics of prisoners, 34-38; defined, 7-8; and disciplinary dispositions, 121-123; and infractions, 119-120; social significance of, 8-10, 147, 170, 214
Race relations: in custodial prisons, 8-9, 214-216; defined, 8; dimensions of, 115, 143; dynamics of, 199-210; and prison reform, 7-10; structure of, 20, 21, 197-198, 212; in therapeutic communities, 218-220
Racism, 97, 102, 184, 203, 210
"Rapping," 92-93, 106
"Rats," 3, 18, 66, 83-84
Rebellion of officers, 59-61
Recreation, 156-163
Reference groups, 6, 87, 103, 142, 148
Rehabilitation: and conflict, 30-31, 51; demands of inmates for, 72; as goal, 28, 33; and therapeutic community, 217-218; views of officers on, 127
Relative deprivation, 86, 143
Repression, 213, 214-216
Research methods, 11-20
Resources: of black prisoners, 130-135; of

correctional officers, 115-116; and discipline, 135-143 passim; financial and manpower, 28-30; mobilization of, 9, 101, 132-135; of white prisoners, 137-141
"Revolutionaries," and conflict, 108-111, 200-201; and conflict resolution, 188-190; as social type, 103-104
Rewards, 115, 148
Riot, conspiracy to, 198-199
"Ripper," 184-185
Role conflict, 52
Role distance, 73
Roles: in drugs, 176; of guard, 52, 56; in homosexuality, 78-79; of inmate social system, 3-4, 85; and social type analysis, 63-64
Rules: absence of written, 32, 116; enforcement, 123-124

San Quentin, 199, 211
Schatzman, Leonard, 14
Schwartz, Charlotte, 13
Schwartz, Morris, 13
Segregation, racial: attitudes of prisoners toward, 147-148; in cell assignments, 154-155; in drug traffic, 174; in gym, 159-161; in "hanging out," 168; at movies, 161-163; in organizations, 163-165; on public occasions, 194-195; at work, 153
Sexual assault, 182-186
Sexual deprivation, 77-78
Shared threat, 9
Sherif, Muzafer, 217
"Signifying," 93
Simmel, Georg, 201
Singer, L., 92
Smith, Luke M., 8
Social types: among black prisoners, 98-112; defined, 63-64; among white prisoners, 64-84
Solidarity: absence of, 83, 89; of black prisoners, 97-102, 132, 147, 166, 193; calculated, 85; code of, 3, 5, 67, 147; convict, 8, 85, 102; and group size, 38; and humanitarian reform, 6, 85-88; inmate, 3; and prejudice, 147; and "ratting," 84
"Soul": aspects of, 91-95; conflict with nationalism, 97-98; and "halfsteppers," 105-108
"Sounding," 93, 105, 106
Spencer, Herbert, 201
Staff-inmate relations: discipline as aspect of, 115; race and, 8-9, 115-116
"Stand-up guy," 64-67, 85

Strategic replacements, 48-49, 50
Strauss, Anselm, 14
Street, David, 6
Strong, Samuel, 63
Subculture, 4, 9, 85, 127, 167
Superordinate goals, 9, 20, 173, 217
Sykes, Gresham M., 3, 9, 47, 63, 64, 65, 131, 151, 215

Therapeutic community, 217-220
Third world, 97
Tittle, Charles R., 4, 7
"Toms," 111-113, 131, 180
Total institution, 3-4
Transfers of prisoners, 198-199, 209-210

Treatment orientation, 6, 9, 30-31, 48-49

Vinter, Robert, 6
Vocational training, 30, 44, 49, 51, 86, 104

Wainwright, Louie, 1
Ward, David A., 5
Weber, Max, 201
Wheeler, Stanton, 3
Williams, Robin M., Jr., 148, 213
Wilson, Thomas P., 6
"Wise guys," 68-71, 82-89 *passim,* 138-140
Work assignments, 116, 139-140, 150-153
Work release, 44, 50, 51, 86, 116

About the Author

Leo Carroll received the Ph.D. in sociology from Brown University. He is Professor of Sociology and Chairman of the Department of Sociology and Anthropology at the University of Rhode Island where he teaches courses in criminology and in race and ethnic relations. Professor Carroll's research involves racial discrimination in criminal justice. His writings have appeared in such professional journals as *American Sociological Review, Criminology, Justice Quarterly,* and *Law and Society Review.*